A REFORMATION
SOURCEBOOK

A REFORMATION SOURCEBOOK

DOCUMENTS FROM AN
AGE OF DEBATE

EDITED BY MICHAEL BRUENING

UNIVERSITY OF TORONTO PRESS

Higher Education Division

www.utppublishing.com

LIBRARY AND ARCHIVES CANADA CATALOGUING IN PUBLICATION

Bruening, Michael W. (Michael Wilson), author
   A Reformation sourcebook : documents from an age of debate / Michael Bruening.

Includes bibliographical references.
Issued in print and electronic formats.

ISBN 978-1-4426-3569-2 (hardback).—ISBN 978-1-4426-3568-5 (paperback).—
ISBN 978-1-4426-3570-8 (html).—ISBN 978-1-4426-3571-5 (pdf).

       Reformation—Sources. I. Title.

BR301.B78 2017   274'.06   C2016-904727-X
                                         C2016-904728-8

We welcome comments and suggestions regarding any aspect of our publications—please feel free to contact us at news@utphighereducation.com or visit our Internet site at www.utppublishing.com.

North America
5201 Dufferin Street
North York, Ontario, Canada, M3H 5T8

2250 Military Road
Tonawanda, New York, USA, 14150

UK, Ireland, and continental Europe
NBN International
Estover Road, Plymouth, PL6 7PY, UK
ORDERS PHONE: 44 (0) 1752 202301
ORDERS FAX: 44 (0) 1752 202333
ORDERS E-MAIL: enquiries@nbninternational.com

ORDERS PHONE: 1-800-565-9523
ORDERS FAX: 1-800-221-9985
ORDERS E-MAIL: utpbooks@utpress.utoronto.ca

This book is printed on paper containing 100% post-consumer fiber.

The University of Toronto Press acknowledges the financial support for its publishing activities of the Government of Canada through the Canada Book Fund.

Printed in the United States of America.

For my colleagues and fellow alumni of the University of Arizona's Division for Late Medieval and Reformation Studies

Contents

Preface

"Age of Debate" is not a term frequently used to describe the Reformation, yet it is, I would argue, appropriate. For the first time in history, Europeans from the ruling classes down to the peasantry were engaged in a prolonged debate that altered the course of European history. This debate was about the correct way to think about and practice the Christian faith. Never before had so many different kinds of people from so many different social classes, careers, educational backgrounds, and geographical locations in Europe weighed in on a topic of such importance.

This sourcebook aims to present the debates of the Reformation era through a range of primary source documents. To that end, it presents the texts in groups rather than individually. Each chapter begins with a general introduction addressing the background and issues relevant to the entire chapter, and sections within the chapter introduce groups of related documents, offering focus questions to help you think about what they mean and how they are related.

This sourcebook adopts a fairly broad operative definition of the word "debate." Some of the documents present actual, formal debates that took place during the Reformation, such as the First Zurich Disputation (§XIII), the Marburg Colloquy (§XIV), or the Iwie Debate on slavery (§XL). Others represent informal debates or disputes, with one text responding directly to the other. These include the treatises by Martin Luther and Erasmus on free will (§IX) and the arguments by Thomas More and William Tyndale on translating the Bible (§XXI). Still other sections present texts that were not necessarily written as a challenge or response to a particular viewpoint, but which nonetheless offer divergent approaches to or perspectives on specific ideas or topics. These too were part of the century-long debate that characterized the Reformation.

One of the reasons the Reformation is such a fascinating period is that its debates are at once so relevant to and so distant from those of the present day. Particularly for those actively involved in a Christian church, many debates of the Reformation are still very much alive. Protestants and Catholics still disagree about the source(s) of religious authority, the role of the pope, the status of the saints, and a variety of other issues; Lutherans still disagree with some Reformed Christians about the nature of the Eucharist. For those interested in these ongoing debates, this book should help you understand their historical origins during the Reformation.

At the same time, the sixteenth century was an entirely different world from that of the twenty-first century. Much has changed in the 500 years since Martin Luther wrote the Ninety-Five Theses in 1517. His was a world in which modern ideas about religious freedom, democracy, gender and social equality, secularism, and relativism did not yet exist. To understand the people of the Reformation and their conflicts, we must strive to practice historical empathy, putting ourselves in the shoes of the people of the sixteenth century. Empathy is one of the "real world" skills that historical inquiry, and hopefully this sourcebook, can help foster. In order really to understand the past, the student of history must mentally enter that world. To understand the Reformation, one must understand both sides of the debates that took place at the time; this sourcebook will help you do just that.

This book would not have been possible without the assistance and advice of many individuals. My spring semester 2015 Reformation class "test drove" the earliest version of this reader. The anonymous reviewers of both the book proposal and especially those who read the entire manuscript made many important corrections and offered excellent suggestions for texts to include, many of which I have tried to incorporate. My wife Jeanine read all of the introductory material and always improves my prose immeasurably. And the editors at the University of

Toronto Press have been enthusiastic and incredibly supportive through the whole process; I would like to mention in particular Natalie Fingerhut, Anna Del Col, Ashley Rayner, and freelance copy editor Kerry Fast. Finally, this book is dedicated to my wonderful group of colleagues and friends from the University of Arizona's Division for Late Medieval and Reformation Studies, where we spent long hours poring over the primary sources of the Reformation during my doctoral studies. My thanks to you all.

How to Read a Primary Document

The Reformation was the first mass movement to make extensive and effective use of the printing press. For the first time, the written word, which had always been important for conveying ideas among the elites, helped to influence a popular movement. Church reformers saw the invention of the printing press as nothing less than providential: a gift of God for conveying his message of renewal within the church. Thus, while one should never underestimate the power of the oral transmission of ideas, or of other media that were increasingly used during the Reformation, such as woodcut illustrations and music, the printed word was central to the period, and it remains our principal access to the mindset, worldview, and debates of the Reformation.

A primary source is a source produced during the time being studied. A secondary source, by contrast, is usually produced later and is about the period being studied. Thus, a treatise written by Martin Luther is a primary source for the Reformation period; a modern biography of Martin Luther is a secondary source. Primary documents are the raw materials of the historian. They are what historians use to "do history." Our understanding of the Reformation—or of any period—shifts over time, not principally because we learn about new facts or events, but because we discover new primary sources or bring new questions to well-known primary documents. Thus, the better you understand how to read, interpret, and analyze these documents, the better you will be as an historian in your own right.

The historian's task in analyzing primary sources is to extract from them as much information about the past as possible. We do this by evaluating what lies behind each word and phrase and considering their implications. Take, for instance, Martin Luther's Ninety-Five Theses, a foundational text of the Reformation. Figure 0.1 demonstrates how a careful student of history might read the first few lines.

To analyze text effectively, it can be helpful to keep in mind the "Five Ws": *Who, What, When, Where,* and *Why*.

Who wrote the text, and who is the intended audience? First, consider the author's background, perspective, and motivations. Every author is shaped by his or her historical context, educational background, social status, and outlook on the world. In the Reformation, the most obvious difference will be adherence to one religious sect or another. Lutherans will have a different perspective from Catholics, for example. But consider other factors as well: Is the author an individual or a collective, such as a council or legislative body? A university-trained theologian or a commoner? A scholastic theologian or a humanist? A king or a judge?

No doubt, you already recognize the problem of bias. You have likely been taught, for good reason, to be suspicious of bias, but suspicion does not justify rejection. To begin with, if you were simply to ignore all the authors who were biased in some way, you would have nothing left to read. A sophisticated analysis, therefore, does not merely state *that* an author is biased, but explains *how* an author is biased, how that bias affects the argument he or she is making, and what effect this has on how we should read the text today.

One should also consider the author's motivations and intended audience. Think, for example, about how you would read a consumer agency warning about the dangers of a particular product and how you would read an advertisement for the same product. The very different goals of these two texts would shape the language, credibility, and appeal of each. The former might tell the reader something about the status of research in a particular field, the role of government agencies, the concerns of

Martin Luther was an Augustinian friar and a university professor at a time when universities were church institutions. He was using the disputation—a standard format for public debate among Christian scholars—and openly inviting others to participate. These facts indicate that he was acting as a member of the church, not as an outsider or opponent to it. They also suggest that he did not regard his actions as subversive.

The church sold indulgences with the understanding that the purchaser could expect forgiveness of his own or another's sins and thus a reduction in the time spent in purgatory. Luther's focus is on the "power and efficacy" of indulgences, indicating that he questions whether purchase of them indeed brings forgiveness.

Luther begins by indicating his purpose or motivation for composing his theses. His reference to "love for the truth and a desire to bring it to light" implies that he believes the truth to have been obscured in some way.

Martin Luther, *Disputation of Doctor Martin Luther on the Power and Efficacy of Indulgences,* 1517

Out of love for the truth and the desire to bring it to light, the following propositions will be discussed at Wittenberg, under the presidency of the Reverend Father Martin Luther, Master of Arts and of Sacred Theology, and Lecturer in Ordinary on the same at that place. Wherefore he requests that those who are unable to be present and debate orally with us, may do so by letter.

In the Name our Lord Jesus Christ. Amen.

Our Lord and Master Jesus Christ, when He said, "Repent," willed that the whole life of believers should be repentance.

This word cannot be understood to mean sacramental penance, i.e., confession and satisfaction, which is administered by the priests.

He names Wittenberg as the location for the disputation. Wittenberg was a university town in Electoral Saxony, which was ruled by Frederick the Wise. It is far from Rome and not nearly as important at the University of Paris for theological matters. His call for both oral and written debate indicates that he foresees a lengthy exchange of views.

Luther's invocation of Jesus is further evidence that he does not understand himself to be in opposition to Christian teachings.

As the first thesis, this one likely holds particular significance. It relies on the authority of Scripture, rather than on the remarks of any theologian or church leader. In particular, it highlights the words of Jesus. Luther's quotation of Jesus in the first thesis indicates that Luther assigned a high priority to the Gospels in evaluating theological questions.

Luther asserts that the word repent cannot refer to the practice of making one's confession to a priest. This is a radical statement. Does he mean to do away with confession given by a priest or simply to add to it? What effect would this have on the sacrament of penance? Would people go more or less often? What does it say about the power of the priesthood? Would this statement be seen as a threat by church authorities like the pope? Why or why not? If Luther wants to see repentance outside of the church's sacrament, what form would that take? What effect would it have on the life of regular Christians?

People in the Middle Ages were expected to confess their sins at least once a year, usually just before Easter. Luther's claim that the "whole life of believers should be repentance" suggests that this practice is insufficient.

Figure 0.1

This illustration demonstrates that every line, from the author and title through the entire text, demands critical evaluation. This is the approach you should take when reading historical primary documents, for you are not simply reading stories; you are analyzing text.

officials or consumers. The latter would more likely reveal information about economic conditions and consumer values or desires. The same differences in purpose affect historical documents, so it is important to consider the objectives that lie behind a text: Is the author trying to convey information? To persuade an audience to take action? To convince opponents to shift their way of thinking? To establish law? To forge closer ties with an ally? The list of possible objectives could go on. The point is that to understand a historical text properly, one must understand what the author was trying to accomplish in writing it.

Intended audience is important too. You probably write differently when texting your friends than when writing papers for classes because your intended audience is different in each case. In the same way, the intended audiences of Reformation-era texts varied. Was the author writing for highly educated theologians or poorly educated commoners? For trained legal specialists or a broader audience of townspeople? In the Reformation period, one clue for answering this question can be found in the language of the original text. If the author was writing in Latin, the intended audience was probably a highly educated one. Authors generally wrote in the vernacular, by contrast, to reach educated commoners.

Next, consider *what* the author is saying. This may sound obvious, but many a text has been misinterpreted simply because the reader did not fully understand it. Sometimes understanding what the author is saying is simply a matter of looking up unfamiliar words in a dictionary—a task that takes just seconds if you use an online dictionary. Looking up unfamiliar words is not only key to understanding a text but also a way to improve your own writing skills.

In many cases, however, understanding a text demands that you seek more comprehensive background information than a dictionary can provide. For example, the debates of the Reformation often revolve around theological concepts like predestination, or religious terms such as "Eucharist," which may be unfamiliar to many students. Your professor will no doubt discuss many of these in class, but you may need to do some background reading in a textbook or elsewhere to fully understand the issues discussed in primary source texts.

Next, *when* and *where* was the text written? Documents can only be understood properly within their historical context. Consider, for example, Martin Luther King, Jr.'s "I Have a Dream" speech. Imagine if a reader thought it was written in nineteenth-century Russia rather than in the United States in 1963; that person would completely misunderstand the text! Just as an understanding of Dr. King's speech demands a familiarity with the context of the American civil rights movement and the March on Washington, so also you must understand the context of the documents produced during the Reformation period. Many were written in response to specific events or discussions. The introductions to the individual sections in this book briefly discuss the contexts in which the works were produced. Be sure to read those introductions and

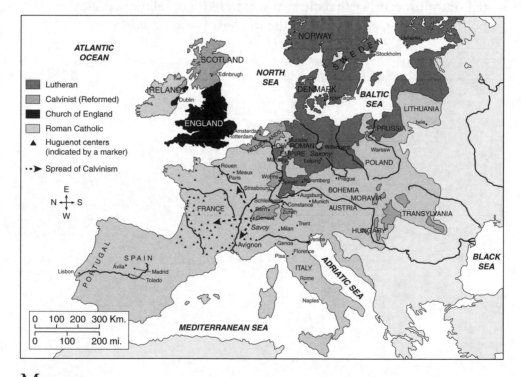

Map 0.1

Europe by Religion, c. 1600

note carefully any additional information provided by your instructor or your textbook.

Finally, ask yourself: *Why* are these texts significant? Literally thousands upon thousands of documents were produced during the period of the Reformation, yet this book contains selections from only 86 of them. Consider what might make each of these few documents important enough to have been selected for this book. A document may be considered particularly significant for a variety of reasons: It could be the first text to put forth a radical new idea. It may state a widely held position so clearly and forcefully that it was reprinted repeatedly and read widely. It may have led to a major shift in ideology or culture. Whatever the specific reason, the documents in this book were not chosen at random. They each illustrate key aspects of the religious upheaval of the sixteenth century that did so much to reorient religion, philosophy, politics, culture, and society in the modern Western world.

I

The Late Medieval Background to the Reformation

The Reformation forever changed Christianity in Western Europe. In order to understand and appreciate exactly how it changed, we must first try to understand the late medieval church. This chapter explores the elements of late medieval Christianity that the Reformation would affect most profoundly, namely, the papacy, Christian theology, and lay piety.

As the texts in this chapter will demonstrate, there was plenty of debate in the years before Martin Luther arrived on the scene. It is a mistake, therefore, to think of the late medieval Catholic Church as a monolithic, all-powerful entity that brooked no dissent from the pope. To be sure, the church took a hard line on what it considered outright heresy (see §II), but there was significant disagreement in the fifteenth century over the authority of the pope (§I), the best means to explore and understand religion (§III), and the proper way for common people to practice their faith (§IV).

The sources in this chapter make clear that there was a strong push to reform the Catholic Church long before Luther's posting of the Ninety-Five Theses in 1517. As you read the documents, think about what was driving these calls for reform. Consider as well the rationales of those who defended the status quo. Bear in mind your conclusions, for you will want to consider the same things when you read Martin Luther in the next chapter.

I. PAPAL AUTHORITY

At the head of the Catholic Church stood—and still stands today—the pope. The pope held a number of different titles in the late Middle Ages: Bishop of Rome, holder of the Apostolic See, Servant of the Servants of Christ, Vicar of St. Peter, and even Vicar of Christ. The pope's power over the church was first seriously called into question, at least in the West, in the late Middle Ages.

The first text below is Pope Boniface VIII's papal bull[1] *Unam Sanctam*, which he wrote in the course of his quarrels with King Philip IV of France. The two men had a long struggle over whether the king had the right to tax the clergy and try them in secular courts. The pope insisted that the king had no such right; the king strongly disagreed and took repeated action to limit the flow of money from France to Rome. After six years of quarreling with the king, Boniface (r. 1294–1303) issued *Unam Sanctam*, one of the strongest statements of papal power ever written.

Just a few years later, however, the pope's power was seriously compromised. First, Boniface's successors moved from Rome to Avignon in present-day France. From 1309 to 1377, seven successive Bishops of Rome did not reside in Rome, a situation referred to by the Italian humanist Francesco Petrarch as the "Babylonian Captivity" of the church. Worse, the death of Pope Gregory XI (r. 1370–78) shortly after he finally returned to Rome provoked such confusion that Western Christendom ended up with two (and later three!) popes in what is known as the Western (or Great) Schism.

---

[1] A papal bull is a declaration published by the pope; the word "bull" comes from the Latin *bulla*, meaning *seal*.

When pressure to resolve the schism grew overwhelming, the pope at Pisa, John XXIII, convoked the Council of Constance (1414–18). Included here are its two most famous decrees, *Haec Sancta* (also known as *Sacrosancta*) and *Frequens*. Together they form the institutional basis for a model of church governance known as conciliarism. Conciliarism holds that the ultimate authority in the church is not the pope but the whole people of the church represented in a general council, to which popes themselves are subject.

The Council of Constance did, in fact, end the Great Schism, but conciliarism had a short life as the dominant principle of church governance. In 1459, Pope Pius II (r. 1458–64), who had formerly been a conciliarist himself, issued the third document below, the papal bull *Execrabilis*, which rejected the chief tenets of conciliarism. While conciliarism died a quick official death, no one forgot its chief tenets, and it continued to be a threat to papal power well into the Reformation. Popes were always aware that further councils, particularly in times of crisis, might once again try to assert their authority over the papacy.

Focus Questions

1. What are the chief bases for Pope Boniface VIII's claims for papal power? What does he conclude about the necessity of obedience to the pope?
2. What are the chief principles of conciliarism as expressed in *Haec Sancta* and *Frequens*?
3. On what basis does Pius II overturn conciliarism?
4. Based on these texts, how secure was the pope's authority on the eve of the Reformation?
5. What different definitions of "the church" do you find in these documents?
6. What parallels do you see between the papal and conciliar models of authority, on the one hand, and monarchical and republican models of political governance, on the other? What are the advantages and disadvantages of each?

1. Pope Boniface VIII, *Unam Sanctam*, 1302[2]

The true faith compels us to believe that there is one, holy, catholic, apostolic Church, and this we firmly believe and plainly confess. And outside of her there is no salvation or remission of sins, as the Bridegroom says in the Song of Solomon: "My dove, my perfect one, is the only one, the darling of her mother, flawless to her that bore her" [S. of S. 6:9], which represents the one mystical body whose head is Christ, but the head of Christ is God [1 Cor. 11:3]. In this Church there is "one Lord, one faith, one baptism" [Eph. 4:5]. For in the time of the flood there was only one ark, that of Noah, prefiguring the one Church, and it was "finished to a cubit above" [Gen. 6:16], and had but one helmsman and master, namely, Noah. And we read that all things on earth outside of this ark were destroyed....

Therefore, there is one body of the one and only Church, and one head, not two heads, as if the Church were a monster. And this head is Christ and his vicar, Peter, and his successor, for the Lord himself said to Peter, "Feed my sheep" [John 21:16]. And he said "my sheep" in general, not these or those sheep in particular, from which it is clear that all were committed to Peter. If, therefore, the Greeks[3] or anyone else say that they are not subject to Peter and his successors, they thereby necessarily confess that they are not of the sheep of Christ. For the Lord says in the Gospel of John that there is one fold and only one shepherd [John 10:16].

By the words of the Gospel, we are taught the two swords, namely, the spiritual authority and the temporal, are in the power of the Church. For when the Apostles said, "Here are two swords" [Luke 22:38]—that is, in the Church, since it was the Apostles who were speaking—the Lord did not answer, "It is too much," but, "It is enough." Whoever denies that the temporal sword is in the power of Peter does not properly understand the word of the Lord when he said, "Put your sword back into its sheath" [John 18:11]. Both swords, therefore, the spiritual and the temporal, are in the power of the Church. The former is to be used by the Church, the latter for the Church; the one by the hand of the priest, the other by the hand of kings and knights but at the command and permission of the priest....

For the truth itself declares that the spiritual power must establish the temporal power and pass judgment on it if it is not good. Thus, the prophecy of Jeremiah concerning the Church and the ecclesiastical power is fulfilled: "See, today I appoint you over nations and over kingdoms, to pluck up and to pull down, to destroy and to overthrow, to build and to plant" [Jer. 1:10].

Therefore, if the temporal power err, it will be judged by the spiritual power, and if a lower

---

[2] Source: Frederic Austin Ogg, ed., *A Source Book of Mediæval History* (New York: American Book Company, 1907), 385–88, text modernized.

[3] That is, the Greek Orthodox Church.

spiritual power err, it will be judged by its superior. But if the highest spiritual power err, it cannot be judged by men, but by God alone. For the Apostle says, "Those who are spiritual discern all things, and they are themselves subject to no one else's scrutiny" [1 Cor. 2:15]. Now this authority, although it is given to man and exercised through man, is not human but divine. For it was given by the word of the Lord to Peter, and the rock was made firm to him and his successors in Christ himself, whom he had confessed. For the Lord said to Peter, "Whatever you bind on earth shall be bound in heaven, and whatever you loose on earth shall be loosed in heaven" [Matt. 16:19].

Therefore, whoever resists this power thus ordained by God resists the ordinance of God [Rom. 13:2].... We, therefore, declare, say, and affirm that submission of all to the Bishop of Rome is altogether necessary for their salvation.

2. The Council of Constance[4]

A. Haec Sancta, 1415

This holy synod of Constance, constituting a general council for the extirpation of the present schism and the union and reformation of the Church of God in head and members, legitimately assembled in the Holy Ghost, to the praise of omnipotent God, in order that it may the more easily, safely, effectively, and freely bring about the union and reformation of the Church of God, hereby determines, decrees, ordains, and declares what follows:

It first declares that this same council, legitimately assembled in the Holy Ghost, forming a general council and representing the Catholic Church militant, has its power immediately from Christ, and everyone, whatever his position or rank, even if it be the papal dignity itself, is bound to obey it in all those things which pertain to the faith, to the healing of the schism, and to the general reformation of the Church of God in head and members.

It further declares that anyone, whatever his position, station, or rank, even if it be the papal, who shall contumaciously refuse to obey the mandates, decrees, ordinances, or instructions which have been, or shall be, issued by this holy council, or by any other general council legitimately summoned, which concern or in any way relate to the abovementioned objects, shall, unless he repudiate his conduct, be subject to appropriate penance and be suitably punished, having recourse, if necessary, to the other resources of the law.

---

[4] Source: James Harvey Robinson, *Readings in European History*, abridged ed. (Boston: Ginn & Company, 1906), 216–18, text modernized.

B. Frequens, *1417*

A frequent celebration of general councils is an especial means for cultivating the field of the Lord and effecting the destruction of briars, thorns, and thistles: that is, heresies, errors, and schism, and of bringing forth a most abundant harvest. The neglect to summon these councils fosters and develops all these evils, as may be plainly seen from a recollection of the past and a consideration of existing conditions. Therefore, by a perpetual edict, we sanction, decree, establish, and ordain that general councils shall be celebrated in the following manner, so that the next one shall follow the close of this present council at the end of five years. The second shall follow the close of that at the end of seven years, and councils shall thereafter be celebrated every ten years in such places as the pope shall be required to designate and assign, with the consent and approbation of the council, one month before the close of the council in question, or which, in his absence, the council itself shall designate. Thus, with a certain continuity, a council will always be either in session, or be expected at the expiration of a definite time.

This term may, however, be shortened on account of emergencies, by the Supreme Pontiff, with the counsel of his brothers, the cardinals of the Holy Roman Church, but it may not be hereafter lengthened. The place, moreover, designated for the future council may not be altered without evident necessity.

3. Pope Pius II, *Execrabilis*, 1459[5]

The execrable and hitherto unknown abuse has grown up in our day, that certain persons, imbued with the spirit of rebellion, and not from a desire to secure a better judgment, but to escape the punishment of some offence which they have committed, presume to appeal from the pope to a future council, in spite of the fact that the pope is the Vicar of Jesus Christ and to him, in the person of St. Peter, the following was said: "Feed my sheep" [John 21:16] and "Whatever you shall bind on earth shall be bound in heaven" [Matt. 16:18]. Wishing, therefore, to expel this pestiferous poison from the Church of Christ and to care for the salvation of the flock entrusted to us, and to remove every cause of offence from the fold of our Savior, with the advice and consent of our brothers, the cardinals of the Holy Roman Church, and of all the prelates, and of those who have been trained in the canon and civil law, who are at our court, and with our own sure knowledge, we condemn all such appeals and prohibit them as erroneous and detestable.

---

[5] Source: Oliver J. Thatcher and Edgar H. McNeal, eds., *A Source Book for Mediaeval History* (New York: Charles Scribner's, 1905), 332, text modernized.

II. LATE MEDIEVAL HERESY

Christian orthodoxy has faced challenges virtually from the beginning of its existence. The church labels as heretics those who challenge it by spreading contrary teachings. In the later Middle Ages, the threat of heresy began to grow in Western Europe. First, the Cathars and Waldensians developed and grew in the twelfth century. Then, in the fourteenth and fifteenth centuries, two important groups of heretics developed with teachings similar to those later adopted by Luther: the English Lollards, who followed John Wyclif, and the Bohemian Hussites, who followed Jan Hus. While considered heretics by the Catholic Church, they are generally embraced by Protestants as forerunners of the Reformation.

John Wyclif (or Wycliffe, c. 1330–84) was a professor at the University of Oxford who attacked some core doctrines of medieval Christianity, notably the authority of the church. He called instead for scripture to be the ultimate judge of all doctrine, and he wanted the Bible to be translated into the vernacular so that laypeople could read it. His followers, who became known as Lollards, took up Wyclif's project and produced the first English translation of the Bible.

Jan (or John) Hus (or Huss, c. 1372–1415) was a Czech reformer active in Prague, who appears to have been influenced by Wyclif but who developed his own ideas as well. He preached against indulgences, simony (the buying of church offices), and the power of the papacy. His criticism of the papacy and late medieval ecclesiology are printed below, taken from perhaps his best known work, *The Church* (or *De Ecclesia*). Church officials frequently lumped Hus and Wyclif together as likeminded heretics. In 1414, Hus was summoned to the Council of Constance (see above, §I) and was granted safe conduct. Instead of being given a chance to debate or to defend his views, he was told to recant, thrown in prison, and finally—in clear violation of the grant of safe conduct—burned at the stake as a heretic. The second document below is the Council's condemnation. Wyclif had died already in 1384, but the Council condemned him for heresy as well, and Pope Martin V later ordered his body exhumed and burned.

Focus Questions

1. What are Hus's arguments against the six points about church governance that he lists at the start of the document?
2. What does Hus indicate should be the bases for finding the truth in religion?
3. Does Hus attack the theology of the late medieval church, the morals of the pope and other officials, or both? Provide examples.
4. What are the bases of the condemnation of Hus at the Council of Constance?
5. What are the advantages and disadvantages of quashing dissent within the ranks of any institution?

4. Jan Hus, *The Church*, 1413[6]

In regard to these follies of the Unlearned, I find these points: 1) The pope is the head of the holy Roman church. 2) The College of Cardinals is the body of the holy Roman church. 3) The pope is manifestly and truly the successor of the prince of the apostles, Peter. 4) Cardinals are manifest and true successors of the college of Christ's other apostles. 5) For the government of the church throughout the whole world, there should always be manifest and true successors of the same kind in the office of the prince of the apostles and in the office of Christ's other apostles. 6) Such successors are not to be found or procured on the earth, other than the pope, the existing head, and the College of Cardinals, the existing body of the church.

Against all these six points, the argument in brief runs thus: All truth in the religion of Christ is to be followed, and only that is truth which is known by the bodily senses, or discovered by an infallible intelligence, or made known through revelation, or laid down in sacred Scripture. But none of these six points is truth known by the bodily senses, or discovered by an infallible intelligence, or known through revelation, or laid down in divine Scripture. Therefore, none of these six points is truth in the religion of Jesus Christ which is to be followed....

It is clear that religious faith is not held by the ecclesiastical doctors so far as these points are concerned unless they prove them plainly or show them to be founded in sacred

---

[6] Source: John Huss, *The Church (De Ecclesia)*, trans. Davis S. Schaff (New York: Charles Scribner's Sons, 1915), 130, 132–35, 137–41, 143, 147–50, text modernized.

Scripture or in clear reasoning.... Then similarly, as to the point that the pope is always and uniformly to be regarded as the head of the Roman church, and that the church is the bride of Christ built upon Christ "against which the gates of hell cannot prevail," we must argue thus: No pope is the most exalted person of the catholic church but Christ himself; therefore, no pope is the head of the catholic church besides Christ....

In the same way, it is not of necessity to salvation for all Christians, living together, that they should believe expressly that anyone is head of any church whatsoever unless his evangelical life and works plainly moved them to believe this.... Likewise, if we examine in the light of the feeling and influence with which we influence inferiors and, on the other hand, examine by the mirror of Scripture, according to which we should regulate our whole life, then we would choose rather to be called servants and ministers of the church than its heads. For it is certain that if we do not fulfil the office of a head, we are not heads.... Blessed, therefore, be the head of the church, Christ, who cannot be separated from his bride which is his mystical body, as the popes have often been separated from the church by heresy.

The second point is this: the College of Cardinals is the body of the holy Roman church.... Again, the body of the holy Roman church is made up of all the predestined, and the college by itself does not include all these. The first part of this statement appears from the words of the apostle, who spoke as the representative of the predestined: "We, who are many, are one body in Christ" (Rom. 12:5). And showing the unity of the body, he does not make the college of the apostles the body of the church (1 Cor. 12:28), but he says, "God has appointed in the church first apostles, second prophets, third teachers; then deeds of power, then gifts of healing," etc.... The second part of this statement, that all the predestined are not that college, is evident of itself. Therefore, the doctors would better have said that Christ is the head of the holy Roman church, and each of the predestined a member and that all together are the body, which is the church, than to have said that the pope is the head of the Roman church and the college of cardinals the body....

The third point is this: the pope is the manifest and true successor of the prince of the apostles.... A man is the vicar of the person whose place he fills and from whom, in a legitimate way, he receives governing power. But no one truly occupies the place of Christ, or Peter, unless he follows him in his life, for no other kind of following is more fitting; nor does anyone otherwise receive governing power. If, therefore, the pope is a most humble man, depending little upon mundane honors and the gain of this world, if he is a shepherd deriving his name from the pasturage of God's Word, of which pasturage the Lord said to Peter, "Feed my sheep" (John 21:17), if he feed the sheep by the Word and the example of his virtues being made example of the flock with his whole heart, as Peter says (1 Peter 5:3), if he is meek, patient, chaste, laboring anxiously and solicitously in the service of the church, esteeming all temporal things as dung—then, without doubt, he is the true vicar of Jesus Christ, manifest to God and men, so far as the judgment of the outward senses can determine. But if he lives at discord with these virtues—for there is "no agreement between Christ and Belial" (2 Cor. 6:15), and as Christ himself said, "Whoever is not with me is against me" (Matt. 12:30)—how can he be the true and manifest vicar of Christ or of Peter and not rather the vicar of antichrist, seeing he resists Christ in morals and in life?

Therefore, when Peter was opposed to Christ in will and words and after Christ had promised him the keys, Christ called Peter "Satan," that is, "adversary," and said, "Get behind me, Satan! You are a stumbling block to me; for you are setting your mind not on divine things but on human things" (Matt. 16:23). If, therefore, Peter, chosen to be Christ's first vicar by Christ and deputed to serve the church in spiritual matters, was called "Satan" by Christ, Peter out of affectionate love having tried to dissuade him from submitting to the sentence of death, why should not another one, more opposed to Christ in his life, not be called Satan and consequently antichrist or antichrist's vicar or antichrist's chief minister?…

From these and other sayings, it is evident that no pope is the manifest and true successor of Peter, the prince of the apostles, if in morals he lives at variance with the principles of Peter; and if he is avaricious, then he is the vicar of Judas, who loved the reward of iniquity and sold Jesus Christ.

And by the same kind of proof the cardinals are not the manifest and true successors of the college of Christ's other apostles, unless the cardinals live after the manner of the apostles and keep the commands and counsels of our Lord Jesus Christ. For if they climb up by another way

than by the door of our Lord Jesus Christ, then they are thieves and robbers, just as the Savior himself declared when of all such he said, "All who came before me are thieves and bandits" (John 10:8)….

Hence, if the cardinals heap up to themselves ecclesiastical livings and barter with them and take money for their sale either themselves or through others, and so devour and consume in luxurious living the good of the poor, and if they do not do miracles or preach the Word of God to the people or pray sincerely or fill the place of deacons—whom the apostles appointed, Acts 6—by not performing their duties or living their lives—in how far, I ask, are they the vicars of the apostles?…

By the same method of proof the sixth point is set forth which is: "there are not to be found or given on earth other such successors than the pope, the present head, and the College of Cardinals, the present body of the Roman church." On this point I note in the first place that Christ is a most sufficient head as he proved during three hundred years or more, when his church prospered and his law was most efficient for the closing of ecclesiastical cases, the end for which God gave his law. For Christ and his law did not fail for the governing of the church, seeing devoted priests ministered this law unto the people, who followed the judgment of holy doctors, which judgment they issued by the indwelling of the Holy Spirit, as is clear from the cases of St. Augustine, St. Jerome, St. Gregory, and St. Ambrose, who were given after the apostles' death to the church to teach her. Hence, it is not to be doubted that St. Augustine was more profitable to the church than many popes, and in matters of doctrine much more profitable than all the cardinals, from the first cardinals down to those now in office. For, in the government of the church, he knew the Scriptures of Christ better than they and also defined the nature of the catholic faith better by clearing the church of heretical errors and correcting them. Why, therefore, were those four doctors not true vicars of the apostles and their manifest successors, nay, even more true and reliable, so far as the people go, than any modern pope with his cardinals who shine before the people neither by virtue of a holy life nor by doctrine?

5. Council of Constance, Sentence against Jan Hus, 1415[7]

Because by the witness of the Truth a bad tree customarily bears bad fruit, for that reason the man of damned memory, John Wyclif, like a poisoned root, by means of his death-bearing doctrine bore many pestiferous sons, whom he left as successors of his perverse dogmas....

Thus when at the general Council recently held in Rome[8] it was decreed that the teaching of John Wyclif of damned memory be condemned, and his books, containing that kind of teaching, be burned as heretical; and the teaching itself was [actually] condemned and his books comprising such insane and pestiferous doctrines were burned; all these decrees were approved by the authority of this sacred Council. Nonetheless, a certain John Hus in this sacred Council here personally present, a disciple not of Christ but rather of the heresiarch John Wyclif, with temerity dared to oppose himself to it thereafter and contrary to the condemnation and the decree, by having taught, asserted, and preached his [Wyclif's] many errors and heresies.... He[9] also asserted and publicly declared that certain articles, hereafter described and many others meriting condemnation, are catholic, which are notoriously contained in the books and minor works of that John Hus.

On that account, having first been fully informed of the said matters, and after a diligent deliberation by the most reverend fathers in Christ of the holy Roman Church, ... this sacrosanct Synod of Constance declares and defines that the articles hereafter described are not catholic, nor are to be taught as such, but many of them are erroneous, others scandalous, others offensive to pious ears, and many of

---

7 Source: Matthew Spinka, ed. and trans., *John Hus at the Council of Constance*, Records of Civilization, Sources and Studies (New York: Columbia University Press, 1965), 295–98.

8 The Rome council took place in 1412.

9 Now the text is referring to Hus.

them are rash and seditious, and several of them are notoriously heretical.... They have been already long ago reprobated and condemned by the holy fathers and general Councils, and strictly prohibited to be preached, taught, or approved in any manner. But because the hereafter articles are expressly contained in his books and his treatises, namely, in the book entitled *De Ecclesia*[10] and others of his minor works; therefore, the above-named books and his teachings and every other treatise and minor work... this sacrosanct Synod reprobates and condemns, and decrees and defines that they be solemnly and publicly burned in the presence of the clergy and the people of the city of Constance....

By these testimonies of the witnesses it is most plainly evident that he, John Hus, had taught many evil, offensive, seditious, and dangerous heresies and had publicly preached them during the course of many years. Therefore, invoking the name of Christ, this sacrosanct Synod of Constance, having God alone before its eyes and being legitimately assembled by the Holy Spirit, by this definitive sentence set forth in these presents[11] pronounces, decrees, and declares the said John Hus to have been and still to be a veritable and manifest heretic and that his errors and heresies have long ago been condemned by the Church of God, and are now condemned, and that he had taught and publicly preached many things scandalous, offensive to pious ears, rash and seditious, to the unmitigated offense of the divine Majesty and of the universal Church, to the detriment of the catholic faith. He had also despised the keys of the Church and ecclesiastical censures, in which he had persisted for many years in an obdurate spirit, offending Christ's faithful by his excessive obstinacy, contemning the due ecclesiastical process by resorting to an appeal to the Lord Jesus Christ as to the supreme judge, and stating in it many false, injurious, and offensive things in contempt even of the Apostolic See as well as of ecclesiastical censures and keys....

Truly on account of these things that this sacred Synod has seen and heard, it recognizes that John Hus is obstinate and incorrigible, and as such does not desire to return into the bosom of the holy mother Church, nor is willing to recant the heresies and errors publicly defended and preached by him, but even now defends and preaches them. For that reason, this sacred Council declares and decrees that John Hus be deposed and degraded from the priestly order....

This sacrosanct Synod of Constance, seeing that the Church of God has nothing more it can do with John Hus, relinquishes him to the secular judgment and decrees that he be relinquished to the secular court.

----

[10] *The Church* (see previous text, doc. 4).

[11] I.e., in this proclamation.

III. SCHOLASTICISM AND HUMANISM

The dominant form of theological education and discussion in the late Middle Ages is known as scholastic theology, or simply scholasticism. Scholasticism emerged in the eleventh and twelfth centuries as a way to understand Christian doctrine through the use of reason and philosophy. As St. Anselm famously wrote, it was an exercise in "faith seeking understanding" (*fides quaerens intellectum*).

The best known practitioner of this kind of theology was St. Thomas Aquinas (1225–74), whose enormous *Summa Theologica* explores nearly every facet of Christian belief and practice in great detail and with rigorous systematic thought. Every question in the *Summa* follows the same format: Question, objections, contrary proof text, Aquinas's answer, reply to objections; you will see this illustrated in the text below (doc. 6). The excerpt from the *Summa* included here is on transubstantiation, for the interpretation of the Eucharist was arguably the single most divisive issue of the Reformation. It pitted Protestants against each other as well as against the Catholic Church. Aquinas neatly sets out here the basic position that the Catholic Church would retain and reaffirm during the Reformation. It is based on an Aristotelian distinction between "substance" (the essence or true nature of a thing) and "accidents" (the way it appears to the senses).

By the time of the Reformation, scholasticism faced a powerful new challenge from humanism, an entirely different method of study that emerged during the Renaissance. Humanism was an attempt to revive the *studia humanitatis*, or the humanities. Humanists believed that more profit could be derived from reading classical literature and studying rhetoric, history, and moral philosophy than from studying scholastic theology. To the humanists, the scholastics were obsessed with absurd questions like "How many angels can dance on the head of a pin." Humanists like Francesco Petrarch, by contrast, believed that "it is better to will the good than to know the truth" of such meaningless questions.

Erasmus of Rotterdam (c. 1466–1536) is known as the "Prince of the Humanists" and was tremendously popular during his time. Several of Erasmus's texts are included in this reader, for he was the most important voice for church reform in the period before Luther and well into the early years of the Reformation. The famous maxim has it that "Erasmus laid the egg that Luther hatched." Partly, he is said to have done so through his biting critiques of the church and "superstition" (see below, doc. 9). But Erasmus was also instrumental in setting the stage for Luther through his biblical scholarship and calls to follow the "philosophy of Christ." The second text below, Erasmus's *Paraclesis* (which means "exhortation"), was the preface to his *Novum Instrumentum*, the first-ever printed edition of the Greek New Testament.

Focus Questions

1. What does the doctrine of transubstantiation hold?
2. How does Erasmus justify the use of vernacular Bible translations?
3. How would you summarize Erasmus's "philosophy of Christ"?
4. What criticism of theologians does Erasmus offer? According to him, what should a true theologian teach?
5. How do Thomas Aquinas's and Erasmus's writing styles and argumentative methods differ?
6. Based on these two texts, what would you say are the key differences between scholasticism and humanism? Which do you find more attractive, and why?

6. Thomas Aquinas, *Summa Theologica*, III.75(2), Transubstantiation, 1274[12]

Question: Whether in this sacrament [of the Eucharist] the substance of the bread and wine remains after the consecration?

Objection 1. It seems that the substance of the bread and wine does remain in this sacrament after the consecration: because

---

[12] Source: St. Thomas Aquinas, *The "Summa Theologica" of St. Thomas Aquinas, Part III*, trans. The Fathers of the English Dominican Province (New York: Benziger Brothers, 1914), 3:266–68, text modernized.

John of Damascus says, "Since it is customary for men to eat bread and drink wine, God has wedded his Godhead to them, and made them His body and blood"; and further on: "The bread of communication is not simple bread, but is united to the Godhead." But wedding together belongs to things actually existing. Therefore, the bread and wine are at the same time in this sacrament with the body and the blood of Christ.

Objection 2. Further, there ought to be conformity between the sacraments. But in the other sacraments the substance of the matter remains, like the substance of water in Baptism, and the substance of chrism in Confirmation. Therefore, the substance of the bread and wine remains also in this sacrament.

Objection 3. Further, bread and wine are made use of in this sacrament, inasmuch as they denote ecclesiastical unity, as "one bread is made from many grains and wine from many grapes," as Augustine says in his book on the Creed. But this belongs to the substance of bread and wine. Therefore, the substance of the bread and wine remains in this sacrament.

On the contrary, Ambrose says: "Although the figure of the bread and wine be seen, still, after the consecration, they are to be believed to be nothing else than the body and blood of Christ."

I answer that, Some have held that the substance of the bread and wine remains in this sacrament after the consecration. But this opinion cannot stand: first of all, because by such an opinion the truth of this sacrament is destroyed, to which it belongs that Christ's true body exists in this sacrament, which, indeed, was not there before the consecration. Now a thing cannot be in any place, where it was not previously, except by change of place, or by the conversion of another thing into itself, just as fire begins anew to be in some house, either because it is carried there or because it is generated there. Now, it is evident that Christ's body does not begin to be present in this sacrament by local motion. First of all, because it would follow that it would cease to be in heaven, for what is moved locally does not come anew to some place unless it quit the former one. Secondly, because every body moved locally passes through all intermediary spaces, which cannot be said here. Thirdly, because it is not possible for one movement of the same body moved locally to be terminated in different places at the same time, whereas the body of Christ under this sacrament begins at the same time to be in several places. Consequently, it remains that Christ's body cannot begin to be anew in this sacrament except by change of the substance of bread into itself. But what is changed into another thing no longer remains after such change. Hence, the conclusion is that, saving the truth of this sacrament, the substance of the bread cannot remain after the consecration.

Secondly, because this position is contrary to the form of this sacrament, in which it is said: "This is my body," which would not be true if the substance of the bread were to remain there, for the substance of bread never is the body of Christ. Rather should one say in that case: "Here is my body."

Thirdly, because it would be opposed to the veneration of this sacrament, if any substance were there, which could not be adored with adoration of *latria*.[13]

Fourthly, because it is contrary to the rite of the Church, according to which it is not lawful to take the body of Christ after bodily food, while it is nevertheless lawful to take one consecrated host after another. Hence, this opinion [that the bread and wine remain after consecration] is to be avoided as heretical.

Reply to Objection 1. God "wedded his Godhead," i.e. his divine power, to the bread and wine,

not that these may remain in this sacrament, but in order that he may make from them his body and blood.

Reply to Objection 2. Christ is not really present in the other sacraments, as in this; therefore, the substance of the matter remains in the other sacraments but not in this.

Reply to Objection 3. The species which remain in this sacrament, as shall be said later, suffice for its signification; because the nature of the substance is known by its accidents.

7. Erasmus of Rotterdam, *Paraclesis*, 1516[14]

[I]n the first place it is not pleasing to renew at the present time this complaint, not entirely new but, alas, only too just—and perhaps never more just than in these days—that when men are devoting themselves with such ardent spirit to all their studies, this philosophy of Christ alone is derided by some, even Christians, is neglected by many, and is discussed by a few, but in a cold manner (I shall not say insincerely). Moreover, in all other branches of learning which human industry has brought forth, nothing is so hidden and obscure which the keenness of genius has not explored, nothing is so difficult which tremendous exertion has not overcome. Yet

how is it that even those of us who profess to be Christian fail to embrace with the proper spirit this philosophy alone? Platonists, Pythagoreans, Academics, Stoics, Cynics, Peripatetics, Epicureans not only have a deep understanding of the doctrines of their respective sects, but they commit them to memory, and they fight fiercely in their behalf, willing even to die rather than abandon the defense of their author. Then why do not we evince far greater spirit for Christ, our Author and Prince?... Certainly He alone was a teacher who came forth from heaven, He alone could teach certain doctrine, since it is eternal wisdom, He alone, the sole author of

---

[13] The medieval church distinguished between two kinds of veneration: *latria* or true worship, which could be offered only to God, and *dulia* or honor or reverence, which could be offered to the saints.

[14] Source: John C. Olin, ed., *Christian Humanism and the Reformation: Selected Writings of Erasmus*, rev. ed. (New York: Fordham University Press, 1965), 94–98.

human salvation, taught what pertains to salvation, He alone fully vouches for whatsoever He taught, He alone is able to grant whatsoever He has promised....

Why, then, out of pious curiosity do we not investigate, examine, explore each tenet [of this philosophy]? Especially since this kind of wisdom, so extraordinary that once for all it renders foolish the entire wisdom of this world, may be drawn from its few books as from the most limpid springs with far less labor than Aristotle's doctrine is extracted from so many obscure volumes.... Indeed, here there is no requirement that you approach equipped with so many troublesome sciences. The journey is simple, and it is ready for anyone. Only bring a pious and open mind, possessed above all with a pure and simple faith. Only be docile, and you have advanced far in this philosophy.... This doctrine in an equal degree accommodates itself to all, lowers itself to the little ones, adjusts itself to their measure, nourishing them with milk, bearing, fostering, sustaining them, doing everything until we grow in Christ.... It casts aside no age, no sex, no fortune or position in life. The sun itself is not as common and accessible to all as is Christ's teaching. It keeps no one at a distance, unless a person, begrudging himself, keeps himself away.

Indeed, I disagree very much with those who are unwilling that Holy Scripture, translated into the vulgar tongue, be read by the uneducated, as if Christ taught such intricate doctrines that they could scarcely be understood by very few theologians, or as if the strength of the Christian religion consisted in men's ignorance of it. The mysteries of kings, perhaps, are better concealed, but Christ wishes his mysteries published as openly as possible. I would that even the lowliest women read the Gospels and the Pauline Epistles. And I would that they were translated into all languages so that they could be read and understood not only by Scots and Irish but also by Turks and Saracens. Surely the first step is to understand in one way or another. It may be that many will ridicule, but some may be taken captive. Would that, as a result, the farmer sing some portion of them at the plow, the weaver hum some parts of them to the movement of his shuttle, the traveller lighten the weariness of the journey with stories of this kind! Let all the conversations of every Christian be drawn from this source. For in general our daily conversations reveal what we are. Let each one comprehend what he can, let him express what he can. Whoever lags behind, let him not envy him who is ahead; whoever is in the front rank, let him encourage him who follows, not despair of him. Why do we restrict a profession common to all to a few? For it is not fitting, since Baptism is common in an equal degree to all Christians, wherein there is the first profession of Christian philosophy, and since the other sacraments and at length the reward of immortality belong equally to all, that doctrines alone should be reserved for those very few whom today the crowd call theologians or monks, the very persons whom, although they comprise one of the smallest parts of the Christian populace, yet I might wish to be in greater measure what they are styled. For I fear that one may find among the theologians men who are far removed from the title they bear, that is, men who discuss earthly matters, not divine, and that among the monks who profess the poverty of Christ and the contempt of the world you may find something more than worldliness. To me he is truly a theologian who teaches not by skill with intricate syllogisms but by a disposition of mind, by the very expression and the eyes, by his very life that riches should be disdained, that the Christian should not put his trust in the supports of this world but must rely entirely on heaven, that a wrong should not be avenged, that a good should be wished for those wishing ill, that we should deserve well of those deserving ill, that all good men should be loved and cherished equally as members of the same body, that the evil should be tolerated if they cannot be corrected, that those who are stripped of their goods, those who are turned away from possessions, those who mourn are blessed and should not be deplored, and that death should even be desired by the devout, since it is nothing other than a passage to immortality. And if anyone under the inspiration of the spirit of Christ preaches this kind of doctrine, inculcates it, exhorts, incites, and encourages men to it, he indeed is truly a theologian, even if he should be a common laborer or weaver. And if anyone exemplifies this doctrine in his life itself, he is in fact a great doctor. Another, perhaps, even a non-Christian, may discuss more subtly how the angels understand, but to persuade us to lead here an angelic life, free from every stain, this indeed is the duty of the Christian theologian.

IV. LAY PIETY

In the first three sections we looked at late medieval religion from the perspective of the elites. In this section, we examine instead the religion of the common people. The surviving evidence suggests that many late medieval lay people were deeply and increasingly engaged with their faith in the years before the Reformation.

Central to late medieval piety was the notion that the divide between heaven and earth could be bridged by holy people (the saints) and objects (relics). The saints were seen as intercessors between humans and God and were believed to have great power. Thus, people prayed to them, took pilgrimages to their shrines, and venerated their relics. The first text below illustrates the belief in the power of relics.

The author, Caesarius of Heisterbach (c. 1180–1240), was a Cistercian monk who wrote a collection of stories illustrating the power of relics and the saints, entitled the *Dialogue on Miracles*. These stories, also known as *exempla* (examples), would often be inserted into late medieval sermons to illustrate points the preacher wanted to make to his congregation.

The second text is from Erasmus (see also above, §III), who takes a satirical view of pilgrimages and relics. Note that he wrote this text after Luther had arrived on the scene. Erasmus never joined the Protestant movement, but he continued his attacks on what he saw as the superstition of much Christian practice. This text is from his *Colloquies*, a popular collection of stories told in dialogue, many of which mocked the practices of late medieval Catholicism.

Focus Questions

1. Compare Caesarius's and Erasmus's treatments of saints and relics. How do their perspectives differ? Do they seem to agree or disagree on how relics were actually used and viewed by the common people in the Middle Ages?
2. Why does Caesarius extol the power of relics?
3. On what bases does Erasmus criticize them? Rather than building expensive shrines and going on pilgrimages, what does he suggest Christians would be better off doing?
4. People still make pilgrimages of all kinds, both religious and secular. The pilgrimage trail to the shrine of St. James in Santiago de Compostela, Spain, for example, is still frequently traveled. A baseball fan might make a "pilgrimage" to Cooperstown, New York to see the Hall of Fame and its "relics." What similarities and differences do you see between medieval and modern pilgrimages? Between sacred and secular ones? Why does traveling to shrines of various sorts elicit such a powerful human response?

8. Caesarius of Heisterbach, *Dialogue on Miracles*, Early Thirteenth Century[15]

A. *"Virgin in Place of a Nun Who Had Fled from the Convent"*

Not many years ago, in a certain monastery of nuns, of which I do not know the name, there lived a virgin named Beatrix. She was beautiful in form, devout of mind, and most fervent in the service of the Mother of God. As often as she could offer secretly to the Virgin special prayers and supplications, she held them for her dearest delight. Indeed, having been made custodian, she did this more devoutly because more freely.

A certain cleric, seeing and lusting after her, began to tempt her. When she spurned the words of lust, and on that account he insisted the more strenuously, the old serpent enkindled her breast so vehemently that she could not bear the flames of love. Therefore, coming to the altar of the Blessed Virgin, the patroness of the oratory, she spoke thus: "Mistress, I have served you as devoutly as I could; behold, I resign your keys to you; I cannot withstand the temptations of the flesh any longer." And, having placed the keys on the altar, she secretly followed the cleric.

When that wretched man had corrupted her, he abandoned her after a few days. Since she had no means of living and was ashamed to return to the convent, she became a harlot. After she had continued in that vice publicly for fifteen years, she came one day in a lay habit to the door of the monastery. She said to the doorkeeper, "Did you know Beatrix, formerly custodian of this oratory?" The latter replied, "I knew her very well. For she is an honest and holy woman, and from infancy even to the present day she has remained in this monastery without fault." When she, hearing the words but not understanding them, wished to go away, the Mother of Mercy appeared in her well-known image and said to her, "During the fifteen years of your absence, I have performed your task; now return to your place and do penance; for no one knows of your departure." In fact, in the form and dress of that woman, the Mother of God had performed the duties of custodian. Beatrix entered at once and returned thanks as long as she lived, revealing through confession what had been done for her.

B. *"Concerning a Merchant to Whom a Harlot Sold the Arm of St. John the Baptist"*

Not long ago a certain merchant of our country, crossing the sea, saw the arm of St. John the

---

[15] Source: Department of History of the University of Pennsylvania, *Translations and Reprints from the Original Sources of European History* (Philadelphia: University of Pennsylvania Press, [1897?–1907?]), vol. 2, no. 4:4–5; 11–13, text modernized.

Baptist in his hospital and desired it. Knowing that the custodian of the relics was following a certain woman, and knowing that there is nothing which women of that class cannot extort from men, he approached her and said, "If you will procure for me the relics of St. John the Baptist of which your lover has the charge, I will give you a hundred and forty pounds of silver." She, craving the sum offered, refused to consent to the Hospitaler until he obtained the sacred arm. This she immediately delivered to the merchant and received the promised weight of silver.

Do you perceive how great a mockery? Just as formerly the head of St. John was delivered by Herod to a lascivious girl as a reward for dancing, and by her was given to an adulterous mother [cf. Mark 6:14–29], so at this time, the Hospitaler, no less wicked than Herod, gave the arm of the same saint to a base woman as the price of fornication, and by her it was sold to the merchant. The latter, not consigning it to the ground like Herodias, but wrapping it in purple, fled almost to the extremities of the earth and arrived at the city of Gröningen, which is situated at the entrance to Frisia. There he built a house and, hiding the arm in one of the columns, began to grow exceedingly wealthy. One day when he was sitting in his shop, someone said to him, "The city is burning and the fire is now approaching your house." He replied, "I do not fear for my house; I have left a good guardian there." Nevertheless he arose and entered his house. When he saw the column unmoved he returned to his shop. All wondered what the cause of his great confidence was.

When questioned about the guardian of his house, he replied ambiguously, but when he realized that his fellow citizens noted it, fearing that they might employ violence against him, he took out the arm and delivered it into the care of a certain hermitess. She, unable to keep the secret, told a man of her charge, and he told the citizens. They immediately took the relics and carried them to the church. When the merchant tearfully requested his relics, they replied harshly. When they asked him which saint these relics were from, not wishing to betray the facts, he said he did not know. Nevertheless, in grief he deserted the city and, falling into poverty, he became very ill not long after. When he feared death, he disclosed to his confessor what the relics were and how he had obtained them.

When the citizens learned this, they made a receptacle in the form of an arm, of silver and gold, adorned with precious stones, and placed the relics in it. I saw the same arm two years ago, and it is covered with skin and flesh. I also saw there among the relics a small gold cross of Frederick the Emperor, which had been given to the above mentioned merchant at the same time as the arm.

Novice: Since no one of the saints is believed to be greater than St. John the Baptist, why is it that we do not read of any miracle in his life?

Monk: So that God may show that holiness does not consist in miracles, but in right living. For after death he was illustrious by innumerable and great miracles. The aforesaid citizens, in truth, fearing for the relics of St. John, built of planks a very strong little house behind the altar, and by night they had a priest sleep in the top of it. The house was so shaken under him on the first night that he felt no slight horror. In the second night, truly it struck him when asleep and hurled him onto the pavement. When one of the rulers of the city fell sick, at his request Theodoric, the priest of the church, carried the arm to his house and unwrapped it. He found the arm, as well as the purple in which it was wrapped, covered with fresh blood. He told me this with his own mouth. A priest cut off a small piece of flesh from the same arm, and when he carried it off secretly in his hand, he felt as much heat from it as if he had been carrying burning coal. Many miracles and hearings indeed were wrought in that city by the same relics through the merits of St. John the Baptist.

9. Erasmus, *Colloquies*, "The Religious Pilgrimage," 1526[16]

Dialogue Characters: Menedemus, Ogygius

[Ogygius tells Menedemus about his trip to the shrine of the Virgin Mary in England]

OGYGIUS: [W]e turned to the heavenly milk of the Blessed Virgin.

MENEDEMUS: O Mother most like her Son! He left us so much of his blood on earth; she left so much of her milk that it's scarcely credible a woman with only one child could have so much, even if the child had drunk none of it.

OGYGIUS: The same thing is said about the Lord's cross, which is exhibited publicly and privately in so many places that if the fragments were joined together they'd seem a full load for a freighter. And yet the Lord carried his whole cross.

MENEDEMUS: Doesn't it seem amazing to you, too?

OGYGIUS: Unusual, perhaps, but by no means amazing, since the Lord, who multiplies these things as he wills, is omnipotent.

MENEDEMUS: You explain it reverently, but for my part I'm afraid many such affairs are contrived for profit.

OGYGIUS: I don't think God will stand for anybody mocking him in that way.

MENEDEMUS: On the contrary, though Mother and Son and Father and Spirit are robbed by the sacrilegious, sometimes they don't even bestir themselves slightly enough to frighten off the criminals by a nod or a noise. So great is the mildness of divinity.

OGYGIUS: That's true. But hear the rest. This milk is kept on the high altar, in the midst of which is Christ; on the right, for the sake of honor, is his Mother. For the milk represents his Mother.

[16] Source: Erasmus, *Colloquies*, Collected Works of Erasmus 39–40, trans. Craig R. Thompson, 2 vols. (Toronto: University of Toronto Press, 1997), 2:632–33, 641, 642–44, 650.

MENEDEMUS: So it's in plain sight.

OGYGIUS: Enclosed in crystal, that is.

MENEDEMUS: Therefore liquid.

OGYGIUS: What do you mean, liquid, when it flowed fifteen hundred years ago? It's hard; you'd say powdered chalk, tempered with white of egg.

MENEDEMUS: Why don't they display it exposed?

OGYGIUS: To save the virginal milk from being defiled by the kisses of men.

MENEDEMUS: Well said, for in my opinion there are those who would bring neither clean nor chaste mouths to it.

OGYGIUS: When the guide saw us, he rushed up, donned a linen vestment, threw a sacred stole around his neck, prostrated himself devoutly, and adored. Next he held out the sacred milk for us to kiss. We prostrated ourselves devoutly on the lowest step of the altar and, after first saluting Christ, addressed to the Virgin a short prayer I had prepared for this occasion: "Virgin Mother, who hast had the honor of suckling at thy maidenly breast the Lord of heaven and earth, thy Son Jesus, we pray that, cleansed by his blood, we may gain that blessed infancy of dovelike simplicity which, innocent of all malice, deceit, and guile, longs without ceasing for the milk of gospel doctrine until it attains to the perfect man, to the measure of the fullness of Christ, whose blessed company thou enjoyest forever, with the Father and Holy Spirit. Amen."

MENEDEMUS: Certainly a devout intercession. What response did she make?

OGYGIUS: Mother and Son both seemed to nod approval, unless my eyes deceived me. For the sacred milk appeared to leap up, and the Eucharistic elements gleamed somewhat more brightly. Meanwhile the custodian approached us, quite silent, but holding out a board, like those used in Germany by toll collectors on bridges.

MENEDEMUS: Yes, I've often cursed those greedy boards when travelling through Germany.

OGYGIUS: We gave him some coins, which he offered to the Virgin. Next, through an interpreter who understands the language well,... I inquired as civilly as I could what proof he had that this was the Virgin's milk. I wanted to know this clearly for the pious purpose of stopping the mouths of certain unbelievers who are accustomed to laugh at all these matters. At first the guide frowned and said nothing. I told the interpreter to press him, but even more politely. He did so with the utmost grace, such that if with words of that sort he had entreated the Mother herself, recently out of childbed, she would not have taken offence. But the guide, as if possessed, gazed at us in astonishment, and as though horrified by such blasphemous speech, said, "What need is there to inquire into that when you have an authentic record?" And it looked very much as if he would throw us out as heretics, except that we calmed the fellow's wrath with a bit of money....

MENEDEMUS: Did you overlook Thomas, archbishop of Canterbury?[17]

OGYGIUS: By no means. No pilgrimage is more devout.

MENEDEMUS: I long to hear about it, if that's not too much trouble.

OGYGIUS: Oh, no, I want you to hear.... Iron screens prevent you from going further, but they permit a view of the space between the end of the building and the choir, as it is called. This is ascended by many steps, under which a certain vault gives access to the north side. A wooden altar sacred to the Holy Virgin is shown there, a very small one, not worth seeing except as a monument of antiquity, a rebuke to the luxury of our times. There the holy man is said to have spoken his last farewell to the Virgin when death was at hand. On the altar is the point of the sword with which the crown of the good bishop's head was cut off, and his brain smashed, evidently to make death come more quickly. Out of love for the martyr we reverently kissed the sacred rust of his sword.

Leaving this place, we went down into the crypt. It has its own custodians. First is shown the martyr's skull, pierced through. The top of the cranium is bared for kissing; the rest covered with silver.... The hairshirt, girdle, and drawers by which the bishop used to subdue his flesh hang in the gloom there—horrible even to look at and a reproach to our softness and delicacy.

MENEDEMUS: Perhaps to the monks themselves, too.

OGYGIUS: I can neither affirm nor deny that, nor is it any of my business.

MENEDEMUS: Very true.

OGYGIUS: From here we return to the choir. On the north side mysteries are laid open. It is wonderful how many bones were brought forth—skulls, jaws, teeth, hands, fingers, whole arms, all of which we adored and kissed. This would have gone on forever if my fellow pilgrim, an unobliging chap, had not cut short the enthusiasm of the guide.

MENEDEMUS: Who was this?

OGYGIUS: An Englishman named Gratian Pullus,[18] a learned and upright man but

---

[17] Thomas Becket, archbishop of Canterbury from 1162 to 1170, was murdered in Canterbury Cathedral, possibly on the order of King Henry II. He was almost instantly proclaimed a martyr, and his shrine in the cathedral became a popular pilgrimage destination. The shrine was destroyed and the gold melted down by Henry VIII a few years after this text was written, and so Erasmus's description of the site here is one of the best ones available.

[18] Probably intended to refer to John Colet (*pullus* means colt), dean of St. Paul's Cathedral in London and a fellow humanist. Erasmus refers in at least two other places in his writings to his visit to Canterbury with Colet.

less respectful towards this side of religion than I liked.

MENEDEMUS: Some Wycliffite,[19] I suppose.

OGYGIUS: I don't think so, although he had read his books. Where he got hold of them isn't clear.

MENEDEMUS: Did he offend the custodian?

OGYGIUS: An arm was brought forth, with the bloodstained flesh still on it. He shrank from kissing this, looking rather disgusted. The custodian soon put his things away. Next we viewed the altar table and ornaments; then the objects that were kept under the altar—all of them splendid; you'd say Midas and Croesus were beggars if you saw the quantity of gold and silver....

Next we were led up above, for behind the high altar you ascend as though into a new church. There in a small chapel is shown the entire countenance of the saint, gilded and ornamented with many jewels. Here a certain unlooked-for accident almost upset all our good luck.

MENEDEMUS: I'm waiting to hear what misfortune you mean.

OGYGIUS: My friend Gratian was far from gracious on this occasion. After a short prayer he asked the keeper, "I say, good father, is it true, as I've heard, that in his lifetime Thomas was most generous to the poor?"

"Very true," the man replied, and began to rehearse the saint's many acts of kindness to them.

Then Gratian: "I don't suppose his disposition changed in this matter, unless perhaps for the better."

The custodian agreed.

Gratian again: "Since, then, the saint was so liberal towards the needy, though he was still poor himself and lacked money to provide for the necessities of life, don't you think he'd gladly consent, now that he's so rich and needs nothing, if some poor wretched woman with hungry children at home, or daughters in danger of losing their virtue because they have no money for dowries, or a husband sick in bed and penniless— if, after begging the saint's forgiveness, she carried off a bit of all this wealth to rescue her family, as though taking from one who wanted her to have it, either as a gift or a loan?" When the keeper in charge of the gilded head made no reply to this, Gratian, who's impulsive, said, "For my part, I'm convinced the saint would rejoice that in death, too, he could relieve the wants of the poor by his riches." At this the custodian frowned and pursed his lips, looking at us as with Gorgon eyes, and I don't doubt he would have driven us from the church with insults and reproaches had he not been aware that we were recommended by the archbishop. I managed to placate the fellow somehow by smooth talk, affirming that Gratian hadn't spoken seriously but liked to joke; and at the same time I gave him some coins.

MENEDEMUS: I quite approve of your sense of duty. But seriously, I wonder sometimes

---

[19] A reference to John Wyclif (see above, the introduction to §II).

what possible excuse there could be for those who spend so much money on building, decorating, and enriching churches that there's simply no limit to it. Granted that the sacred vestments and vessels of the church must have a dignity appropriate to their liturgical use; and I want the building to have grandeur. But what's the use of so many baptistries, candelabra, gold statues? What's the good of the vastly expensive organs, as they call them? (We're not content with a single set, either.) What's the good of that costly musical neighing when meanwhile our brothers and sisters, Christ's living temples, waste away from neglect and starvation?…

OGYGIUS: But look here: don't you itch to go on these pilgrimages?

MENEDEMUS: Maybe I'll itch after you've finished talking. As matters stand now, I have enough to do by going on my Roman stations.

OGYGIUS: Roman? You, who've never seen Rome?

MENEDEMUS: I'll tell you. Here's how I wander about at home. I go into the living room and see that my daughters' chastity is safe. Coming out of there into my shop, I watch what my servants, male and female, are doing. Then to the kitchen, to see if any instruction is needed. From here to one place and another, observing what my children and my wife are doing, careful that everything be in order. These are my Roman Stations.

OGYGIUS: But St. James will look after these affairs for you.

MENEDEMUS: Sacred Scripture directs me to take care of them myself. I've never read any commandment to hand them over to saints.

FURTHER READING

Augustijn, Cornelis. *Erasmus: His Life, Works, and Influence.* Erasmus Studies 10. Toronto: University of Toronto Press, 1991.

Christianson, Gerald, Thomas M. Izbicki, and Christopher M. Bellitto, eds. *The Church, the Councils, and Reform: The Legacy of the Fifteenth Century.* Washington, DC: Catholic University of America Press, 2008.

Duffy, Eamon. *The Stripping of the Altars: Traditional Religion in England, c.1400–c.1580.* New Haven, CT: Yale University Press, 1992.

Fudge, Thomas A. *Jan Hus: Religious Reform and Social Revolution in Bohemia.* New York: Palgrave Macmillan, 2010.

Jardine, Lisa. *Erasmus, Man of Letters: The Construction of Charisma in Print.* Princeton, NJ: Princeton University Press, 1993.

Lahey, Stephen E. *John Wyclif.* Oxford: Oxford University Press, 2009. http://dx.doi.org/10.1093/acprof:oso/9780195183313.001.0001.

Lambert, Malcolm. *Medieval Heresy: Popular Movements from the Gregorian Reform to the Reformation*, 3rd ed. Oxford: Blackwell, 2002.

Oakley, Francis. *The Conciliarist Tradition: Constitutionalism in the Catholic Church, 1300–1870*. Oxford: Oxford University Press, 2003.

Oakley, Francis. *The Western Church in the Later Middle Ages*. Ithaca, NY: Cornell University Press, 1979.

Rummel, Erika. *The Humanist-Scholastic Debate in the Renaissance and Reformation*. Harvard Historical Studies 120. Cambridge, MA: Harvard University Press, 1995.

Šmahel, František, ed. *A Companion to Jan Hus*. Brill's Companions to the Christian Tradition 54. Leiden: Brill, 2015.

Tracy, James. *Erasmus of the Low Countries*. Berkeley: University of California Press, 1996.

II

The Development of Martin Luther's Thought

Martin Luther (1483–1546) started the Protestant Reformation and shaped most of the teachings that would be embraced by Protestants everywhere. These included justification by grace alone (*sola gratia*) through faith alone (*sola fide*), the belief in the Bible as the sole basis of religious truth (*sola scriptura*), and the priesthood of all believers. They also entailed the rejection of the Catholic sacramental system, the cult of the saints, the veneration of relics, purgatory, indulgences, and perhaps above all, the papacy. Almost all Protestants of the Reformation period would share these ideas of Luther, even if they sometimes disagreed about their finer points or corollary doctrines. Thus, we must begin with an extensive examination of Luther's thought, especially in its early years, as it moved from a simple rejection of indulgences to a wholesale rejection of the late medieval religious system. As you read this chapter, ask yourself what was new in Luther's teachings, what he took from reformers before him, and why his ideas were so threatening to his Catholic opponents.

V. THE INDULGENCE CONTROVERSY

Traditionally, the Reformation is said to have begun on October 31, 1517, when Luther allegedly posted the Ninety-Five Theses to the castle church door in Wittenberg. There is some doubt about whether

Luther actually posted his theses to the door, but he did use that date on the letter he sent to Archbishop Albrecht of Mainz along with the theses. The theses themselves are not included here, for they are just that: a long list of individual statements intended to be debated, with no explanations attached to them.[1] Instead, the first text below is one of Luther's early elaborations on the theme of the Ninety-Five Theses, namely, the criticism of indulgences. An indulgence was an official statement from the church that removed the need to make satisfaction for one's sins in the sacrament of penance or helped to shorten a deceased loved one's time in purgatory. They had been offered for many years to those who performed good works, such as making pilgrimages or going to confession at certain times and places, particularly during Jubilee years. But by the sixteenth century, they were simply being sold outright. "When the coin in the coffer rings," quipped the indulgence sellers, "the soul from purgatory springs."

Luther's theses were prompted by the 1517 indulgence sale, initiated by Pope Leo X in order to raise money for rebuilding St. Peter's basilica in Rome (the church that still stands there today). Luther's *Sermon on Indulgences and Grace* was his first "bestseller"; it went through 14 editions in 1518 alone. Luther wrote the *Sermon* in German, in an early and largely successful effort to have his ideas read by commoners as well as educated churchmen. The person responsible for selling indulgences in and around Wittenberg, Johann Tetzel, is the author of the second document, which is a direct rebuttal of Luther's *Sermon* and, thus, a defense of indulgences.

Focus Questions

1. On what bases does Luther criticize indulgences and the sacrament of penance in the *Sermon on Indulgences and Grace*?

---

[1] The Ninety-Five Theses are easily found online.

2. What is Luther's attitude toward good works? What about purgatory, the pope, and the scholastic theologians?

3. What seems to be Luther's attitude toward the Catholic Church at this point? Does he seem to consider himself still a member of it or has he broken away from it?

4. What are Tetzel's chief arguments against Luther?

5. On what authorities do Luther and Tetzel rely? What do their choices reveal?

6. What does Tetzel predict will happen if people follow Luther's arguments?

10. Martin Luther, *Sermon on Indulgences and Grace*, 1518[2]

First, you should know that various new teachers such as the Master of the Sentences,[3] St. Thomas,[4] and their followers ascribe three parts to penance, namely contrition, confession, and satisfaction. And although this distinction according to their opinion is with difficulty or not at all to be found substantiated in Holy Scripture or in the ancient holy Christian teachers, nevertheless we will let it stand now as it is and speak in their manner....

Fourth, it is unquestioned by all of them that indulgence takes away those same works of satisfaction obligated by or imposed for sins. Thus, since it is supposed to take away all of these works, there would remain nothing else good for us to do....

Ninth, I say, even if the Christian church right now would decide and declare that indulgence removes more than the works of satisfaction, it would still be a thousand times better, if no Christian would buy or desire an indulgence but would rather do the works and bear the suffering. For indulgence is nothing else, and cannot become anything else, than a release from good works and wholesome suffering. Men should rightly welcome these rather than avoid them, in spite of the fact that some modern preachers have invented two kinds of suffering: remedial and satisfactory, that is, some suffering is for satisfaction, some for amending one's ways. But we have more freedom to disdain this and all such prattle (Thanks be to God!) than they do

---

[2] Source: Dewey Weiss Kramer, trans., *Johann Tetzel's Rebuttal against Luther's Sermon on Indulgences and Grace* (Atlanta: Pitts Theology Library, 2012), 12–32.

[3] Peter Lombard, author of the *Sentences*, the primary theological textbook of the late Middle Ages.

[4] St. Thomas Aquinas.

to invent it. For all suffering, indeed everything that God inflicts, is beneficial and useful for Christians....

Thirteenth, it is a great error that anyone would think that he would himself make satisfaction for his sins, since God forgives those same sins at all times for free, out of his inestimable grace, demanding nothing but that one live well from thence forward. Christianity, to be sure, does demand something, thus it can and should also cease doing this and not impose difficult and unbearable things....

Fifteenth, it would be far more positive and beneficial for a person to give to the building of St. Peter, or to whatever project is named, solely for the sake of God than to get an indulgence for so doing. For it is dangerous to make such a gift for the sake of an indulgence and not for the sake of God.

Sixteenth, far better is the good work shown a needy person than that given to a building. It is also far better than the indulgence granted for it. For as it is said: "Better is a good work done than much remitted." The indulgence, however, is the remittance of many good works, or else nothing is remitted.

Indeed, so that I instruct you correctly, pay attention. You should above all things (considering neither St. Peter's nor indulgence) give to your poor neighbor, if you want to give anything. But if it should happen that there is no one else in your city who needs help (which unless God will it, will never happen), then you should give as you will, to the churches, altars, jewels, chalices in your city. And when that too is now no longer necessary, then and only then may you give as you will to the building of St. Peter's or to anything

else. Nonetheless, that also you ought not to do for the sake of indulgences. For St. Paul says, "Whoever does not do good to his closest neighbor is no Christian and worse than a heathen" [1 Tim. 5:8]. And keep this in mind: whoever tells you otherwise is deceiving you or is really seeking your soul in your purse. And if he finds a penny therein, he would prefer that to every soul.

If you then declare, "Then I will never more buy an indulgence," I reply, "I have already said earlier that my will, desire, request, and advice is that no one seek an indulgence. Let lazy and sleepy Christians buy indulgences. You go your own way."...

Eighteenth, whether souls are drawn out of purgatory by indulgences, I do not know. Still, I do not believe so, although various modern scholars say so. But it is impossible for them to prove it, and furthermore, the Church has not yet come to a conclusion. Therefore, for greater certainty it is better that you pray for them and labor for them. For this is more proven and is certain.

Nineteenth, in these points I have no doubts and they are sufficiently grounded in Scripture. Therefore, you should also have no doubt and let the Scholastic Doctors remain Scholastics. Taken all together they are not enough with their opinions to substantiate a sermon.

Twentieth, whether some people reproach me as a heretic (for such a truth is quite injurious for their money boxes), I pay little heed to such babblings inasmuch as no one does so except some muddled brains who have never sniffed a Bible, have never read the Christian teachers, have never understood their own teachers but rather are decaying in their riddled and fragmented opinions. For if they had understood them, they would know that they should defame no one without hearing and challenging him.

Nonetheless, may God give them and us right understanding. Amen.

11. Johann Tetzel, *Rebuttal* against Luther's *Sermon on Indulgences and Grace*, 1518[5]

So that Christians not be unduly upset and misled by a sermon of twenty erroneous articles, presumptuously attacking aspects of the sacrament of penance and the truth of indulgences, which was printed and distributed during Lent, the title of which reads, *A Sermon on Indulgences and Grace*... I, Brother Johannes Tetzel, the Order of Preachers' inquisitor of heretics, have had that same sermon of twenty erroneous articles printed, together with its title, opening, and conclusion. And I refute each article of the named sermon with constant reference to Holy Scripture, as everyone will judge from the following pages....

[Luther's first article] is rebutted thusly in a Christian manner and on solid foundation: First, it is erroneous and unfounded, when it claims that the three parts of penance are not founded on Holy Scripture and on the ancient Christian teachers, wherein truth resides. For Scripture and the ancient and modern holy doctors, of whom there are many thousand, maintain that Almighty God wishes to have repayment and satisfaction for sin. For Christ our Lord commands sinners in the Gospel, "Bear fruit worthy of repentance" [Matt. 3:8]. This is interpreted and understood by all the holy doctors of the whole world to mean satisfying penance....

Priests, however, can neither recognize a person's contrition nor give them contrition. They possess merely the key of their office. Therefore, no matter how greatly a person repents of his sins or carries the cross, if he scorns confession or satisfaction as elements of the sacrament of penance, the pain due his sins will never be forgiven him....

[Luther's fourth article] is rebutted in this Christian manner: The plenary indulgence remits the works of satisfaction to this extent: whoever is granted complete remission of pain is freed through papal power so that he is no longer obligated to do those works of satisfaction ... which had been imposed upon him for repented and confessed sins. Yet after the complete forgiveness of sins and pain, a person is no less tempted by the devil, his own flesh, and the world than he was before forgiveness. And evil habits and the possibility of falling quickly into sin again remain after forgiveness of sins and suffering. Therefore, in order to resist the devil, the flesh and the world and to subdue evil, sinful habit, inclination, and the possibility of falling quickly into sin again, a

---

[5] Source: Kramer, *Johann Tetzel's Rebuttal*, 12–32.

man, after complete forgiveness of sins and suffering, dare not refrain from penitential works that are salvific for him and a medicine for his spiritual weakness and also helpful toward gaining eternal life.

Also, no papal or episcopal brief of indulgence maintains that people who earn an indulgence should refrain henceforth from good works and from making satisfaction. In fact, we owe it to the honor of the eternal Godhead to do good works, even had we not sinned, solely because of his creation. And when we have accomplished all the good works that are possible for us, then we should [still] say, "We are useless servants of God" [Luke 10:17]. For this reason, this article is completely erroneous and misleading, and fabricated solely to the disadvantage of indulgences....

[*On Luther's ninth article*] This erroneous article also indicates that no person should desire an indulgence, but also that the indulgence remits more from that person than the penance imposed by priest or canon law. These words contradict Christian truth. For with them the article maintains that a person may have an indulgence without contrition. Thus, it also separates the indulgence from contrition and the production of the good works for which indulgence is given. That can nevermore be substantiated in Christian doctrine. For those who earn an indulgence are living in a state of genuine contrition and in the love of God, which state does not allow them to remain lazy and slothful. Rather, it enflames them to serve God and do great works to honor him. For it is as clear as day that Christian, God-fearing, pious people, and not loose and lazy persons, earn indulgences with fervent desire....

[Luther's thirteenth article] is rebutted in Christian manner thusly: First, it is unfounded and misleading, for God, along with the Church, as shown repeatedly above, desires satisfaction for sins. This has been the conclusion of the ancient and modern doctors of Holy Church, of whom there are thousands and of whom many count among the saints in heaven. They all say that no matter how great contrition is, if a person scorns confession and acts of penance, then contrition alone will not help.... However, this erroneous article does not count as new, for Wycliffe and Johannes Hus also maintained this error: specifically, the idea that confession, in which acts of satisfaction are imposed upon a person, is not necessary. And for this reason Johannes Hus was burned at the stake by the ecumenical Council of Constance and Wycliffe died as a heretic.

[Luther's fifteenth article] is rebutted thusly in Christian manner: First, it is totally bare and naked and fabricated without any proof based on Holy Scripture, when it implies in its conclusion that a person could give alms merely for the sake of an indulgence and not for the sake of God. As though anyone would give alms for the sake of an indulgence without thereby also praising God! For just as surely as a person gives alms for an indulgence, so too he gives it for the sake of God. Indeed, all indulgences are given first of all for the glory of God....

[Luther's sixteenth article] is rebutted in Christian manner thusly: First, it is unfounded and entirely obscure, since it considers one matter and leaves the other matter unmentioned. For giving alms to a poor person is more beneficial for the earning of salvation, yet buying a

34

plenary—or indeed any indulgence—is more beneficial for the speedier satisfaction of punishment due to sin. Further, everyone should know that buying an indulgence is also a work of mercy. For whoever buys an indulgence takes pity on his soul and makes himself well-pleasing to God thereby....

[Luther's eighteenth article] is refuted thusly in Christian manner: First, it is full of malicious guile, when it claims that the Church has not concluded that souls can be delivered from purgatory through indulgences. For the tradition of the Roman Church does maintain that souls are delivered from purgatory by an indulgence. There are also very many altars, churches, and chapels in Rome, where souls are released by celebrating Masses or by doing other good works. This is so because the popes have granted plenary indulgences to these very places to release souls, whenever Mass is celebrated there or other good works are carried out, as is the practice in Rome. The pope and the Roman Church would not permit this release of souls in such manner in Rome, if it were not thoroughly established. For the pope and the holy See, as well as the papal office, do not err in matters that concern the faith.

Now indulgences also concern faith, for whoever does not believe that the pope can grant indulgences and plenary indulgences to the living and the dead—as long as they remain in God's love—that person maintains that the pope has not received complete authority from the Lord Christ over Christian believers, which contradicts sacred canon law....

[Luther's nineteenth article] is refuted in Christian manner accordingly: First, this article and all the articles cited are totally ungrounded in Scripture. For the articles contradict the practice of the holy Roman Church and the teaching of all modern, venerable Christian teachers....

[T]he holy Roman Church together with the whole community of sacred Christendom are in unanimous agreement that the revered venerable *"Doctores Scholasticos"*[6] buttress the holy Christian faith against the heretics with their truly salvific teaching based on solid Christian doctrine. And what is more, they are certainly able to preach a sermon! Thus this article makes sport of them quite unfairly and shamefully and contrary to all reason and truth.

Further, all the erroneous articles are characterized by abruptness and obscurity, perhaps because they are intended to be interpreted however one will and in any direction. The great scandal that they elicit, however, ought to have been considered beforehand. For because of them many people will hold the *magisterium* and jurisdiction of His Papal Holiness and the holy Roman See in contempt. The works of sacramental reparation will also cease. People will no longer believe preachers and theologians. Everyone will want to interpret Holy Scripture according to his own whim. Through this, all of holy Christendom must come into great spiritual danger, since each person will believe what best pleases him. In time,

---

[6] The Scholastic Doctors.

as the deceptive article announces, the modern revered theologians, in whom for many centuries Christianity has placed great confidence, shall no longer be considered credible. For these reasons this article is entirely erroneous.

[Luther's twentieth article is] refuted in a Christian and well-grounded manner: First, it is totally erroneous, and it requires no riddled brain to know who is a heretic....

From all this it will also become clear who "has a confused brain, who has never sniffed a Bible, never read the Christian masters, has never understood his own teachers." Therefore, I offer all of this rebuttal and my position that I have written regarding these matters for the consideration and judgment of His Holiness the Pope, the holy Roman Church, all trustworthy Christian universities, and doctors with sure trust in the truth, with the commitment to suffer whatever they judge just, [if any of it be heretical], be it through imprisonment, the stocks, drowning, or burning at the stake.

VI. LUTHER'S THREE TREATISES, PART 1:
ADDRESS TO THE CHRISTIAN NOBILITY
AND THE PRIESTHOOD OF ALL BELIEVERS

Luther hit his stride and developed his mature theology in a string of powerful works from 1520: *The Address to the Christian Nobility of the German Nation, The Babylonian Captivity of the Church*, and *The Freedom of a Christian*. These deservedly remain three of his best-known works. Together, they set forth for the first time the core elements of Luther's teachings: the priesthood of all believers, the rejection of the Catholic sacramental system, and justification by faith alone.

In the first of these treatises, the *Address to the Christian Nobility*, Luther again wrote in German rather than in Latin to the elite laity of Germany. In the excerpt below, he attacks the "three walls of the Romanists" that the pope and his followers have constructed to block efforts to reform the institutional church. Luther lays out his doctrine of the priesthood of all believers in this text and uses it as a basis for encouraging the German nobles to ignore the Romanists' "walls" and take church reform into their own hands.

Johannes Eck (1486–1543), a professor of theology at the University of Ingolstadt and a lifelong opponent of Luther, wrote the most popular sixteenth-century Catholic handbook for refuting Protestant teaching.

His *Enchiridion*, first published in 1525, appeared in 46 editions through 1576. In the excerpt below, Eck defends the Catholic understanding of the ordained priesthood.

Focus Questions

1. Identify Luther's "three walls," and summarize his argument against each.
2. The *Address to the Christian Nobility* contains an explanation of the doctrine of the priesthood of all believers. Explain it in your own words.
3. What is Eck's position with regard to the priesthood and the laity?
4. Why did Luther address this text to the German nobles and not to theologians or the clergy? Is he pandering? Were his goals realistic?
5. How do you think the German nobles would have received this text?
6. The term "vocation" literally means "calling," but we often use it today simply to mean "job." How might Luther's teaching have influenced this shift in meaning?

12. Luther, *Address to the Christian Nobility of the German Nation*, 1520[7]

The Three Walls of the Romanists

The Romanists, with great adroitness, have built three walls about them, behind which they have hitherto defended themselves in such a way that no one has been able to reform them, and this has been the cause of terrible corruption throughout all Christendom.

First, when pressed by the temporal power, they have made decrees and said that the temporal power has no jurisdiction over them, but, by contrast, that the spiritual is above the temporal power. Second, when the attempt is made to reprove them out of the Scriptures, they raise the objection that the interpretation of the

---

[7] Source: Henry Eyster Jacobs et al., eds., *Works of Martin Luther: With Introductions and Notes* (Philadelphia: A. J. Holman Company, 1915), 2:65–79, text modernized.

Scriptures belongs to no one except the pope. Third, if threatened with a council, they answer with the fable that no one can call a council but the pope.

In this way they have slyly stolen from us our three rods, so that they may go unpunished, and have ensconced themselves within the safe stronghold of these three walls, that they may practice all the knavery and wickedness which we now see.... Now God help us, and give us one of the trumpets with which the walls of Jericho were overthrown, that we may blow down these walls of straw and paper and may set free the Christian rods for the punishment of sin, bringing to light the craft and deceit of the devil, to the end that through punishment we may reform ourselves, and once more attain God's favor.

Against the first wall we will direct our first attack. It is pure invention that pope, bishops, priests, and monks are to be called the "spiritual estate" and princes, lords, artisans, and farmers the "temporal estate." That is indeed a fine bit of lying and hypocrisy. Yet no one should be frightened by it, and for this reason—namely, that all Christians are truly of the "spiritual estate," and there is among them no difference at all but that of office, as Paul says in I Corinthians 12:12, we are all one body, yet every member has its own work, whereby it serves every other, all because we have one baptism, one Gospel, one faith, and are all alike Christians; for baptism, Gospel, and faith alone make us "spiritual" and a Christian people.

But that a pope or a bishop anoints, confers tonsures, ordains, consecrates, or prescribes dress unlike that of the laity, this may make

hypocrites and graven images, but it never makes a Christian or "spiritual" man. Through baptism all of us are consecrated to the priesthood, as St. Peter says in I Peter 2:9, "You are a royal priesthood, a holy nation," and the book of Revelation says, "By your blood you have made them to be a kingdom and priests serving our God" (Rev. 5:10)....

To make it still clearer: If a little group of pious Christian laymen were taken captive and set down in a wilderness and had among them no priest consecrated by a bishop, and if there in the wilderness they were to agree in choosing one of themselves, married or unmarried, and were to charge him with the office of baptizing, saying Mass, absolving and preaching, such a man would be as truly a priest as though all bishops and popes had consecrated him. That is why in cases of necessity anyone can baptize and give absolution, which would be impossible unless we were all priests....

Therefore, a priest in Christendom is nothing else than an officeholder. While he is in office, he has precedence; when deposed, he is a peasant or a townsman like the rest. Beyond all doubt, then, a priest is no longer a priest when he is deposed. But now they have invented "indelible" characters and prate that a deposed priest is nevertheless something different from a mere layman. They even dream that a priest can never become a layman or be anything else than a priest. All this is mere talk and man-made law....

Therefore, just as those who are now called "spiritual"—priests, bishops or popes—are neither different from other Christians nor superior to them, except that they are charged with the administration of the word of God and the sacraments, which is their work and office, so it is with the temporal authorities; they bear sword and rod with which to punish the evil and to protect the good.…

On this account the Christian temporal power should exercise its office without let or hindrance, regardless whether it be pope, bishop, or priest whom it affects; whoever is guilty, let him suffer.… So then, I think this first paperwall is overthrown, since the temporal power has become a member of the body of Christendom, and is of the spiritual estate, though its work is of a temporal nature.…

The second wall is still more flimsy and worthless. They wish to be the only masters of the Holy Scriptures, even though in all their lives they learn nothing from them. They assume for themselves sole authority, and with insolent juggling of words they would persuade us that the pope, whether he be a bad man or a good man, cannot err in matters of faith, and yet they cannot prove a single letter of it.…

But not to fight them with mere words, we will quote the Scriptures. St. Paul says in I Corinthians 14:30: "If a revelation is made to someone else sitting nearby, let the first person be silent." What would be the use of this commandment, if we were only to believe him who does the talking or who has the highest seat? Christ also says in John 6:45 that all Christians shall be taught of God. Thus, it may well happen that the pope and his followers are wicked men and not true Christians, not taught of God, not having true understanding. On the other hand, an ordinary man may have true understanding; why then should we not follow him? Has not the pope erred many times? Who would help

Christendom when the pope errs, if we were not to believe another who had the Scriptures on his side more than the pope?

Therefore it is a wickedly invented fable, and they cannot produce a letter in defense of it, that the interpretation of Scripture or the confirmation of its interpretation belongs to the pope alone. They have themselves usurped this power, and although they allege that this power was given to Peter when the keys were given to him, it is plain enough that the keys were not given to Peter alone, but to the whole community. Moreover, the keys were not ordained for doctrine or government, but only for the binding and loosing of sin, and whatever further power of the keys they arrogate to themselves is mere invention.…

The third wall falls of itself when the first two are down. For when the Pope acts contrary to the Scriptures, it is our duty to stand by the Scriptures to reprove him and to constrain him, according to the word of Christ in Matthew 18:15[–17]: "If another member of the church sins against you, go and point out the fault when the two of you are alone. If you are not listened to, take one or two others along with you; if the member refuses to listen to them, tell it to the church; and if the offender refuses to listen even to the church, let such a one be to you as a Gentile and a tax collector." Here every member is commanded to care for every other. How much rather should we do this when the member that does evil is a ruling member, and by his evil-doing is the cause of much harm and offense to the rest! But if I am to accuse him before the Church, I must bring the Church together.

They have no basis in Scripture for their contention that it belongs to the pope alone to call a council or confirm its actions, for this is based merely upon their own laws, which are valid only in so far as they are not injurious to Christendom or contrary to the laws of God. When the pope deserves punishment, such laws go out of force, since it is injurious to Christendom not to punish him by means of a council.

Thus we read in Acts 15:6 that it was not St. Peter who called the Apostolic Council, but the apostles and elders. If, then, that right had belonged to St. Peter alone, the council would not have been a Christian council, but an heretical *conciliabulum*.[8] Even the Council of Nicaea—the most famous of all—was neither called nor confirmed by the Bishop of Rome, but by the Emperor Constantine, and many other emperors after him did the like, yet these councils were the most Christian of all. But if the pope alone had the right to call councils, then all councils must have been heretical. Moreover, if I consider the councils which the pope has created, I find that they have done nothing of special importance.

Therefore, when necessity demands, and the pope is an offense to Christendom, the first man who is able, a faithful member of the whole body, should do what he can to bring about a truly free council. No one can do this so well as the temporal authorities, especially since now they also are fellow-Christians, fellow-priests, "fellow-spirituals," fellow-lords-over-all-things, and whenever it is needful or profitable, they should give free course to office and work in which God has put them above every man. Would it not be an unnatural thing, if a fire broke out in a city, and everybody were to stand by and let it burn on and on and consume everything that could burn, for the sole reason that nobody had the authority of the burgomaster, or because, perhaps, the fire broke in the burgomaster's house? In such a case, is it not the duty of every citizen to arouse and call the rest? How much more should this be done in the spiritual city of Christ, if a fire of offense breaks out, whether in the papal government, or anywhere else?…

Thus I hope that the false, lying terror with which the Romans have this long time made our conscience timid and stupid has been allayed. They, like all of us, are subject to the temporal sword; they have no power to interpret the Scriptures by mere authority, without learning; they have no authority to prevent a council or, in sheer wantonness, to pledge it, bind it, or take away its liberty; but if they do this, they are in truth the communion of Antichrist and of the devil, and have nothing at all of Christ except the name.

---

[8] *Conciliabulum* literally means "little council," but it was frequently used to denounce councils that the church rejected as heretical.

13. Johannes Eck, *Enchiridion*, "The Sacrament of Holy Orders," 1555[9]

Thirteen hundred years ago, Tertullian taught that those Lutheran ordinations were common among the heretics. For they turn priests into laymen and give to laymen the duties of a priest. The way Luther tries to make priests is no different from how Pharaoh and the heathen made them. And in the same way, Scripture tells of Jeroboam, who created brand new priests from among the common people (1 Kings 12[:31]) and prohibited them from going to Jerusalem, just as Luther now forbids going to Rome.

The heretics claim, "All Christians are priests and are anointed into the priesthood through baptism." Catholics respond: It is clear that all the faithful are priests, just as they are all kings, but only in a spiritual manner. For God reigns in them through freely given love, and they in turn rule their senses and the power of their souls through the anointing of the Holy Spirit. But besides these needy "kings," there are also external kings and rulers in the Church. And so all the faithful are spiritual priests because they offer their faith and prayers to God, and this priesthood also has its ceremonies. But besides this internal priesthood, there is an external priesthood in the Church that has been bestowed upon certain individuals. Take another example: The faithful Christian is the temple of God, for Paul says, "You are God's holy temple" (1 Cor. 3[:16]).

But besides this "temple," there is the physical temple built in a certain place, where the faithful gather....

Hence, St. Augustine explains Revelation 20[:6] ("But they will be priests of God and of Christ, and they will reign with him a thousand years"), saying, "This refers not only to bishops and presbyters, who are now properly called priests in the church, but as we call all believers *Christians* on account of the mystical chrism, so we call all *priests* because they are members of the one Priest. Of them the Apostle Peter says, 'A holy people, a royal priesthood'[1 Peter 2:9]."...

Thus, there is an enormous difference between a priest and the priesthood, between the laity and the church hierarchy. The Lutherans sin, for they are deceived by a false equivalency and do not understand how in Holy Scripture the words *priest* and *priesthood* are used in some places to refer to those who are taken from among the people in order to perform the duties of praying and sacrificing for their own sins and for those of the people, and in other places, they refer to those over whom these priests are placed and for whom they sacrifice and pray.

The heretics say, "'For in the one Spirit we were all baptized into one body and we were all made to drink of one Spirit' (1 Cor. 12[:13]). It follows that we are all equally priests." Catholics

---

[9] Source: Johannes Eck, *Enchiridion locorum communorum adversus Lutherum et alios hostes Ecclesiae* (Lyon: Theobaldum Paganum, 1555), 93–96, translated by the editor.

respond: The heretics twist this passage, for even if we are all one body in Christ, how stupid would it be to infer that we are all hands, or that we are all feet, when there are differences even within the members themselves? Therefore, the different members stand together in the unity of the body.

We acknowledge that all Christians, even the laity, can make spiritual offerings and thus can be considered mystical priests, for they have built an altar of affection for God within themselves. But it does not follow that they are external, hierarchical priests.

VII. LUTHER'S THREE TREATISES, PART 2: *THE BABYLONIAN CAPTIVITY* AND THE SACRAMENTS

Luther followed the *Address to the Christian Nobility* with the *Babylonian Captivity of the Church*, which is an attack on the Catholic sacramental system. Luther addresses each of the Catholic Church's seven sacraments (baptism, the Eucharist, penance, confirmation, marriage, holy orders, and extreme unction), trying to show that each one either is not actually a sacrament or has been badly misunderstood and abused by the Catholic Church. The excerpt printed here focuses on the sacrament of the Eucharist. Bear in mind that in the medieval church, only the bread was given to the laity during communion, for fear that the common people might "spill the blood of Christ" if given the wine. Luther and all Protestants would argue instead for "communion in both kinds," giving both the bread and wine to all. Note, too, that the Catholic Church interpreted the Mass as a sacrifice; in essence, Jesus was believed to be offered up once again as a sacrifice "in an unbloody manner" as he once was offered on the cross. As such, this sacrifice of the Mass was also a "good work" which could be offered on behalf of souls in purgatory, and many Christians in their wills endowed masses to be said for their souls.[10]

We are fortunate to have a direct response to this text from a somewhat surprising source: King Henry VIII of England. While it is unlikely that Henry actually wrote the text,[11] it was published under his name

---

[10] For a much fuller discussion of this, see the Council of Trent's statement on the Mass as sacrifice (see below, doc. 48).

[11] The leading candidates for actual authorship of the text are Bishop John Fisher and Sir Thomas More.

and won for him—ironically in view of his later break from Rome—the title "Defender of the Faith" from the pope.

Focus Questions

1. What are the three "captivities" by which Luther says the Catholic Church has perverted the proper understanding of the Eucharist, and how does he refute them?
2. What position does Luther take on the proper understanding of the sacrament in general and on the presence of Christ's body in the Eucharist in particular?
3. Why does Luther believe that the interpretation of the Mass as a sacrifice has been so harmful?
4. How does Henry VIII attempt to refute Luther on each of the three captivities? Does he have the same position as Thomas Aquinas (see above, doc. 6)? What is Henry's general attitude toward Luther?
5. Why would a European monarch have wanted to get involved in a theological debate like this at the time?

14. Luther, *The Babylonian Captivity of the Church*, 1520[12]

Preface

At the outset, I must deny that there are seven sacraments, and hold for the present to but three—baptism, penance, and the bread. These three have been subjected to a miserable captivity by the Roman curia, and the Church has been deprived of all her liberty....

The Sacrament of the Bread

Now there are two passages that do clearly bear upon this matter: The Gospel narratives of the institution of the Lord's Supper and Paul in 1 Corinthians 11. Let us examine these.

Matthew, Mark, and Luke agree that Christ gave the whole sacrament to all the disciples, and

---

[12] Source: Jacobs et al., *Works of Martin Luther*, 2:177, 179–80, 186–90, 194, 199, 209–12, text modernized.

it is certain that Paul delivered both kinds. No one has ever had the temerity to assert the contrary. Further, Matthew reports that Christ did not say of the *bread*, "All of you, eat of it," but of the *cup*, "Drink of it all of you." Mark likewise does not say, "They all *ate* from it," but, "They all *drank* from it." Both Matthew and Mark attach the note of universality to the cup, not to the bread, as though the Spirit saw this schism coming, by which some would be forbidden to partake of the cup, which Christ desired should be common to all.... In the Lord's Supper, I say, the whole sacrament, or communion in both kinds, should either be given only to the priests or also to the laity. If it is given only to the priests, as they would have it, then it is not right to give it to the laity in either kind.... But if it is given also to the laity, then it inevitably follows that it ought not to be withheld from them in either form....

The first captivity of this sacrament, therefore, concerns its substance or completeness, of which we have been deprived by the despotism of Rome....

The second captivity of this sacrament is less grievous so far as the conscience is concerned, yet the very gravest danger threatens the man who would attack it, to say nothing of condemning it. Here I shall be called a Wycliffite and a heretic a thousand times over. But what of that? Since the Roman Bishop has ceased to be a bishop and become a tyrant, I fear none of his decrees, for I know that it is not in his power, nor even in that of a general council, to make new articles of faith. Years ago, when I was delving into scholastic theology, the Cardinal of Cambrai[13] gave me food for thought, in his comments on the fourth Book of the *Sentences*, where he argues with great acumen that to believe that real bread and real wine, and not their accidents only, are present on the altar, is much more probable and requires fewer unnecessary miracles—if only the Church had not decreed otherwise. When I learned later what church it was that had decreed this—namely, the Church of Thomas Aquinas, i.e., of Aristotle—I waxed bolder, and after floating in a sea of doubt, at last found rest for my conscience in the above view—namely, that it is real bread and real wine, in which Christ's real flesh and blood are present, not otherwise and not less really than they assume to be the case under their accidents. I reached this conclusion because I saw that the opinions of the Thomists,[14] though approved by pope and council, remain but opinions and do not become articles of faith, even though an angel from heaven were to decree otherwise. For what is asserted without Scripture or an approved revelation may be held as an opinion but need not be believed. But this opinion of Thomas hangs so completely in the air, devoid of Scripture and reason, that he seems here to have forgotten both his philosophy and his logic. For Aristotle writes about subject and accidents so very differently from St. Thomas, that I think this great man is to be pitied, not only for drawing his opinions in matters of faith from Aristotle, but for attempting to base them

---

[13] The theologian Pierre d'Ailly (1351–1420).
[14] The followers of St. Thomas Aquinas.

on him without understanding his meaning—an unfortunate superstructure upon an unfortunate foundation.

I therefore permit everyone to hold either of these views, as he chooses. My one concern at present is to remove all scruples of conscience, so that no one may fear to become guilty of heresy if he should believe in the presence of real bread and real wine on the altar, and that everyone may feel at liberty to ponder, hold, and believe either one view or the other, without endangering his salvation....

Moreover, the Church had the true faith for more than twelve hundred years, during which time the holy Fathers never once mentioned this "transubstantiation"—certainly, a monstrous word for a monstrous idea—until the pseudo-philosophy of Aristotle became rampant in the Church these last three hundred years....

The third captivity of this sacrament is that most wicked abuse of all, in consequence of which there is today no more generally accepted and firmly believed opinion in the Church than this: that the Mass is a good work and a sacrifice. This abuse has brought an endless host of others in its wake, so that the faith of this sacrament has become utterly extinct and the holy sacrament has truly been turned into a fair, tavern, and place of merchandise. Hence, participations, brotherhoods, intercessions, merits, anniversaries, memorial days, and the like wares are bought and sold, traded and bartered in the Church, and from this priests and monks derive their whole living....

The Mass, according to its substance, is, therefore, nothing else than the words of Christ mentioned above: "Take and eat."... From this you will see that nothing else is needed to have a worthy Mass than a faith that confidently relies on this promise, believes these words of Christ are true, and does not doubt that these infinite blessings have been bestowed upon it....

But you will say, "How is this? Will you not overturn the practice and teaching of all the churches and monasteries, by virtue of which they have flourished these many centuries? For the Mass is the foundation of their anniversaries, intercessions, applications, communications, etc.—that is to say, of their fat income." I answer: This is the very thing that has constrained me to write of the captivity of the Church, for in this manner the praiseworthy testament of God has been subjected to the bondage of a godless traffic, through the opinions and traditions of wicked men, who, passing over the word of God, have put forth the thoughts of their own hearts and misled the whole world. What do I care for the number and influence of those who are in this error? The truth is mightier than they all....

It is certain, therefore, that the Mass is not a work which may be communicated to others, but it is the object, as it is called, of faith, for the strengthening and nourishing of the personal faith of each individual.

But there is yet another stumbling-block that must be removed, and this is much greater and the most dangerous of all. It is the common belief that the Mass is a sacrifice, which is offered to God. Even the words of the canon tend in this direction, when they speak of "these gifts," "these offerings," "this holy sacrifice," and farther on, of "this offering." Prayer also is made, in so many words, "that the sacrifice may be accepted even as the sacrifice of Abel," etc., and hence Christ is termed the "sacrifice of the altar." In addition to this, there are the sayings of the holy Fathers, the great number of examples, and the constant usage and custom of all the world.

We must resolutely oppose all of this, firmly entrenched as it is, with the words and example of Christ. For unless we hold fast to the truth, that the Mass is the promise or testament of Christ, as the words clearly say, we shall lose the whole Gospel and all our comfort. Let us permit nothing to prevail against these words, even though an angel from heaven should teach otherwise. For there is nothing said in them of a work or a sacrifice.

15. King Henry VIII, *Defense of the Seven Sacraments*, 1521[15]

Henry VIII to Pope Leo X

Most Holy Father: I most humbly commend myself to you, and devoutly kiss your blessed feet. Whereas we believe that no duty is more incumbent on a Catholic sovereign than to preserve and increase the Christian faith and religion and the proofs thereof, and to transmit them preserved thus inviolate to posterity, by his example in preventing them from being destroyed by any assailant of the faith or in any way impaired, so when we learned that the plague of Martin Luther's heresy had appeared in Germany and was raging everywhere, without let or hindrance, to such an extent that many, infected with its poison, were falling away, . . . we bent all our thoughts and energies on uprooting in every possible way, this cockle, this heresy from the Lord's flock. . . . We determined to show by our own writing our attitude towards Luther and our opinion of his vile books; to manifest more openly to all the world that we shall ever defend and uphold—not only by force of arms but by the resources of our intelligence and our services as a Christian—the Holy Roman Church. . . .

From our royal palace at Greenwich, the twenty-first day of May, 1521. . . .

Let us therefore begin where he began himself, with the adoration-worthy Sacrament of Christ's Body. . . . Let us truly examine how subtly, under pretense of favoring the laity, he endeavors to stir them up to hatred against the clergy: For when he resolved to render the Church's faith suspicious, that its authority should be of no consequence against him (and so, by opening that gap, he might destroy the chief mysteries of Christianity), he began with that thing, which he foresaw would be praised and applauded by the people: For he touched the old sore, by which Bohemia had been formerly blistered, namely,

---

[15] Source: Henry VIII, *Assertio Septem Sacramentorum, or Defence of the Seven Sacraments*, ed. Louis O'Donovan (New York: Benziger Brothers, 1908), 152, 154, 212–90, text modernized.

that the laity ought to receive the Eucharist under both kinds.[16] . . . And though to me no reasons appear why the Church should not ordain that the sacrament should be administered to the laity under both kinds, yet I do not doubt that what was done in times past, in omitting it, and also in hindering it to be so administered now, is very convenient. . . . It further appears not to be a thing of any such danger, because God not only bestowed heaven upon those men who did this thing themselves and wrote that it ought to be done, but likewise would have them honored on earth by those by whom he is adored himself: Among whom (to omit others) was that most learned and holy man Thomas Aquinas, whom I the more willingly name here because the wickedness of Luther cannot endure the sanctity of this man, but reviles him with his foul lips, him whom all Christians honor. . . .

What I most admire is that Luther should be so angry and passionate for having one kind taken away from the laity in Communion but is not at all moved that children should be barred from both. For he cannot deny that children in the primitive times received Communion. This custom, if it was justly omitted (though Christ said, "Drink of this, all of you" [Matt. 26:27]), and that without doubt for very good reasons (though nobody can now remember them), why should we not think that it was for good and just reasons, unknown at this time, that the primitive custom of the laity's receiving the sacrament in both kinds was taken away? . . .

He makes it a second captivity that any man should be forbidden to believe that the true bread and true wine remain after consecration. So that in this (contrary to the belief of the whole Christian world, both now, and for so many ages past), he endeavors to persuade that the body and blood of Christ are after such a manner in the Eucharist that the substance of true bread and true wine remains still after consecration. I suppose, afterwards, when it pleases him, he will deny the substance of the body and blood to be there, when he has a mind to change his opinion, as he has three times done already. . . .

St. Matthew's words are these, "While they were eating, Jesus took a loaf of bread, and after blessing it he broke it, gave it to the disciples, and said, 'Take, eat; this is my body.' Then he took a cup, and after giving thanks he gave it to them, saying, 'Drink from it, all of you; for this is my blood of the covenant, which is poured out for many for the forgiveness of sins'" [Matt. 26:26–28]. . . . In all these words of the Evangelists, I see none where, after the consecration, the sacrament is called "bread and wine," but only "body and blood." They say that "Christ took bread in his hands," which we all confess; but when the Apostles received it, it was not called "bread" but "body." . . .

For how could Christ have more properly said that no bread and wine remain in the sacrament, than when he said, "This is my body"? For he did not say, "My body is in this," or "With this which you see, is my body," as if it should consist in the

[16] This is a reference to the Hussites in Bohemia, who had also insisted on the administration of both the bread and wine to the laity during communion.

47

bread, or with the bread; but "This (he says) is my body," manifestly declaring (to shut the mouth of every yelping fellow) what he then gave to be his body....

Luther takes a deal of pains to confute the arguments of the Neoteries,[17] by which they endeavored to maintain and prove transubstantiation by philosophical reasons, out of Aristotle's school, in which he troubles himself more than is requisite: For the Church does not believe it because they dispute it so to be, but because it believed so from the beginning and, so that none should stagger about it, decreed that all should so believe....

For it is certain that the faithful, for over a thousand years past, did believe the substance of bread and wine to be truly changed into the body and blood of Jesus Christ, which makes me wonder that Luther is not ashamed of himself to say that this belief of transubstantiation has not been in the Church above three hundred years.... What could be said more to the purpose than this of St. Augustine: "We honor (says he) invisible things, namely, the flesh and blood in the visible form of the bread and wine"? He does not say "in the bread and wine" but "in the form of bread and wine."... Likewise, St. Gregory of Nyssa says, "That before the consecration, it is but bread, but when it is consecrated by mystery, it is made and called the body of Christ."... Moreover, that none should say that the ancient Fathers believed the body of Christ in such manner to be in the Eucharist as that the bread should still remain,... St. Ambrose said that "Although the form of

bread and wine is seen, nevertheless we are to believe that there is nothing else after consecration but the body and blood of Christ."...

Wherefore (to conclude this discourse of transubstantiation) it evidently appears by Christ's words, and by the judgment of the holy Fathers, that the faith of the Church, at the present, is true, by which it is believed that the substance of bread or wine does not remain in the Eucharist; whence it follows that Luther's opinion in teaching the contrary is false and heretical....

After this man, who is free from any evil, has escaped these two captivities, which he imagines to himself, that he may not captivate his mind to the obedience of God, he overcomes (as he pretends) a third captivity, and proposes a liberty by which he may captivate the whole Church. This... endeavors to scatter abroad the Church's most splendid congregation, to extinguish its Pillar of Fire, to violate the Ark of the Covenant, and to destroy the chief and only sacrifice which reconciles us to God, and which is always offered for the sins of the people. For, as much as in him lies, he robs the Mass of all the benefits that flow from it to the people, denying it to be a good work, or to bring them any kind of profit.... He sees, and confesses himself, that the opinions of the holy Fathers are against him, as also the Canon of the Mass with the custom of the universal Church, confirmed by the usage of so many ages and the consent of so many people. What defense then does he oppose against so innumerable, so powerful, and so invincible armies? His accustomed force rages; he strives to breed discord, and move

---

[17] This refers to the recent scholastic theologians.

seditions, to excite the commonalty against the nobility. And that he may the more easily stir them up to a revolt, he, by his foolish and weak policy, falsely pretends that he has Christ for captain of the whole army in his camp, and that the trumpet of the Gospel sounds only for him, which is the most ridiculous strategy that ever was invented. For what man living is so wicked or blockish as to think that . . . Christ, who never abandoned the flesh which once he took, should have cast off the Church, for whose sake he took that flesh; and that he should, for so many ages, absent himself from her, with whom he promised to remain to the end of the world, and should now pass to Luther's side, who is her professed enemy? But pray let us see by what enchantment he makes it appear for truth that Christ is on his side, as he brags. . . .

He says that this sacrament of the Mass is no other thing than the testament of Christ, and the testament is nothing but the promise of eternal heritage giving his body and blood to us Christians, whom he appointed for his heirs, as a sign for the ratifying of his promise. . . . Further, (he says) that the Mass is not a sacrifice, that it is only profitable to the priest, not to the people, that it is nothing available, either to the dead or to the living; that to sing Mass for sins, for any necessity, or for the dead, is an impious error; that fraternities, as also the annual commemorations for the dead, are vain and wicked things; that our voluntary maintaining of priests, monks, canons, brothers, and whatsoever we call religious, is to be abolished. . . .

Not only those things which Christ did first at his Supper belong to the Testament, but also his oblation on the cross. For on the cross he consummated the sacrifice which he began in the Supper. And therefore, the commemoration of the whole thing, to wit, of the consecration in the Supper and the oblation on the cross, is celebrated and represented together in the sacrament of the Mass; so that it is the death that is more truly represented than the Supper. And therefore, the Apostle, when writing to the Corinthians, in these words: "For as often as you eat this bread and drink the cup," adds not, "you shall declare the Lord's Supper," but, "you proclaim the Lord's death" (1 Cor. 11:26). . . .

Since it cannot be denied that Christ wrought a good work in his Last Supper and on the cross, neither can it be denied that the priest represents and performs the same things in the Mass. How can it then be feigned that the Mass is not a good work? . . . The most holy Fathers . . . took all possible care and used their utmost endeavors, that the greatest faith imaginable should be had towards this most propitiatory sacrament, and that it should be worshipped with the greatest honor possible. And for that cause, among many other things, they, with great care, delivered us this also: That the bread and wine do not remain in the Eucharist, but are truly changed into the body and blood of Christ. They taught the Mass to be a sacrifice, in which Christ himself is truly offered for the sins of Christian people. And so far as it was lawful for mortals, they adorned this immortal mystery with venerable worship and mystical rites. They commanded the people to be present in adoration of it, while it is celebrated, for the procuring of their salvation. Finally, lest the laity, by forbearing to receive the sacrament, should, little by little, omit it once and for all, they have established an obligation that everyone shall receive it at least once a year. By those things and many of the like nature, the holy Fathers of the Church, in several ages, have demonstrated their care for the faith and veneration of this adoration-worthy sacrament.

VIII. LUTHER'S THREE TREATISES,
PART 3: *FREEDOM OF A CHRISTIAN* AND JUSTIFICATION BY FAITH ALONE

Luther's *Freedom of a Christian* rounds out the three treatises of 1520 and explores the relationship between faith and good works. The term "justification," which Luther uses throughout the text, is particularly important in the context of the Reformation. Essentially, justification means the state of being just or righteous before God. Thus, Christians who die justified will go straight to heaven. Central to the late medieval concept of justification was the idea that Christians needed not only to confess their sins but also to make satisfaction for them. This could be done through such things as good works, pilgrimages, indulgences, and having masses said for one's soul. Luther argues in this text for one of the central concepts of Protestantism: justification through faith alone (*sola fide*), not by any works. Luther did not want to get rid of good works, but as this text makes clear, he redefines their role in Christian life. Eck's *Enchiridion* once again presents a Catholic position on faith and works.

Focus Questions

1. What is the paradox Luther presents in *Freedom of a Christian*, and how does he resolve it?
2. According to Luther, why are Christians justified by faith alone?
3. How does Luther answer the objection that the Bible contains so many injunctions to do good works?
4. What is Luther's attitude in this text toward good works? Is it any different from his position in the *Sermon on Indulgences and Grace* (doc. 10)?

5. How is Eck's position with regard to faith and works different from Luther's?
6. With what evidence does Eck support his position?

16. Luther, *The Freedom of a Christian*, 1520[18]

That I may open then an easier way for the ignorant—for these alone I am trying to serve—I first lay down these two propositions, concerning spiritual liberty and servitude:

A Christian is the most free lord of all, and subject to none;

A Christian is the most dutiful servant of all, and subject to everyone.

Although these statements appear contradictory, yet, when they are found to agree together, they will serve my purpose excellently. They are both the statements of Paul himself, who says, "Though I am free with respect to all, I have made myself a slave to all" (1 Cor. 9:19), and "Owe no one anything, except to love one another" (Rom. 13:8). Now love is by its own nature dutiful and obedient to the beloved object. Thus, even Christ, though Lord of all things, was yet made of a woman, made under the law, at once free and a servant, at once in the form of God and in the form of a servant.

Let us examine the subject on a deeper and less simple principle. Man is composed of a twofold nature, a spiritual and a bodily. As regards the spiritual nature, which they name the soul, he is called the spiritual, inward, new man; as regards the bodily nature, which they name the flesh, he is called the fleshly, outward, old man. The Apostle speaks of this: "Even though our outer nature is wasting away, our inner nature is being renewed day by day" (2 Cor. 4:16). The result of this diversity is that in the Scriptures opposing statements are made concerning the same man, the fact being that in the same person these two men are opposed to one another, the flesh lusting against the spirit, and the spirit against the flesh (Gal. 5:17).

We first approach the subject of the inward man, that we may see by what means a man becomes justified, free, and a true Christian; that is, a spiritual, new, and inward man. It is certain that absolutely none among outward things, under whatever name they may be reckoned, has any influence in producing Christian righteousness or liberty, nor, on the other hand, unrighteousness or slavery. This can be shown by an easy argument.

What can it profit the soul that the body should be in good condition, free, and full of life; that it should eat, drink, and act according to its

---

[18] Source: Martin Luther, *Concerning Christian Liberty*, Harvard Classics 36, trans. R.S. Grignon (New York, P.F. Collier & Son, 1910), 363–85, text modernized.

pleasure, when even the most impious slaves of every kind of vice are prosperous in these matters? Again, what harm can ill-health, bondage, hunger, thirst, or any other outward evil do to the soul, when even the most pious of men and the freest in the purity of their conscience are harassed by these things? Neither of these states of things has to do with the liberty or the slavery of the soul.

And so it will profit nothing that the body should be adorned with sacred vestments, or dwell in holy places, or be occupied in sacred offices, or pray, fast, and abstain from certain meats, or do whatever works can be done through the body and in the body. Something widely different will be necessary for the justification and liberty of the soul, since the things I have spoken of can be done by any impious person, and only hypocrites are produced by devotion to these things....

One thing, and one alone, is necessary for life, justification, and Christian liberty; and that is the most holy word of God, the Gospel of Christ, as he says, "I am the resurrection and the life. Those who believe in me, even though they die, will live" (John 11:25), and also, "If the Son makes you free, you will be free indeed" (John 8:36), and, "One does not live by bread alone, but by every word that comes from the mouth of God" (Matt. 4:4).

Let us, therefore, hold it for certain and firmly established that the soul can do without everything except the word of God, without which none at all of its needs are provided for. But, having the word, it is rich and lacks nothing, since that is the word of life, of truth, of light, of peace, of justification, of salvation, of joy, of liberty, of wisdom, of virtue, of grace, of glory, and of every good thing....

But you will ask, "What is this word, and by what means is it to be used, since there are so many words of God?" I answer, the Apostle Paul (Rom. 1) explains what it is, namely the Gospel of God, concerning his Son, incarnate, suffering, risen, and glorified, through the Spirit, the Sanctifier. To preach Christ is to feed the soul, to justify it, to set it free, and to save it, if it believes the preaching. For faith alone and the efficacious use of the word of God bring salvation. "If you confess with your lips that Jesus is Lord and believe in your heart that God raised him from the dead, you will be saved" (Rom. 10:9); and again, "Christ is the end of the law so that there may be righteousness for everyone who believes" (Rom. 10:4); and "The one who is righteous will live by faith" (Rom. 1:17). For the word of God cannot be received and honored by any works, but by faith alone. Hence, it is clear that as the soul needs the word alone for life and justification, so it is justified by faith alone, and not by any works. For if it could be justified by any other means, it would have no need of the word, nor consequently of faith....

And so, on the other hand, it is solely by impiety and incredulity of heart that he becomes guilty and a slave of sin, deserving condemnation, not by any outward sin or work. Therefore, the first care of every Christian ought to be to lay aside all reliance on works and strengthen his faith alone more and more, and by it grow in the knowledge, not of works, but of Christ Jesus, who has suffered and risen again for him....

But you ask how it can be the fact that faith alone justifies and affords without works so great a treasure of good things, when so many works, ceremonies, and laws are prescribed to us in the

Scriptures?... It is to be noted that the whole Scripture of God is divided into two parts: precepts and promises. The precepts certainly teach us what is good, but what they teach is not forthwith done. For they show us what we ought to do but do not give us the power to do it. They were ordained, however, for the purpose of showing man to himself, that through them he may learn his own impotence for good and may despair of his own strength. For this reason they are called the Old Testament, and are so....

Now when a man has through the precepts been taught his own impotence, and become anxious by what means he may satisfy the law— for the law must be satisfied, so that no jot or tittle of it may pass away, otherwise he must be hopelessly condemned—then, being truly humbled and brought to nothing in his own eyes, he finds in himself no resource for justification and salvation.

Then comes in that other part of Scripture, the promises of God, which declare the glory of God, and say, "If you wish to fulfill, the law, and, as the law requires, not to covet, lo! believe in Christ, in whom are promised to you grace, justification, peace, and liberty." All these things you shall have, if you believe, and shall be without them if you do not believe.... Thus, the promises of God give that which the precepts exact, and fulfill what the law commands, so that all is of God alone, both the precepts and their fulfilment. He alone commands; He alone also fulfills. Hence, the promises of God belong to the New Testament; nay, *are* the New Testament....

But if man has no need of works, neither has he need of the law; and if he has no need of the law, he is certainly free from the law, and the saying is true, "The law is laid down not for the innocent" (1 Tim. 1:9). This is that Christian liberty, our faith, the effect of which is not that we should be careless or lead a bad life, but that no one should need the law or works for justification and salvation....

Let it suffice to say this concerning the inner man and its liberty, and concerning that righteousness of faith which needs neither laws nor good works; nay, they are even hurtful to it, if any one pretends to be justified by them.

And now let us turn to the other part: to the outward man. Here we shall give an answer to all those who, taking offence at the word of faith and at what I have asserted, say, "If faith does everything, and by itself suffices for justification, why then are good works commanded? Are we then to take our ease and do no works, content with faith?" Not so, impious men, I reply, not so. That would indeed really be the case, if we were thoroughly and completely inner and spiritual persons; but that will not happen until the Last Day, when the dead shall be raised. As long as we live in the flesh, we are but beginning and making advances in that which shall be completed in a future life. On this account the Apostle calls that which we have in this life the first fruits of the Spirit (Rom. 8:23). In the future we shall have the tenths and the fullness of the Spirit. To this part belongs the fact I have stated before: that the Christian is the servant of all and subject to all. For in that part in which he is free he does no works, but in that in which he is a servant he does all works. Let us see on what principle this is so.

Although, as I have said, inwardly, and according to the spirit, a man is amply enough justified by faith, having all that he requires to have, except that this very faith and abundance ought to increase from day to day, even till the future life, still he remains in this mortal life upon earth, in which it is necessary that he should rule his own body and interact with other people. Here then works begin; here he must not take his ease; here he must give heed to exercise his body by fasting, vigils, labor, and other regular discipline, so that it may be subdued to the spirit, and obey and conform itself to the inner man and faith, and not rebel against them nor hinder them, as is its nature to do if it is not kept under. For the inner man, being conformed to God and created after the image of God through faith, rejoices and delights itself in Christ, in whom such blessings have been conferred on it, and hence has only this task before it: to serve God with joy and for nought in free love....

These works, however, must not be done with any notion that by them a man can be justified before God—for faith, which alone is righteousness before God, will not bear with this false notion—but solely with this purpose: that the body may be brought into subjection and be purified from its evil lusts, so that our eyes may be turned only to purging away those lusts. For when the soul has been cleansed by faith and made to love God, it would have all things to be cleansed in like manner, and especially its own body, so that all things might unite with it in the love and praise of God....

A Christian, being consecrated by his faith, does good works, but he is not by these works made a more sacred person or more a Christian. That is the effect of faith alone; no, unless he were previously a believer and a Christian, none of his works would have any value at all; they would really be impious and damnable sins.

True, then, are these two sayings: "Good works do not make a man good, but a good man does good works"; and "bad works do not make a man bad, but a bad man does bad works." Thus, it is always necessary that the substance or person should be good before any good works can be done, and that good works should follow and proceed from a good person. As Christ says, "A good tree cannot bear bad fruit, nor can a bad tree bear good fruit" (Matt. 7:18). Now it is clear that the fruit does not bear the tree, nor does the tree grow on the fruit; but, on the contrary, the trees bear the fruit, and the fruit grows on the trees.

As then trees must exist before their fruit, and as the fruit does not make the tree either good or bad, but on the contrary, a tree of either kind produces fruit of the same kind, so must first the person be good or bad before he can do either a good or a bad work; and his works do not make him bad or good, but he himself makes his works either bad or good....

We do not, then, reject good works; no, we embrace them and teach them in the highest degree. It is not on their own account that we condemn them, but on account of this impious addition to them and the perverse notion of seeking justification by them. These things cause them to be only good in outward show, but in reality not good, since by them men are deceived and deceive others, like ravening wolves in sheep's clothing....

Lastly, we will speak also of those works which he performs towards his neighbor. For man does not live for himself alone in this mortal body, in order to work on its account, but also for all humans on earth; no, he lives only for others, and not for himself. For it is to this end that he brings his own body into subjection, that he may be able to serve others more sincerely and more freely. As Paul says, "We do not live to ourselves, and we do not die to ourselves. If we live, we live to the Lord, and if we die, we die to the Lord; so then, whether we live or whether we die, we are the Lord's" (Rom. 14:7–8). Thus, it is impossible that he should take his ease in this life and not work for the good of his neighbors, since he must speak, act, and converse among others, just as Christ was made in the likeness of men and found in fashion as a man, and had his conversation among humans.

Yet a Christian has need of none of these things for justification and salvation, but in all his works he ought to entertain this view and look only to this object: that he may serve and be useful to others in all that he does, having nothing before his eyes but the necessities and the advantage of his neighbor....

Here is the truly Christian life, here is faith really working by love, when a man applies himself with joy and love to the works of that freest servitude in which he serves others voluntarily and for nothing, himself abundantly satisfied in the fullness and riches of his own faith.

17. Eck, *Enchiridion*, "Faith and Good Works," 1533[19]

Note here that works that are good in and of themselves are pleasing to God and meritorious of eternal life. But this must be understood to refer to living works, that is, those that have their origin in a spiritual life, which is grace and charity. The righteous do such works by "faith working through love" (Gal. 5[:6]). Far different, however, are the works performed by the impious, such as fornicators, adulterers, and the like. Even if they appear to be good on the surface, those works are neither pleasing... nor meritorious of eternal life. For fornicators, adulterers, thieves, and bandits (however much they lie and claim to be evangelicals and followers of Paul), do not have an inheritance in the kingdom of Christ and God, nor do they follow him. But the Lord will judge them....

Nevertheless, in sinners who are not blind and hardened, but who humbly confess their sins and seek forgiveness, good works of this kind, although dead, bestow grace. This is clear in the case of the tax collector who received an indulgence through his humble and devout confession of his sins and "went down to his home justified" (Luke 18[:13-14]). It is also clear in the case of the gentile Cornelius, whose "prayer has been heard and whose alms have been remembered before God." He was baptized by Peter who had been sent to him, along with his relatives and close friends, and the

---

[19] Source: Johannes Eck, *Enchiridion locorum communorum Ioannis Eckii, adversus Lutheranos* (Venice: Ioan. Antonium and Fratres de Sabio, 1533), 24r–v, 26r–v, translated by the editor.

Holy Spirit descended upon them in a visible sign (Acts 10).

Therefore, sinners must be advised to apply their hands immediately to whatever works they can do and not to overthrow or withdraw from good works (which the impious Lutherans do, who are haters of all good). They are especially to exercise them for the true catholic poor, not for the apostate monks and nuns who sacrilegiously fornicate and commit adultery under the honest name of marriage. "Give to the devout, but do not help the sinner. Do good to the humble, but do not give to the ungodly" (Sirach 12:[4-5]). Daniel advised the same thing to Nebuchadnezzar, saying, "Therefore, O king, may my counsel be acceptable to you: atone for your sins with righteousness, and your iniquities with mercy to the oppressed" (Daniel 4[:27])…. The whole error of the Lutherans concerning good works proceeds from ignorance of this distinction made in and founded upon Holy Scripture….

What Augustine said is true: This heresy (for it is not new but very old) comes from Paul's words poorly understood. We acknowledge that "The one who is righteous will live by faith" (Rom. 1[:17]), for faith, as the "assurance of things hoped for" [Heb. 11:1], is the foundation of the spiritual building. But what the heretic adds with his "faith alone" mutilates and falsifies the biblical text, for nowhere does it say, "The one who is righteous will live by faith *alone*."

To believe in God, according to the use of the Scriptures, includes clinging to God through charity, according to Augustine. The younger theologians call this "formed faith," as is clear from St. Paul: "For in Christ Jesus neither circumcision nor uncircumcision counts for anything; the only thing that counts is faith working through love." See, Paul does not say any kind of faith suffices, but faith that works through love….

The heretics object, "'Abraham believed God, and it was reckoned to him as righteousness'" (Gen. 15[:6; Rom. 4:3]). St. James responds, "Was not our ancestor Abraham justified by works when he offered his son Isaac on the altar? You see that faith was active along with his works, and faith was brought to completion by the works." And further down, "You see that a person is justified by works and not by faith alone" (James 2[:21-22, 24]).

IX. LUTHER AND ERASMUS ON FREE WILL

It is a well-known and oft-repeated fact that Luther wanted to reform the church from within. He had no desire to break up the Catholic Church or create his own new church. By 1520, however, it was clear that Luther's reforms went well beyond attacks on indulgences and corruption within the church. Luther's three treatises of 1520 undermined the very pillars of late medieval Catholicism: the papacy, the sacraments, purgatory, and the entire system that had been developed either to speed souls through purgatory or to bypass it completely. Luther threatened the very core of late medieval religious culture, not just church doctrine but also deeply ingrained Christian practices. Thus, it was only a matter of time before the religious and secular authorities took action against him. Pope Leo X excommunicated Luther in the bull *Decet Romanum Pontificem,* January 3, 1521, and Emperor Charles V declared Luther and his followers criminals in the Edict of Worms, issued on May 8, 1521.

While Luther's break from the authorities was predictable enough, he soon developed enemies even among some of his sympathizers. Most prominent among these was Erasmus of Rotterdam. We met Erasmus in chapter 1 (docs. 7 and 9), as one of the loudest voices for reform in the period before Luther became a public figure. Initially, Erasmus showed qualified support for Luther, but he never embraced his teachings wholeheartedly. Nevertheless, Erasmus was widely seen—both by Catholics and by Luther's followers—as being inside Luther's camp. Luther's supporters praised Erasmus for his criticisms of the church, and Luther's enemies blamed him for having started the whole mess.

By the time of Luther's excommunication, Erasmus saw that Luther was going much further in his assaults and in his doctrinal changes than he thought appropriate. Thus, Erasmus used his treatise *On Free Will* not only to challenge Luther on a key issue underlying Luther's theology, but also as a way to distance himself from Luther. Despite the political advantages of criticizing Luther, there is no reason to think his text was disingenuous. Renaissance humanism tended to celebrate the abilities of humans to make a difference in the world, and Luther seemed to be taking free will away from them altogether.

Luther responded to Erasmus with *The Bondage of the Will*, in which he fully acknowledged that humans have no free will in matters of salvation. Luther's response, as you will see, is quite sharply worded, and Erasmus was deeply hurt by it.

One important note on Erasmus's title, the full version of which is *Diatribe or Collection on Free Will:* Luther mocks this title in his text, so it is important to understand his references. The word "diatribe," in the classical sense in which Erasmus uses it, does not mean "a scathing attack," as we tend to use it today. Instead, a diatribe was usually a dialogue on some moral or philosophical theme. Thus, Erasmus is bringing together a number of different views (hence the word "collection," or *collatio*, in the title) to examine the philosophical topic of free will.

Focus Questions

1. What arguments does Erasmus make in support of free will? What implications or dangers does he see in denying free will?
2. What limitations does Erasmus place on human free will?
3. How does Luther respond to Erasmus's arguments?
4. How does Luther respond to Erasmus as a person and theologian?
5. Why does Luther mock Erasmus's title and approach?
6. What are the positions of both men on assertions? On the interpretation of the Bible?

18. Erasmus, *On Free Will*, 1524[20]

[Preface]

Among the many difficulties encountered in Holy Scripture there is hardly a labyrinth more impenetrable than that of free will: this question has long exercised the minds of philosophers and theologians, ancient and modern, to an amazing degree, but has, I feel, demanded more in labour than it has yielded in results....

Now for my part I was well aware how poorly suited I was for this wrestling-match—indeed there is hardly a man less practised in the art than I, for I have always had a deep-seated inner revulsion from conflict, and so have always preferred sporting in the spacious plains of the Muses to engaging in swordplay at close quarters. And I take so little pleasure

---

[20] Source: Erasmus, *A Discussion of Free Will*, Collected Works of Erasmus 76, trans. Peter McCardle (Toronto: University of Toronto Press, 1999), 5, 7–10, 14, 16–17, 19, 21, 36, 74, 79–80, 86–89.

in assertions that I will gladly seek refuge in Scepticism whenever this is allowed by the inviolable authority of Holy Scripture and the church's decrees; to these decrees I willingly submit my judgment in all things, whether I fully understand what the church commands or not.

I prefer, indeed, to have this case of mind than that which I see characterizes certain others, so that they are uncontrollably attached to an opinion and cannot tolerate anything that disagrees with it, but twist whatever they read in Scripture to support the view they have embraced once and for all....

And so, as far as my own position is concerned, I would say that many and various views on free will have been handed down by the ancient writers, and that as yet I have no settled opinion regarding them, beyond a belief that a certain power of free will does exist....

Yet I would be pleased if I could persuade those of average intellect that in discussions of this kind they should not be too persistent in making assertions which may more readily damage Christian harmony than advance true religion. For in Holy Scripture there are some secret places into which God did not intend us to penetrate very far, and if we attempt to do so, the further in we go the less and less clearly we see. This is presumably in order to make us recognize the unsearchable majesty of divine wisdom, and the frailty of the human intellect....

In my opinion, therefore, as far as free will is concerned, what we have learned from the Scriptures should be sufficient: if we are on the path of righteousness, we should move swiftly on to better deeds, forgetting what lies behind. If we are entangled in sin, we should do our best to struggle out; we should approach the remedy of penance and in all ways seek to obtain God's mercy, without which human will and effort are fruitless; we should impute anything bad to ourselves; anything good we should ascribe entirely to the bounty of God, to which we owe the very fact of our being. Moreover we should believe that everything, happy or sad, that befalls us in this life has been sent by God for our salvation; that no wrong can be done us by a God who is righteous by nature, even if things do in some way seem to happen that we have not deserved; and that no one must despair of forgiveness from a God who is by nature most merciful. To know this, I say, would be enough for a good Christian life, and we would not have to penetrate with irreverent curiosity into obscure, indeed otiose topics: whether God foreknows anything contingently; whether our will accomplishes anything in matters pertaining to eternal salvation or simply suffers the action of grace; whether we do—or rather suffer—everything, good or evil, by absolute necessity....

Holy Scripture has its own way of speaking, accommodated to our understanding. Sometimes God is angry, sad, indignant; he raves, threatens, hates; at other times he is merciful, repents, changes his mind; not because such changes really take place in the divine nature, but because this manner of speaking is suited to our weakness and stupidity.... I would therefore be happier convincing my readers not to waste their time or talents in labyrinths of this kind than I would be refuting or confirming Luther's teachings....

59

[Introduction]

If the reader sees that my argument proves a match for that of my opponents, then he should consider whether more weight ought to be given to the judgments already made by very many learned and orthodox men, many saints and martyrs, many ancient and modern theologians, many universities, councils, bishops, and popes, or to the private judgment of one individual or another.... I concede that it is right for the authority of the Holy Scripture alone to outweigh all the decisions of all mortals. But the debate here is not about Scripture itself. Both sides gladly accept and venerate the same Scripture: the quarrel is over its meaning....

But now comes the objection, "What need of an interpreter, when Scripture is perfectly clear?" If it is so clear, why have such distinguished men throughout so many centuries been blind, precisely in a matter of such importance, as Luther and his adherents want us to see it?...

If, in the event of some disagreement over the meaning of Scripture, we quote the interpretation of the ancient orthodox authorities, they immediately sing out, "But they were only men." If asked by what means we can know what the true interpretation of Scripture is, seeing that there are "only men" on both sides, they reply, "By a sign from the Spirit." If you ask why the Spirit should be absent from those men, some of whom have been world-famous for their miracles, rather than from themselves, they reply as though there had been no gospel in the world these thirteen hundred years....

[Passages from the Old Testament Supporting Free Will]

First of all, it cannot be denied that there are many passages in Holy Scripture which clearly seem to support the freedom of the human will; and on the other hand, some which seem to deny it completely. Yet it is certain that Scripture cannot contradict itself, since it all proceeds from the same Spirit. And so, we shall first review those which confirm our opinion; then we shall attempt to explain those which seem to oppose it....

But what point is there in quoting a few passages of this kind when all Holy Scripture is full of exhortations like this: "Turn back to me with all your heart" [Joel 2:12]; "Let every man turn from his evil way" [John 3:8]; "Come back to your senses, you transgressors" [Isa. 46:8]; "Let everyone turn from his evil way, and I will repent the ill that I have thought to do them on account of the evil of their endeavors"; and "If you will not listen to me, to walk in my law" [Jer. 26:3–4]. Nearly the whole of Scripture speaks of nothing but conversion, endeavour, and striving to improve. All this would become meaningless once it was accepted that doing good or evil was a matter of necessity....

[Judgments Concerning Free Will and Grace]

Now, the reason that different scholars have reached different opinions working from the same Scripture is that they directed their attention to different things, and interpreted what they read in the light of their individual aims. Some reflected on the great extent of human religious apathy and on the great evil of despairing of salvation; in the attempt to remedy these ills, they fell unawares into another evil and exaggerated the role of free will. Others, however, considered how destructive it is of true godliness for man to rely on his own strength and merits, and how intolerable is the arrogance of certain parties who display their own good deeds, and even weigh and measure them out for sale to others, like oil and soap. In their valiant efforts to avoid this evil, they have either taken half of free will away, to the extent that it plays no part at all in a good work, or they have destroyed it altogether by propounding the absolute necessity of all events....

In my opinion free will could have been established in such a way as to avoid that trust in our own merits and the other harmful consequences which Luther avoids, as well as those which we mentioned above, yet so as not to destroy the benefits which Luther admires. This I believe is achieved by the opinion of those who ascribe entirely to grace the impetus by which the mind is first aroused, and only in the succeeding process attribute something to human will in that it does not resist the grace of God. Since there are three parts to everything—beginning, continuation, and completion—they ascribe the first and last to grace and allow that free will has an effect only in the continuation, in so far as

in a single, indivisible act there are two causes, divine grace and human will, working together. However, grace is the principal cause and will the secondary cause, unable to do anything without the principal cause, whereas the principal cause is sufficient in itself....

On this moderate view man must ascribe his salvation entirely to the grace of God; for what free will accomplishes in this is very insignificant indeed, and what it can accomplish is itself due to divine grace, which first created free will, then freed and healed it. And this will appease (if they can be appeased) those who believe that there is no good in man which he does not owe to God....

Pelagius seemed to attribute too much to free will; Duns Scotus attributed an ample amount;[21] at first Luther merely mutilated free will by cutting off its right arm, but soon, not content with this, he cut its throat and made away with it altogether. I favour the opinion of those who attribute something to free will, but most to grace....

Why, you may ask, attribute anything at all to free will? To allow the ungodly, who have deliberately fallen short of the grace of God, to be deservedly condemned; to clear God of the false accusation of cruelty and injustice; to free us from despair, protect us from complacency, and spur us on to moral endeavour. For these reasons nearly everyone admits the existence of

---

[21] Pelagius was St. Augustine's chief opponent on the question of free will's role in salvation. Pelagius ascribed much to free will, Augustine very little. John Duns Scotus was a thirteenth-century scholastic theologian.

free will; but, lest we claim anything for ourselves, they assert that it can achieve nothing without the perpetual grace of God....

I know I shall hear the objection, "Erasmus should come to know Christ and bid farewell to human learning. No one understands these matters unless he has the spirit of God." Well, if I still have no understanding of Christ, I have clearly been far off the mark till now! And yet I would be glad to learn what spirit all the Christian doctors and people (for it is likely that the people agreed with the bishops' teaching) have had these last thirteen hundred years, since they too lacked that understanding. I have discussed the issue. Let others pass judgment.

19. Luther, *The Bondage of the Will*, 1525[22]

First of all, I would just touch upon some of the heads of your preface; in which you somewhat disparage our cause and adorn your own. In the first place, I would notice your censuring in me, in all your former books, an obstinacy of assertion, and saying in this book, that you "are so far from delighting in assertions, that you would rather at once go over to the sentiments of the skeptics, if the inviolable authority of the Holy Scriptures, and the decrees of the Church, would permit you: to which authorities you willingly submit yourself in all things, whether you follow what they prescribe, or follow it not." These are the principles that please you.

I consider (as in courtesy bound) that these things are asserted by you from a benevolent mind, as being a lover of peace. But if anyone else had asserted them, I should, perhaps, have attacked him in my accustomed manner. But, however, I must not allow even you, though so very good in your intentions, to err in this opinion. For not to delight in assertions is not the character of the Christian mind; no, he must delight in assertions, or he is not a Christian.... I speak concerning the asserting of those things which are delivered to us from above in the Holy Scriptures....

What shall we say to these things also, where you add, "To which authorities I submit my opinion in all things, whether I follow what they enjoin, or not"? What say you, Erasmus? Is it not enough that you submit your opinion to the Scriptures? Do you submit it to the decrees of the Church also? What can the Church decree that is not decreed in the Scriptures? If it can, where then remains the liberty and power of judging those who make the decrees?...

I have, upon this occasion, expressed myself thus so that henceforth you may cease to accuse our cause of pertinacity or obstinacy. For by

---

[22] Source: Martin Luther, *On the Bondage of the Will, Written in Answer to the Diatribe of Erasmus on Free-Will*, trans. Henry Cole (London: T. Bensley, 1823), 6–7, 10, 12–15, 17–18, 23, 26–27, 32, 51–52, 55–56, 62, 140–41, 374–77, text modernized.

doing so, you only evince that you hug in your heart a Lucian or some other of the swinish tribe of the Epicureans, who, because he does not believe there is a God, secretly laughs at all those who do believe and confess it. Allow us to be assertors and to study and delight in assertions, and you go ahead and favor your Skeptics and Academics until Christ shall have called you also. The Holy Spirit is not a Skeptic, nor are the things he has written on our hearts doubts or opinions but assertions more certain and more firm than life itself and all human experience....

That there are in God many hidden things which we know not, no one doubts.... But that there are in the Scriptures some things incomprehensible and that all things are not quite plain is a report spread abroad by the impious Sophists by whose mouth you speak here, Erasmus. But they never have produced, nor ever can produce, one article whereby to prove this their madness. And it is with such scarecrows that Satan has frightened away men from reading the sacred writings and has rendered the Holy Scripture contemptible, that he might cause his poisons of philosophy to prevail in the church. This, indeed, I confess: that there are many *places* in the Scriptures obscure and hidden, not from the majesty of the thing, but from our ignorance of certain terms and grammatical particulars, but which do not prevent a knowledge of all the *matter* in the Scriptures. For what *matter* of more importance can remain hidden in the Scriptures, now that the seals are broken, the stone rolled from the door of the sepulcher, and that greatest of all mysteries brought to light, Christ made man: that God is Trinity and Unity, that Christ suffered for us and will reign to all eternity? Are not these things known and proclaimed even in our streets? Take Christ out of the Scriptures, and what will you find remaining in them?...

If many things still remain hidden to many, this does not arise from obscurity in the Scriptures, but from the blindness or lack of understanding of those who do not go the way to see the all-perfect clearness of the truth. As Paul says concerning the Jews (2 Cor. 3:15), "A veil lies over their minds." And again, "If our gospel is veiled, it is veiled to those who are perishing. In their case the god of this world has blinded the minds of the unbelievers" (2 Cor. 4:3–4). With the same rashness anyone may cover his own eyes or go from the light into the dark and hide himself, and then blame the day and the sun for being obscure. Let, therefore, wretched men cease to impute with blasphemous perverseness the darkness and obscurity of their own heart to the all-clear Scriptures of God....

But this is still more intolerable: your enumerating this subject of free will among those things that are "useless and not necessary," and drawing up for us, instead of it, a "form" of those things which you consider "necessary unto Christian piety." Such a form as, certainly, any Jew or any Gentile utterly ignorant of Christ might draw up. For of Christ you make no mention in one iota. As though you thought that there may be Christian piety without Christ, if God be but worshipped with all the powers as being by nature most merciful.

What shall I say here, Erasmus? To me, you breathe out nothing but Lucian and draw in the gorging surfeit of Epicurus. If you consider this subject "not necessary" to Christians, away, I pray you, out of the field; I have nothing to do with you. I consider it necessary....

It is not irreligious, curious, or superfluous, but essentially wholesome and necessary, for a Christian to know whether or not the will does anything in those things which pertain unto salvation. Indeed, let me tell you, this is the very hinge upon which our discussion turns. It is the very heart of our subject. For our object is this: to inquire what free will can do, in what it is passive, and how it stands with reference to the grace of God. If we know nothing of these things, we shall know nothing whatever of Christian matters.... For if I know not how much I can do myself, how far my ability extends, and what I can do towards God, I shall be equally uncertain and ignorant how much God is to do, how far his ability is to extend, and what he is to do toward me: whereas it is "God who activates all in everyone" (1 Cor. 12:6). But if I know not the distinction between our working and the power of God, I know not God himself. And if I know not God, I cannot worship him, praise him, give him thanks, nor serve him, for I shall not know how much I ought to ascribe to myself and how much to God. It is necessary, therefore, to hold the most certain distinction between the power of God and our power, the working of God and our working, if we would live in his fear. Hence, you see, this point forms another part of the whole sum of Christianity, on which depends and in which is at stake the knowledge of ourselves and the knowledge and glory of God....

This, therefore, is also essentially necessary and wholesome for Christians to know: That God foreknows nothing by contingency, but that he foresees, purposes, and does all things according to his immutable, eternal, and infallible will. By this thunderbolt, free will is thrown to the ground and utterly dashed to pieces. Those, therefore, who would assert free will must either deny this thunderbolt, or pretend not to see it, or push it from them....

Do you believe that God foreknows against his will, or that he wills in ignorance? If then, he foreknows, willing, his will is eternal and immovable, because his nature is so; and if he wills, foreknowing, his knowledge is eternal and immovable, because his nature is so. From which it follows unalterably, that all things which we do, although they may appear to us to be done mutably and contingently, and even may be done thus contingently by us, are yet, in reality, done necessarily and immutably with respect to the will of God. For the will of God is effective and cannot be hindered....

If, therefore, we are taught and if we believe that we ought not to know the necessary foreknowledge of God and the necessity of the things that are to take place, Christian faith is utterly destroyed, and the promises of God and the whole Gospel entirely fall to the ground, for the greatest and only consolation of Christians in their adversities is the knowing that God does not lie but does all things immutably and that his will cannot be resisted, changed, or hindered....

In the last part of your Preface, where you deter us from this kind of doctrine, you think your victory is almost gained.... "What a floodgate of iniquity," you say, "would these things, publicly proclaimed, open unto men! What bad man would amend his life! Who would believe that he was loved of God! Who would war against his flesh!"...

"Who," you say, "will endeavor to amend his life?" I answer: No one! No one *can*! For God does not regard your self-amenders without the Spirit, for they are hypocrites. But the elect and those who fear God will be amended by the Holy Spirit; the rest will perish unamended....

"Who will believe," you say, "that he is loved of God?" I answer: No one will believe it! No one *can*! But the elect shall believe it; the rest shall perish without believing it, filled with indignation and blaspheming, as you here describe them. Therefore, there will be some who shall believe it. And as to your saying that "by these doctrines the floodgate of iniquity is thrown open unto men," so be it. They pertain to that leprosy of evil to be borne, spoken of before. Nevertheless, by the same doctrines, there is thrown open to the elect and to those who fear God a gate unto righteousness, an entrance into heaven: a way unto God!...

[*In response to Erasmus's assertion that Scripture is full of exhortations:*] The words of the law are spoken, not that they might assert the power of the will, but that they might illuminate the blindness of reason, that it might see that its own light is nothing and that the power of the will is nothing. "Through the law," Paul says, "comes the knowledge of sin" (Rom. 3:20); he does not say "is the abolition of," or "the escape from" sin. The whole nature and design of the law is to give knowledge only, and that of nothing else except sin, but not to discover or communicate any power whatever. For knowledge is not power, nor does it communicate power, but it teaches and shows how great the impotency must be there where there is no power. And what else can the knowledge of sin be but the knowledge of our evil and infirmity? For he does not say, "by the law comes the knowledge of strength or of good." The whole thing that the law does, according to the testimony of Paul, is to make known sin.

And this is the place where I take occasion to enforce my general reply: that man, by the words of the law, is admonished and taught what he *ought* to do, not what he *can* do; that is, that he is brought to know his sin but not to believe that he has any strength in himself. Wherefore, friend Erasmus, as often as you throw in my face the words of the law, so often I throw in yours that of Paul, "By the law is the knowledge of sin," not of the power of the will. Heap together, therefore, out of the large concordances all the imperative words into one chaos, provided that they be not words of the promise but of the requirement of the law only, and I will immediately declare that by them is always shown what men *ought* to do, not what they *can* do or do, in fact, do....

And now, my friend Erasmus, I entreat you for Christ's sake to perform what you promised. You promised "that you would willingly yield to him who should teach you better than you knew." Lay aside all respect of persons. You, I confess, are great and adorned with many gifts of God, and those the most noble (to say nothing of the rest), with talent, with erudition, and with eloquence to a miracle. Whereas I have nothing and am nothing, excepting that I glory in being almost a Christian!

In this, moreover, I give you great praise and proclaim it: You alone in pre-eminent distinction from all others have entered upon the matter itself, that is, the grand turning point of the cause, and have not wearied me with those irrelevant points about popery, purgatory, indulgences, and other like baubles, rather than causes, with which all have hitherto tried to hunt me down, though in vain! You, and you alone, saw what was the grand hinge upon which the whole turned, and therefore you attacked the vital part at once, for which I thank you from my heart. For in this kind of discussion, I willingly engage as far as time and leisure permit me. Had those who have heretofore attacked me done the same and would those still do the same who are now boasting of new spirits and new revelations, we should have less sedition and sectarianism and more peace and concord....

But, however, if you cannot manage this cause otherwise than you have managed it in this *Diatribe*, do, I pray you, remain content with your own proper gift. Study, adorn, and promote literature and languages, as you have done thus far to great advantage and with much credit. In this capacity, you have rendered me also a certain service, so much so that I confess myself to be much indebted to you, and in that character, I certainly venerate and honestly respect you. But as to this our cause: To this, God has neither willed nor given it you to be equal....

Nor is it an unlikely thing that you, being a man, should not rightly understand nor with sufficient diligence weigh the Scriptures or the sayings of the Fathers; under these guides, you imagine you cannot miss the mark. And that such is the case is quite clear from this: your saying that you do not "assert" but "collect." No man would write thus who was fully acquainted with and well understood his subject. On the contrary I, in this book of mine, have "collected" nothing, but have "asserted" and still do "assert"; and I wish none to become judges but all to yield assent. And may the Lord, whose cause this is, illuminate you and make you a vessel to honor and to glory. Amen!

FURTHER READING

Brecht, Martin. *Martin Luther*. Translated by James L. Schaaf. 3 vols. Philadelphia: Fortress Press, 1985–93.

Christ-von Wedel, Christine. *Erasmus of Rotterdam: Advocate of a New Christianity*. Erasmus Studies. Toronto: University of Toronto Press, 2013.

Kolb, Robert, Irene Dingel, and L'Ubomír Batka, eds. *The Oxford Handbook of Martin Luther's Theology*. Oxford Handbooks. Oxford: Oxford University Press, 2014.

Kroeker, Greta Grace. *Erasmus in the Footsteps of Paul: A Pauline Theologian*. Erasmus Studies. Toronto: University of Toronto Press, 2011.

Luther, Martin. *Three Treatises*, rev. ed. Translated by Charles M. Jacobs. Philadelphia: Fortress Press, 1970.

Miller, Clarence, ed. *Erasmus and Luther: The Battle over Free Will*. Indianapolis: Hackett, 2012.

Oberman, Heiko A. *Luther: Man between God and Devil*. Translated by Eileen Walliser-Schwarzbart. New Haven, CT: Yale University Press, 1989.

Swanson, R. N. *Promissory Notes on the Treasury of Merits: Indulgences in Late Medieval Europe*. Brill's Companions to the Christian Tradition 5. Leiden: Brill, 2006.

III

The Early Radical Wing and the German Peasants' War

At the same time that Catholics deemed Luther's theology incompatible with church doctrine, new evangelical opponents attacked him for not pushing reform far enough. This radical wing of the Reformation included reformers such as Andreas Bodenstein von Karlstadt (1486–1541) and Thomas Müntzer (c. 1489–1525), among others. Karlstadt (§X) focused on rapid reform of the liturgy, images, and the Eucharist. Müntzer (§XI) demanded radical social as well as religious reform and became closely associated with the largest peasant rebellion of the sixteenth century, the German Peasants' War (§XII). While the peasants were undoubtedly motivated in large part by economic grievances, their demands were informed by some of Luther's ideas. In all of these developments, Luther saw his movement spinning out of control and lashed out at all of these radicals or "fanatics" (*Schwärmer*), as he preferred to call them.

X. KARLSTADT, LUTHER, AND THE DEBATE OVER IMAGES AND THE SPEED OF REFORM

Andreas Bodenstein von Karlstadt was a colleague of Luther's at the University of Wittenberg who quickly supported his ideas. He debated Johannes Eck alongside Luther at the Leipzig Disputation, and the Edict of Worms mentioned Karlstadt by name as a fellow heretic with Luther.

After the Diet of Worms, Luther was hidden away in the Wartburg, a castle belonging to Luther's prince, Elector Frederick "the Wise" of Saxony (1463–1525).[1] While Luther was in hiding, Karlstadt remained in Wittenberg, where he began to push for more sweeping reforms. At the Christmas Eve Mass in 1521, he distributed both the bread and the wine to the laity and used a much shorter version of the Mass liturgy. Karlstadt also began to speak more forcefully against religious images, which he considered idolatrous. The first text below (doc. 20) contains Karlstadt's call for the removal of images from the churches, which prompted a wave of iconoclasm in Wittenberg.

Writing to his Wittenberg colleagues from the Wartburg, Luther counseled caution, but to no avail. Increasingly concerned about the situation, he eventually risked return to Wittenberg to help restore order. When he got there, he delivered a series of sermons during the week after *Invocavit* Sunday;[2] thus, they are known collectively as the *Invocavit Sermons* (doc. 21). In them, Luther provides his reasons for not moving too swiftly with reform.

Karlstadt left Wittenberg and soon found a position at Orlamünde (about 100 miles southwest of Wittenberg). Soon afterwards, he published a response to Luther's *Invocavit Sermons*, entitled *Whether One Should Proceed Slowly and Avoid Offending the Weak in Matters that Concern God's Will* (doc. 22).

Focus Questions

1. According to Karlstadt, what are the usual justifications for keeping images in the churches? What arguments does he use to try to overturn them?

---

[1] Frederick earned his nickname for refusing the candidacy for the imperial election in 1519.

[2] *Invocavit* Sunday is named for the first word of the entrance verse (or Introit) used in the Mass that day, normally the first Sunday of Lent.

2. What is Luther's position in the *Invocavit Sermons* on the rapid changes that have been taking place in Wittenberg?

3. What are his arguments against Karlstadt on images?

4. What does each conclude about the role of the secular authorities in reform? What does each conclude about the proper pace of reform?

5. Think about another, perhaps modern, example when someone implemented or wanted to implement rapid change. What were the motivations for and obstacles to that change, and how might this help us to understand the context of this debate between Karlstadt and Luther?

20. Karlstadt, *On the Removal of Images*, 1522[3]

1. To have images in churches and houses of God is wrong and contrary to the first commandment, "You shall have no other gods before me" [Ex. 20:3].

2. To have carved or painted idols upon altars is more harmful and devilish still.

3. It is good, necessary, laudable, and godly to do away with them and to give the reasons found in Scripture for their removal....

God said soon after he had given the commandment, "You shall have no other gods. You are not to make carved or hewn images. You shall make no likeness of anything that is in heaven above or in the earth beneath or in the water. You shall not worship these; you shall not honor them. I am your God, a strong and jealous God, a zealous God who punishes the wickedness of the fathers in their sons" [Ex. 20:4].

Note how God prohibits all kinds of images. Because human beings are fickle and might worship them, God states that you shall not worship them or give them honor. Thus God prohibits all homage and destroys the hiding places of the papists who by their slippery ways always violate Scripture, making black what is actually white and evil what is actually good. And if one should say, "I do not worship images and show them no honor on their own account but only because of the saints whom they represent," God answers in short and clear words, "You shall not worship them. You shall not honor them."...

---

3 Source: Edward Furcha, ed., *The Essential Karlstadt*, Classics of the Radical Reformation (Waterloo, ON: Herald Press, 1995), 102, 105, 106–7, 114, 118.

Pope Gregory[4] did not forget his papal nature. He gave to images the honor which God had given to his own word, saying that images are the books of lay persons. Is not this a truly papal teaching and devilish addition, to let the little sheep of Christ use deceptive books or examples?

Christ says, "My little sheep hear my voice" [John 10:27]. He does not say, "They see images of me or my saints."…

It cannot be true therefore that images are the textbooks of lay persons. For they are unable to learn their salvation from them. They can draw nothing from images which serves unto salvation or which is necessary for Christian living.…

I say, therefore, that we should not tolerate images in churches or among believers, even though they indicate a good thing. Just as Baalam had to confess, saying, "There is no image in Jacob and no idol in Israel." Num. 23:21 and Ex. 20:4 openly express this. Therefore, no Christian or believer must accept images, for he has clearly heard, "You shall have no images." A believer must live by these words and heed no appearance, whatever form or name it might have.

If someone should come along and say that images teach and instruct lay persons, just as books do scholars, you must answer, "God prohibited images, therefore, I intend to learn nothing from them." If someone should come along and say that images remind us of, and recall for us, the suffering of the Lord and often cause someone to pray an "Our Father" and think of God when otherwise he would not pray or think on God, you should reply, "God has prohibited images." Similarly, Christ says that God is spirit. Everyone who truly worships God, prays to God in spirit, John 4:24.

All who worship God through images worship falsehood. They are focusing on the appearance and external signs of God. Yet, their heart is far from God, creating its own idol in the heart and being full of lies, as Isa. 44:10 says, "In their foolishness and ignorance they worship them [images], neglecting to say, 'I have falsehood in my right hand.'"…

"You are to do thus to them," says God, Deut. 7:5, "you are to throw over and destroy their altars. You are to smash their images. You are to cut down their linden trees and you are to burn their carved images." These are no divine altars, but only pagan or human ones, as is noted in Ex. 20:4. Thus, in keeping with Scripture, Christians are to do away with them. They are external things. Whenever you intend to honor God in external things, or seek him through ceremonies, you are to follow his ceremonies and his law. The authorities, too, are to put away images and judge or sentence them to the penalty, which Scripture requires.

I had also hoped that the almighty God would have brought to fruition the seed he had sown—a predisposition toward removal of images which would have led to the external work. But so far, no execution thereof has taken place—probably because God allows his anger to trickle down on us with the intent of pouring out his full wrath when we become so blind as to fear that which cannot harm us at all.

I know that the authorities are punished on that account. Scripture never lies.

---

4 Pope Gregory I, called "Gregory the Great" (r. 590–604).

21. Luther, *Invocavit Sermons*, 1522[5]

A. *The First Sermon, March 9, 1522,* Invocavit *Sunday*

Thirdly, there must also be love, and through love we must do unto one another as God has done unto us through faith. For without love, faith is nothing, as St. Paul says, 1 Cor. 13:1–2: "If I could speak with the tongues of angels and of the highest things in faith but do not have love, I am nothing." And here, dear friends, have you not grievously failed? I see no signs of love among you, and I observe that you have not been grateful to God for his rich gifts and treasures....

Dear friends, the kingdom of God—and we are that kingdom—consists not in speech or in words, but in deeds, in works and exercises. God does not want hearers and repeaters of words, but doers and followers who exercise themselves in the faith that works by love. For a faith without love is not enough—rather it is not faith at all, but a counterfeit of faith, just as a face seen in a mirror is not a real face but merely the reflection of a face.

Fourthly, we also need patience. For whoever has faith, trusting in God and showing love to his neighbor, practicing it day by day, must suffer persecution....

And here, dear friends, one must not insist upon his rights but must see what may be useful and helpful to his brother, as St. Paul says, "All things are lawful for me, but not all things are beneficial" [1 Cor. 6:12]. We are not all equally strong in faith; some of you have a stronger faith than I. Therefore, we must not look upon ourselves, or our strength, or our rank, but upon our neighbor.... How does a mother nourish her child? First, she feeds it with milk, then gruel, then eggs and soft food. If she weaned it and at once gave it the ordinary, coarse food, the child would never thrive. So we should also deal with our brother, have patience with him for a time, suffer his weakness and help him bear it.... I would not have gone so far as you have done if I had been here. What you did was good, but you have gone too fast. For there are also brothers and sisters on the other side who belong to us and must still be won....

Therefore, all those have erred who have helped and consented to abolish the Mass—in itself a good undertaking, but not accomplished in an orderly way. You say it was right according to the Scriptures. I agree, but what becomes of order? For it was done in wantonness, with no regard for proper order and with offense to your neighbor. If, beforehand, you had called upon God in earnest prayer, and had obtained the aid of the authorities, one could be certain that it had come from God. I, too, would have taken steps toward the same end if it had been a good thing to do; and if the Mass were not so evil a thing, I would introduce it again....

---

[5] Source: Henry Eyster Jacobs et al., eds., *Works of Martin Luther: With Introductions and Notes* (Philadelphia: A. J. Holman Company, 1915), 2:392–95, 404–6, text modernized.

Here one can see that you do not have the Spirit, in spite of your deep knowledge of the Scriptures. Take note of these two things: *must* and *free*. The *must* is that which necessity requires, and which must ever be unyielding, as, for instance, the faith, which I shall never permit anyone to take away from me, but which I must always keep in my heart and freely confess before everyone. But *free* is that in which I have choice and may use or not, yet in such a way that it profit my brother and not me. Now do not make a *must* out of what is *free*, as you have done, so that you may not be called to account for those who were led astray by your exercise of liberty without love....

B. The Third Sermon, March 11, 1522, Tuesday after Invocavit

But we must come to the images, and concerning them also it is true that they are unnecessary, and we are free to have them or not, although it would be much better if we did not have them. I am not partial to them.... You read in the law, Exodus 20[:4], "You shall not make for yourself an idol, whether in the form of anything that is in heaven above, or that is on the earth beneath, or that is in the water under the earth." There you take your stand; that is your ground. Now let us see! When our adversaries shall say, "The first commandment aims at this, that we should worship one God alone and not any image, even as it is said immediately following, 'You shall not bow down to them or worship them,'" and when they declare that the worship of images is forbidden and not the making of them, they disturb and unsettle our foundation for us. And if you reply, "The text says, 'You shall not make for yourself an idol,'" they answer, "It also says, 'You shall not worship them.'" In the face of such uncertainty, who would be so bold as to destroy the images? Not I.

But let us go farther. Did not Noah, Abraham, and Jacob build altars? And who will deny that? We must admit it. Again, did not Moses erect a bronze serpent, as we read in his fourth book? How can you say Moses forbids the making of images when he himself makes one? It seems to me that such a serpent is an image too. How shall we answer that? Again, do we not read that two cherubim were erected on the mercy-seat [Ex. 25: 18], the very place where God willed that he should be worshipped? Here we must admit that we may make images and have images, but we must not worship them, and when they are worshiped, they should be put away and destroyed, just as King Hezekiah broke in pieces the serpent erected by Moses....

Therefore, it should have been preached that images were nothing and that God is not served by putting them up, and they would have fallen of themselves. That is what I did; that is what Paul did in Athens, when he went into their churches and saw all their idols. He did not strike at any of them but stood in the marketplace and said, "People of Athens, you are all idolatrous" [Acts 17:22–23]. He preached against their idols, but he overthrew none by force. And you would rush in, create an uproar, break down the altars and overthrow the images? Do you really believe you can abolish the images in this way? No, you will only set them up more firmly. Even if you overthrew the images in this place, do you think you have overthrown those in Nuremberg and the rest of the world? Not at all. St. Paul, as we read in Acts [28:11], sat in a ship on whose prow were painted or carved the Twins [Castor and Pollux]. He went on board and did not bother about it at all, neither did he break them off. Why must Luke describe the Twins at this place? Without doubt he wanted to show that outward things could do no harm to faith, if only the heart does not cleave to them nor put its trust in them. This is what we must preach and teach, and let the word alone do the work, as I said before. The word must first capture the hearts of men and enlighten them—we cannot do it.

22. Karlstadt, *Whether One Should Proceed Slowly*, 1524[6]

To my especially beloved brother in Christ, Bartel Bach, city clerk in Joachimstal.... Dear brother, in response to my intimation that several changes have taken place here,[7] you write that you wish to go slowly in your place. By this you give me to understand privately that, in order to avoid offending the weak, one ought not move ahead quickly or suddenly, but slowly. This is nothing other than what the entire world is now doing, shouting, "Weak, weak, sick, sick; not so fast, easy does it, easy does it."... I must say to you that neither in this case nor in other matters which pertain to God should you look to the way the great mass speaks or judges. Rather, you should only look to God's word....

We are to keep all of God's commandments to the best of our ability and are not to wait until the unwise or the weak act on them.... The doing of what God asks of us is commanded of us all, even if the entire world were to hold back and be unwilling to follow....

I ask whether I ought to leave the idols standing, which God commands me to remove until all the weak follow suit by removing idols. Likewise, whether I ought to slander God until all others stop slandering. If you should say yes, the enemies of Christ could say with equal right that murderers can murder, thieves steal, and adulterers commit adultery and knaves commit all sorts of vices until all knaves have become righteous, for the same reasoning and foundation goes for all commandments.... How much harder and more seriously [will the one be hit] who sins against his commandments to please a knave. Paul says, "Have nothing in common with idolaters, adulterers, and the like" [2 Cor. 6:14]. Yet, you tell me that you think one should go easy and depart gradually from evil. I also know that St. Peter will turn the key— which he is supposed to have to open heaven— very slowly; that he will twist and turn it in the lock and will open to them just as slowly as they are approaching....

---

[6] Source: Furcha, *The Essential Karlstadt*, 248, 250–51, 253, 260–61, 267.

[7] Karlstadt was in the city of Orlamünde at this time.

Here then you have clear grounds that we were not obliged, either in word or deed, to hold back in doing God's commandments until our neighbors and those gluttons at Wittenberg are prepared to follow suit....

It is wrong to use the giving of offense and brotherly love as excuses for maintaining idols and allowing the mass and other blasphemies to blossom and flourish.... [I]dols are more perdicious in Christendom than are carnal houses of pleasure, and they lead more quickly to spiritual adultery than any whore or knave. Therefore, those who bid us keep idols (which lay persons call saints) in God's houses, atop mountains, in valleys, and at crossroads under the pretext of fraternal love until the weak become strong do not exemplify genuine brotherly love. They preach fraternal harm and not fraternal service or love....

We ought to take such harmful things away from the weak and tear them out of their hands with no regard to whether they might cry, shout, or flee because of it. For the time will come when those who now curse and swear at us will thank us.... Now I ask you, when I see a small infant holding a sharp, pointed knife in its hands, one which it would love to keep, do I show brotherly love toward the child when I yield to its will and leave the harmful knife, so that it might hurt and kill itself, or rather when I break its will and take away the knife? You will have to say, when you take away from the child what could harm it, you do a fatherly or brotherly Christian deed.... What they call brotherly love is in fact brotherly harm and offense. Their love is the kind of love which senseless mothers show who let their children have their own will, thus leading them to the gallows....

Look to God's commandments and teaching, and you will find this. Destroy all places at which the Gentiles (whom you shall conquer) served their idols—be it on hills or mountains or under green trees—break up and devastate, do away with, etc. [Deut. 12:2–3]. God never commanded the Jews to first preach to the Gentiles ere they removed their idols. And what more than double Gentiles are our idolatrous Christians? It is unnecessary to teach them first before removing from them what might destroy them. Even though they may be angry now, they will rejoice later. God did not order the Jews to do it in the entire world, but only in the places which they were to conquer and in which they were to rule. Accordingly, the conclusion is that where Christians rule, they are not to look to any magistrate, but are to strike out freely and of their own and throw down whatever is against God even without preaching.

XI. THOMAS MÜNTZER, SPIRITUALISM, AND SOCIAL REVOLUTION

More dangerous than Karlstadt in Luther's eyes was Thomas Müntzer. Müntzer had been a Catholic priest who came into contact with Luther and Karlstadt in Wittenberg around 1518–19. He became more prominent, however, in 1520, when he started preaching in Zwickau, which like

Wittenberg was in Saxony. Müntzer preached about being guided by the direct influence of the Holy Spirit, rather than by the careful interpretation of the Scriptures. This approach, which would come be known as Spiritualism, was a major departure from Luther's teaching, and the two men became increasingly hostile to one another. Like Karlstadt, Müntzer believed reform had to go further and move more swiftly than Luther was taking it. Moving well beyond Karlstadt, Müntzer believed true religious reform had to entail the complete reordering and "cleansing" of society. In the text below (doc. 23), Müntzer appeals to the local German nobility to take up the sword to do exactly that.

Luther believed Müntzer to be the chief of the *Schwärmer* (fanatics) and calls on the princes to restrain him (doc. 24).

Focus Questions

1. How does Müntzer characterize the present age?
2. What points of Müntzer's theology does Luther's letter criticize?
3. What is meant by "testing the spirits," and how does Luther propose it should be done?
4. What do Müntzer and Luther each ask the princes to do?
5. What ideas do Müntzer and Luther seem to have about the proper relationship between church and state?

23. Thomas Müntzer, *Sermon before the Princes*, 1524[8]

It is true, and [I] know it to be true, that the Spirit of God is revealing to many elect, pious persons a decisive, inevitable, imminent reformation [accompanied] by great anguish, and it must be carried out to completion....

[T]he fifth [symbolized by the iron and clay feet,][9] is this which we have before our eyes, which is also of iron and would like to coerce. But it is matted together with mud, as we see before [our] discerning eyes—vain, pretentious

---

[8] Source: George Huntston Williams, ed., *Spiritual and Anabaptist Writers*, Library of Christian Classics (Philadelphia: Westminster Press, 1957), 62–66, 68–69.

[9] Müntzer is referring to the series of kingdoms prophesied in the book of Daniel.

schemes of hypocrisy which writhe and wriggle over the whole earth. One sees nicely now how the eels and the vipers all in a heap abandon themselves to obscenities. The priests and all the wicked clerics are the vipers, as John the baptizer of Christ calls them (Matt. 3:7), and the temporal lords and princes are the eels, as is figuratively represented in Leviticus (ch. 11:10–12) by the fishes, etc.... Therefore, you much beloved and esteemed princes, learn your judgments directly from the mouth of God and do not let yourselves be misled by your hypocritical parsons nor be restrained by false consideration and indulgence.... The poor laity [of the towns] and the peasants see it much more clearly than you. Yea, God be praised, it has become so great [that] already, if other lords or neighbors should wish to persecute you for the gospel's sake, they would be driven back by their own people!... Therefore, you esteemed princes of Saxony... seek only straightway the righteousness of God, and take courageously the cause of the gospel!... For the pitiable corruption of holy Christendom has become so great that at the present time no tongue can tell it all. Therefore a new Daniel must arise and interpret for you your vision and this [prophet], as Moses teaches (Deut. 20:2), must go in front of the army. He must reconcile the anger of the princes and the enraged people. For if you will rightly experience the corruption of Christendom and the deception of the false clerics and the vicious reprobates, you will become so enraged at them that no one can think it through.... For they have made fools of you so that everyone swears by the saints that the princes are in respect to their office a pagan people. They are said to be able to maintain nothing other than a civil unity. O beloved, yea, the great Stone

there is about to fall and strike these schemes of [mere] reason and dash them to the ground, for he says (Matt. 10:34): I am not come to send peace but a sword. What should be done, however, with the same? Nothing different from [what is done with] the wicked who hinder the gospel: Get them out of the way and eliminate them, unless you want to be ministers of the devil rather than of God, as Paul calls you (Rom. 13:4). You need not doubt it. God will strike to pieces all your adversaries who undertake to persecute you.... Now if you want to be true governors, you must begin government at the roots, and, as Christ commanded, drive his enemies from the elect. For you are the means to this end. Beloved, don't give us any old jokes about how the power of God should do it without your application of the sword. Otherwise may it rust away for you in its scabbard!... Therefore let not the evil-doers live longer who make us turn away from God (Deut. 13:5). For the godless person has no right to live when he is in the way of the pious.... [The ancient Jews] did not conquer the land by the sword but rather through the power of God. But the sword was the means, as eating and drinking is for us the means of living. In just this way, the sword is necessary to wipe out the godless (Rom. 13:4). That this might now take place, however, in an orderly and proper fashion, our cherished fathers, the princes, should do it, who with us confess Christ. If, however, they do not do it, the sword will be taken from them (Dan. 7:26f.). For they confess him all right with words and deny him with the deed (Titus 1:16).... The weeds must be plucked out of the vineyard of God in the time of the harvest....

Without doubt inexperienced people will to such an extent anger themselves over this little book for the reason that I say with Christ (Luke 19:27; Matt. 18:6) and with Paul (1 Cor. 5:7, 13) and with the instruction of the whole divine law that the godless rulers should be killed, especially the priests and monks who revile the gospel as heresy for us and wish to be considered at the same time as the best Christians.... In the last days the lovers of pleasures will indeed have the form of godliness, but they will denounce its power. Nothing on earth has a better form and mask than spurious goodness. For this reason all corners are full of nothing but hypocrites, among whom not a one is so bold as to be able to say the real truth. Therefore in order that the truth may be rightly brought to the light, you rulers—it makes no difference whether you want to or not—must conduct yourselves according to the conclusion of this chapter (Dan. 2:48f.), namely that Nebuchadnezzar made the holy Daniel an officer in order that he might execute good, righteous decisions, as the Holy Spirit says (Ps. 58:10f.). For the godless have no right to live, except as the elect wish to grant it to them....

24. Luther, *Letter to the Princes of Saxony Concerning the Rebellious Spirit*, 1524[10]

Grace and peace in Christ Jesus our Savior. God's holy word, when it arises, always has the good fortune to excite Satan with all his might against it. At first, the devil rages with his fist and wicked power; then, if that does no good, he attacks with evil tongues and extravagant spirits and doctrines, so that what he could not crush with power he may suffocate with venomous lies.... Now, Satan knows that the rage of pope and emperor will accomplish nothing against us; indeed, he feels that, as is the way with God's word, the more it is oppressed the more it spreads and grows, and therefore, he now attacks it with false spirits and sects. We must, therefore, consider and not err, for it must be so; as Paul says to the Corinthians, "Indeed, there have to be factions among you, for only so will it become clear who among you are genuine" [1 Cor. 11:19]. And so, as Satan, having been driven out, has now wandered two or three years through dry places, seeking rest and finding none [Matt. 12:43], he has at last settled down in your Grace's electorate and made himself a nest at Allstedt[11] and plans under our peace, protection, and guardianship to fight against us....

Now, it is an especial joy that our followers did not begin this heresy, as the sectarians themselves boast that they did not learn it from us, but directly from heaven, and that they hear God speak to them directly as to the angels. It is a simple fact that at Wittenberg, only faith, love, and the cross of Christ are taught. God's voice,

---

[10] Source: Preserved Smith and Charles Jacobs, ed. and trans., *Luther's Correspondence and Other Contemporary Letters* (Philadelphia: Lutheran Publication Society, 1918), 2:241–47, text modernized.

[11] This is a reference to Müntzer, who was living in Allstedt at the time.

they say, you must hear yourself, and suffer and feel God's work in you to know your own weight; indeed, they make nothing of Scripture, which they call "Bible-Booble-Babel."...

The sole reason for my writing this letter to your Graces is that I have gathered from the writings of these people that this same spirit will not be satisfied to make converts by word only, but intends to take up arms and set himself with power against the government, and will soon raise a riot. Here Satan lets the cat out of the bag; that is, he makes too much public. What will this spirit do when he has won the support of the mob? Truly, here at Wittenberg, I have heard from the same spirit that his business must be carried through with the sword. I then marked that their plans would come out, namely, to overturn the civil government and themselves become lords of the world. But Christ says his kingdom is not of this world [John 18:36] and teaches the apostles not to be like the rulers of the earth [Matt. 10:25]....

Their boasting about the spirit counts for nothing, for we have the saying of St. John, bidding us to "test the spirits to see whether they are from God" [1 John 4:1]. Now this spirit has not yet been tested and goes about with turbulence and makes a disturbance according to his own sweet will. If he were a good spirit, he would first humbly submit to be tested and judged, as does the Spirit of Christ.... But the spirit of Allstedt shuns that sort of thing as the devil shuns the cross, and yet in his own nest he speaks the most unterrified language, as though he were full of three Holy Ghosts, and this unseemly boasting is a fine proof of who this spirit is. For in his book he offers to appear before a harmless assembly and to stake life and soul upon it, but not privately, in the presence of two or three persons.... What kind of spirit is that who is afraid of two or three people and cannot endure an assembly that may do him harm? I shall tell you. He smells the roast; he has been with me once or twice in my cloister at Wittenberg and had his nose punched; so he does not like the soup and will not appear except where his own followers are present who will say, "Yes!" to his swelling words....

I have said these things to your Graces, so that your Graces may not be afraid of this spirit or delay action, but enjoin them strictly to refrain from violence and stop their destroying of monasteries and churches and their burning of saints' images, commanding them that if they wish to prove their spirit, to do so in a proper manner and first submit to investigation, either by us or by the papists....

To sum it up, gracious lords, your Graces must not interfere with the office of the word. Let them go on boldly and confidently preaching what they can and against whom they will; for, as I have said, there must be divisions, and the word of God must take the field and fight.... If their spirit is true, he will not fear us and will hold the field; if our spirit is true, he will not be afraid of him or of anybody. Let the spirits fight it out. If some are led astray, that is the fortune of war; when there is a battle, some must fall and be wounded, but he who fights bravely will receive the crown. But if they will fight with anything more than the word, if they will break and smite with the fist, then your Graces should interfere, whether it is we or they who do it, forbid the offenders the land, and say, "We shall gladly look on and allow you to fight with the word, so that the true doctrine may be preserved, but keep your fists to yourselves, for that is our affair; or else get out of the land." We, whose concern is with the word of God, must not fight with the fist. It is a spiritual battle that wins hearts and souls from the devil.... Our duty is to preach and to suffer, not to strike and defend ourselves with the fist.

Christ and his apostles destroyed no churches and broke up no images, but they won men's hearts with God's word, and the churches and images fell of themselves....

Your Graces' obedient,
Dr. Martin Luther

XII. THE GERMAN PEASANTS' WAR

The German Peasants' War (1524–26) was the largest peasant rebellion in Europe before the French Revolution. It was an utter catastrophe for the peasants, over 100,000 of whom were killed in the fighting. Peasant revolts were not uncommon in Europe in the late Middle Ages, but what made the German Peasants' War different was, first, its scale, and second, its ties to the Reformation. Some radical Protestant leaders, such as Thomas Müntzer, saw the Reformation as an opportunity for widespread social reform and encouraged the peasants in their rebellion. Others, including Luther, firmly opposed it.

The first text below, the *Twelve Articles of the Peasants* (doc. 25) is the fullest written explanation we have of the peasants' grievances. They were drawn up by a group of peasant representatives in southern Germany in March 1525 and were widely printed in Germany.

At the initial outbreak of hostilities, Luther published his *Admonition to Peace*, urging both sides to come to an agreement. But as the violence spread, he became increasingly frustrated with the peasants and turned viciously against them. The title of the second text succinctly conveys Luther's attitude: *Against the Robbing and Murdering Hordes of the Peasants.*

Focus Questions

1. How would you characterize the demands of the peasants in the Twelve Articles? Are they chiefly economic or religious grievances? On what basis do you arrive at that conclusion?

2. What does Luther advise the princes of Germany to do with the peasants?

3. What do the attitudes of both the peasants and Luther convey about their understanding of secular authority? Since Luther himself was also under the emperor's ban in the Edict of Worms, was he hypocritical in calling for the rigorous enforcement of the law against the peasants? Why or why not?

25. The Twelve Articles of the Peasants, 1525[12]

There are many evil writings put forth of late which take occasion, on account of the assembling of the peasants, to cast scorn upon the Gospel, saying, "Is this the fruit of the new teaching, that no one should obey but all should everywhere rise in revolt and rush together to reform, or perhaps destroy altogether, the authorities both ecclesiastic and lay?" The articles below shall answer these godless and criminal faultfinders and serve, in the first place, to remove the reproach from the word of God and, in the second place, to give a Christian excuse for the disobedience or even the revolt of the entire peasantry.... Therefore, Christian reader, read the following articles with care and then judge. Here follow the articles:

The First Article. First, it is our humble petition and desire, as also our will and resolution, that in the future we should have power and authority so that each community should choose and appoint a pastor, and that we should have the right to depose him should he conduct himself improperly. The pastor thus chosen should teach us the Gospel pure and simple, without any addition, doctrine, or ordinance of man. For to teach us continually the true faith will lead us to pray God that through his grace this faith may increase within us and become part of us. For if his grace does not work within us, we remain flesh and blood, which avails nothing, since the Scripture clearly teaches that only through true faith can we come to God. Only through his mercy can we become holy. Hence, such a guide and pastor is necessary and in this fashion grounded upon the Scriptures.

The Second Article. According as the just tithe is established by the Old Testament and fulfilled in the New, we are ready and willing to pay the fair tithe of grain. The word of God plainly provided that, in giving according to right to God and distributing to his people, the services of a pastor are required. We will that,

---

[12] Source: *Translations and Reprints from the Original Sources of European History*, Reformation Number (Philadelphia: Department of History of the University of Pennsylvania, 1897), 2:19–24, text modernized.

for the future, our church provost, whomsoever the community may appoint, shall gather and receive this tithe. From this he shall give to the pastor elected by the whole community a decent and sufficient maintenance for him and his household, as shall seem right to the whole community. What remains over shall be given to the poor of the place, as the circumstances and the general opinion demand. Should anything farther remain, let it be kept lest anyone should have to leave the country on account of poverty. Provision should also be made from this surplus to avoid laying any land tax on the poor.... The small tithes, whether ecclesiastical or lay, we will not pay at all, for the Lord God created cattle for the free use of man. We will not, therefore, continue to pay an unseemly tithe which is of man's invention.

The Third Article. It has been the custom hitherto for men to hold us as their own property, which is pitiable enough, considering that Christ has delivered and redeemed us all, without exception, by the shedding of his precious blood, the lowly as well as the great. Accordingly, it is consistent with Scripture that we should be free and wish to be so. It's not that we would wish to be absolutely free and under no authority. God does not teach us that we should lead a disorderly life in the lusts of the flesh, but that we should love the Lord our God and our neighbor. We would gladly observe all this as God has commanded us in the celebration of the communion. He has not commanded us to disobey the authorities, but rather to be humble, not only towards those in authority, but towards everyone. We are, thus, ready to yield obedience according to God's law to our elected and regular authorities in all proper things becoming to a Christian. We, therefore, take it for granted that you will release us from serfdom as true Christians, unless it should be shown to us from the Gospel that we are serfs.

The Fourth Article. In the fourth place it has become the custom that no poor man should be allowed to catch venison or wild fowl or fish in flowing water, which seems to us quite unseemly and unbrotherly as well as selfish and not agreeable to the word of God. In some places the authorities preserve the game to our great annoyance and loss, recklessly permitting the unreasoning animals to destroy to no purpose our crops, which God allows to grow for the use of man, and yet we must remain quiet. This is neither godly or neighborly. For when God created man he gave him dominion over all the animals, over the birds of the air and over the fish in the water. Accordingly, it is our desire that if a man holds possession of waters, he should prove from satisfactory documents that his right has been acquired by purchase. We do not wish to take it from him by force, but his rights should be exercised in a Christian and brotherly fashion. But whoever cannot produce such evidence should surrender his claim with good grace.

The Fifth Article. In the fifth place we are aggrieved in the matter of woodcutting, for the noble folk have appropriated all the woods to themselves alone. If a poor man requires wood he must pay double for it. It is our opinion in regard to wood which has fallen into the hands of a lord, whether spiritual or temporal, that unless it was duly purchased it should revert again to the community. It should, moreover, be free to every member of the community to help himself to such firewood as he needs in his home. Also, if a man requires wood for carpenter's purposes, he should have it free, but with the knowledge of a person appointed by the community for that purpose. Should, however, no such forest be at the disposal of the community, let that which has been duly bought be administered in a brotherly and Christian manner. If the forest, although unfairly appropriated in the first instance, was later duly sold, let the matter be adjusted in a friendly spirit and according to the Scriptures.

The Sixth Article. Our sixth complaint is in regard to the excessive services demanded of us which are increased from day to day. We ask that this matter be properly looked into so that we shall not continue to be oppressed in this way but that some gracious consideration be given us, since our forefathers were required only to serve according to the word of God.

The Seventh Article. Seventh, we will not hereafter allow ourselves to be further oppressed by our lords but will let them demand only what is just and proper according to the word of the agreement between the lord and the peasant. The lord should no longer try to force more services or other dues from the peasant without payment, but permit the peasant to enjoy his holding in peace and quiet. The peasant should, however, help the lord when it is necessary, and at proper times when it will not be disadvantageous to the peasant and for a suitable payment.

The Eighth Article. In the eighth place, we are greatly burdened by holdings which cannot support the rent exacted from them. The peasants suffer loss in this way and are ruined, and we ask that the lords may appoint persons of honor to inspect these holdings and fix a rent in accordance with justice, so that the peasants shall not work for nothing—"for the worker deserves his wages" [Luke 10:7].

The Ninth Article. In the ninth place, we are burdened with a great evil in the constant making of new laws. We are not judged according to the offense, but sometimes with great ill will, and sometimes much too leniently. In our opinion we should be judged according to the old written law so that the case shall be decided according to its merits, and not with partiality.

The Tenth Article. In the tenth place, we are aggrieved by the appropriation by individuals of meadows and fields which at one time belonged to a community. These we will take again into our own hands. It may, however, happen that the land was rightfully purchased. When, however, the land has unfortunately been purchased in this way, some brotherly arrangement should be made according to circumstances.

The Eleventh Article. In the eleventh place we will entirely abolish the due called *Todfall* [death tax] and will no longer endure it, nor allow widows and orphans to be thus shamefully robbed against God's will and in violation of justice and right, as has been done in many places and by those who should shield and protect them. These have disgraced and despoiled us, and although they had little authority, they assumed it. God will suffer this no more, but it shall be wholly done away with, and for the future no man shall be bound to give little or much.

Twelfth Article and Conclusion. In the twelfth place it is our conclusion and final resolution, that if one or more of the articles set forth here should not be in agreement with the word of God, as we think they are, such article we will willingly recede from when it is proved really to be against the word of God by a clear explanation of the Scripture. Or if articles should now be conceded to us that are hereafter discovered to be unjust, from that hour they shall be dead and null and without force. Likewise, if more complaints should be discovered which are based upon truth and the Scriptures and relate to offenses against God and our neighbor, we have determined to reserve the right to present these also, and to exercise ourselves in all Christian teaching. For this we shall pray God, since he can grant these, and he alone. May the peace of Christ abide with us all.

26. Luther, *Against the Robbing and Murdering Hordes of Peasants*, 1525[13]

In my preceding pamphlet I had no occasion to condemn the peasants, because they promised to yield to law and better instruction, as Christ also demands (Matt. 7:1). But before I can turn around, they go out and appeal to force, in spite of their promises, and rob and pillage and act like mad dogs. From this it is quite apparent what they had in their false minds, and that what they put forth under the name of the Gospel in the *Twelve Articles* was all vain pretense. In short, they practice mere devil's work, and it is the arch-devil himself who reigns at Mühlhausen,[14] indulging in nothing but robbery, murder, and bloodshed; as Christ says of the devil in John 8:44, "He was a murderer from the beginning." Since, therefore, those peasants and miserable wretches allow themselves to be led astray and act differently from what they declared, I likewise must write differently concerning them and first bring their sins before their eyes, as God commands [Isa. 58:1; Ezek. 2:7], whether perchance some of them may come to their senses; and, further, I would instruct those in authority how to conduct themselves in this matter.

With threefold horrible sins against God and men have these peasants loaded themselves, for which they have deserved a manifold death of body and soul.

First, they have sworn to their true and gracious rulers to be submissive and obedient, in accord with God's command, "Give, therefore, to the emperor the things that are the emperor's" [Matt. 22:21], and, "Let every person be subject to the governing authorities" [Rom. 13:1]. But since they have deliberately and sacrilegiously abandoned their obedience and, in

---

[13] Source: James Harvey Robinson, *Readings in European History*, 2 vols. (Boston: Ginn & Company, 1906), 2:106–8, text modernized.

[14] A reference to Thomas Müntzer.

addition, have dared to oppose their lords, they have thereby forfeited body and soul, as perfidious, perjured, lying, disobedient wretches and scoundrels are accustomed to do. Wherefore St. Paul judges them, saying, "Those who resist will incur judgment" [Rom. 13:2]. The peasants will incur this sentence sooner or later, for God wills that fidelity and allegiance shall be sacredly kept.

Second, they cause uproar and sacrilegiously rob and pillage monasteries and castles that do not belong to them, for which, like highway robbers and murderers, they deserve the two-fold death of body and soul. It is right and lawful to slay at the first opportunity a rebellious person who is known as such, for he is already under God's and the emperor's ban. Everyone is at once judge and executioner of a public rebel, just as when a fire starts, he who can extinguish it first is the best fellow. Rebellion is not simply vile murder but is like a great fire that kindles and devastates a country; it fills the land with murder and bloodshed, makes widows and orphans, and destroys everything, like the greatest calamity. Therefore, whoever can, should smite, strangle, and stab, secretly or publicly, and should remember that there is nothing more poisonous, pernicious, and devilish than a rebellious man. Just as one must slay a mad dog, so, if you do not fight the rebels, they will fight you, and the whole country with you.

Third, they cloak their frightful and revolting sins with the Gospel, call themselves Christian brothers, swear allegiance, and compel people to join them in such abominations. By this they become the greatest blasphemers and violators of God's holy name, and serve and honor the devil under the semblance of the Gospel, so that they have ten times deserved death of body and soul, for never have I heard of uglier sins. And I believe also that the devil foresees the judgment day, that he undertakes such an unheard-of measure, as if he said, "It is the last, and therefore, it shall be the worst; I'll stir up the dregs and knock the very bottom out." May the Lord restrain him! Lo, how mighty a prince is the devil; how he holds the world in his hands and can put it to confusion. Who else could so soon capture so many thousands of peasants, lead them astray, blind and deceive them, stir them to revolt, and make them the willing executioners of his malice?

FURTHER READING

Blickle, Peter. *The Revolution of 1525: The German Peasants' War from a New Perspective.* Translated by Thomas A. Brady, Jr., and H. C. Erik Midelfort. Baltimore: Johns Hopkins University Press, 1981.

Burnett, Amy Nelson. *Karlstadt and the Origins of the Eucharistic Controversy: A Study in the Circulation of Ideas.* New York: Oxford University Press, 2011. http://dx.doi.org/10.1093/acprof:oso/9780199753994.001.0001.

Eire, Carlos M.N. *War against the Idols: The Reformation of Worship from Erasmus to Calvin.* Cambridge: Cambridge University Press, 1986. http://dx.doi.org/10.1017/CBO9780511528835.

Goertz, Hans-Jürgen. *Thomas Müntzer: Apocalyptic, Mystic, and Revolutionary.* Translated by Jocelyn Jaquiery. Edinburgh: T&T Clark, 1993.

Müntzer, Thomas. *The Collected Works of Thomas Müntzer.* Edited by Peter Matheson. Edinburgh: T & T Clark, 1988.

Scott, Tom, and Bob Scribner, eds. *The German Peasants' War: A History in Documents.* Atlantic Highlands, NJ: Humanities Press, 1991.

Stayer, James. *The German Peasants' War and the Anabaptist Community of Goods.* Montreal: McGill-Queen's University Press, 1991.

William, George H. *The Radical Reformation,* 3rd ed. Kirksville, MO: Truman State University Press, 2000.

IV

Ulrich Zwingli, the Reformed Tradition, and Swiss Anabaptism

Soon after Luther started the Reformation in Germany, a Swiss priest named Ulrich (or Huldrych) Zwingli spearheaded a similar movement in Zurich (§XIII). Zwingli adopted many of the same theological positions as Luther; they agreed, for example, on the doctrines of *sola gratia, sola fide, sola scriptura*, and the priesthood of all believers. There were two areas, however, in which they sharply disagreed. The first was on the proper interpretation of the Eucharist; Zwingli adopted a symbolic understanding of the sacrament, while Luther insisted on the real presence of Christ in the bread and wine. The second was that Zwingli believed a more thorough reform of church practice was necessary, including the removal of images, music, and clerical vestments from the churches. For this reason, the movement he started is referred to as the Reformed tradition, in contrast to Lutheranism. The division between the two Protestant traditions was sealed at the 1529 Colloquy of Marburg, where Zwingli and Luther met but could not agree on the doctrine of the Eucharist (§XIV).

Like Luther, Zwingli faced opposition from both Catholics and radicals. While the early radicals in Germany tended toward Spiritualism (see above, §XI), those in Switzerland focused on believers' baptism and separation from sinful society. Since they believed Christians had to be baptized as adult believers, even if they had been baptized as infants (as most of them had), they were labeled *Anabaptists*, or "rebaptizers." Zwingli turned just as harshly against the Anabaptists (§XV) as Luther had against Müntzer and his followers.

XIII. ZWINGLI AND THE REFORMATION IN ZURICH

Ulrich Zwingli (1484–1531) was a Catholic priest who had received a humanist education at the University of Basel. In 1518, he became pastor of Zurich and began preaching reform of the church. The first key event of the Zurich Reformation took place in 1522, when Zwingli encouraged some followers to ignore the prohibition on eating meat during Lent (see below, doc. 63), based on the same notion of Christian freedom preached by Luther (see above, doc. 16). The Zurich city council, which was independent of feudal lordship,[1] subsequently took an active role in introducing the Reformation in the canton. An early act of the council was to call for a religious disputation to determine whether or not Zwingli was preaching heresy in the city. The document below is an account of this religious disputation in Zurich, which took place in January 1523. Zwingli prepared 67 articles for debate at the disputation. The city council invited the canton's clergy and the bishop of Constance, in whose diocese Zurich lay. Approximately 600 people were in the city hall for the debate. Zwingli's chief opponent in the disputation was Johann Fabri, the vicar-general of the diocese of Constance. The account of the debate was written down by Erhard Hagenwald, a schoolteacher in Zurich, and edited by Zwingli himself. The disputation was an

---

[1] All the cantons of the Swiss Confederation were governed by city councils rather than by feudal lords. One should also note that Switzerland was not yet a unified nation state. Instead, the Swiss Confederation was an alliance of independent cantons, one of which was Zurich. Representatives of the cantons would meet regularly at diets, but the diets' decisions did not have the force of law in the individual cantons.

important victory for Zwingli, but it would be another two years before the Zurich council abolished the Mass, in 1525.

Focus Questions

1. Explain the disagreement over the venue for this disputation. Why does Zwingli support holding it in the Zurich town hall? Where does Fabri think it should be held, and why? What does this say about their ideas of religious authority?
2. What is Fabri's chief argument against Zwingli and the reformers generally?
3. How does Zwingli defend himself?
4. What are their positions on the intercession of the saints, and how do they justify them?
5. What does the city council finally decide at the end of the debate?
6. A high percentage of independent cities like Zurich adopted the Protestant faith. Why do you think such cities—as opposed to those ruled by a lord—might have been particularly open to reform?

27. The First Zurich Disputation, January 1523[2]

[*The motivation for and legitimacy of the disputation*]

ZWINGLI: Although I know that for the past five years I have preached in this city of Zurich nothing but the true, pure, and clear word of God, the holy Gospel, the joyous message of Christ, the Holy Scripture, not by the aid of man, but by the aid of the Holy Ghost, still all this did not help me. But I am maligned by many as a heretic, a liar, a deceiver, and one disobedient to the Christian Church, which facts are well known to my lords of Zurich. I made complaint of these things before them as my lords; I have often entreated and begged

---

[2] Source: Samuel Macauley Jackson, ed., *Selected Works of Huldreich Zwingli (1484–1531), the Reformer of German Switzerland* (Philadelphia: University of Pennsylvania, 1901), 48–51, 54–55, 64–69, 79–80, 92–94, text modernized.

of them in the public pulpit to grant me permission to give an account of my sermons and preaching (delivered in their city) before all men, learned or not, spiritual or secular, also before our gracious lord, the Bishop of Constance, or his representative.... At such request of mine, my lords, perhaps by divine will, you have granted me permission to hold a discussion in German before the assembled council, for which privilege I thank you especially as my lords.... I hope and am confident, indeed I know, that my sermons and doctrine are nothing else than the holy, true, pure Gospel, which God desired me to speak by the intuition and inspiration of his Spirit.... Therefore, I offer here to anyone who thinks that my sermons or teachings are unchristian or heretical to give the reasons and to answer kindly and without anger. Now let them speak in the name of God. Here I am....

VICAR-GENERAL JOHANN FABRI: If there is a desire to dispute and oppose good old customs, the ways and usages of the past, then in such case I say that I shall not undertake to dispute anything here at Zurich. For, as I think, such matters are to be settled by a general Christian assembly of all nations, or by a council of bishops and other scholars as are found at universities, just as occurred in times past among the holy apostles in Jerusalem, as we read in Acts 15....

ZWINGLI: As to claiming that such matters should be settled by a Christian assembly of all nations, or by a council of bishops, etc., I say that

here in this room is without doubt a Christian assembly. For I hope that the majority of us here desire from divine will and love to hear, to further, and to know the truth, which wish Almighty God will not deny us if we desire it to his honor with right belief and right hearts. For the Lord says, "Where two or three are gathered in my name, I am there among them" [Matt. 18:20]....
As to the council which is said to be announced at Nuremberg, it seems to me that the thing is proposed only to put off the common people desirous of God's word.... For pope, bishops, prelates, and the "big wigs" will allow no council in which the divine Scriptures were set forth in their clarity and purity....

[*The intercession of the saints*]

FABRI: Since I have been summoned to answer by Master Ulrich, I will say that some hundreds of years ago it happened, my dear sirs, that heresy and dissention arose in the Church, the causes and beginners of which were Novatians, Montanists, Sabellians, Ebionites, Marcionites,[3] and others, under whose false teachings and error many articles like these of our times were planted in men, and by their teachings many believing folk went astray. Among these some asserted that praying to the dear saints and their intercession, as also of the mother of God, and that purgatory, too, did not exist, but were man's invention, and the like. In order to close up such misleading roads and ways of error, many pious bishops and fathers met in many places, at one time in Asia, then in Africa,

---

[3] All early Christian heretics.

then somewhere in Greece, that they might hold synods and councils, and avoid and stop heresy and such things. And afterward, constitutions (that is, ordinances and decisions) were made, prescribed, and commanded about these matters by the holy fathers and the popes that such heretical views should not be held, having been rejected by the Christian Church. And although this was firmly and irrevocably ratified a long time ago by decrees of the popes and bishops, and considered wrong in Christian churches, still later schisms, dissenting parties, and sects have sprung up in Europe, as, to mention their names, the Bohemians, Picards, who were led astray by such heretics as Wyclif and Hus, living contrary to the decrees and ordinances of the holy popes, acting contrary to the regulations of the Christian Church, and not putting any faith in the intercession of the saints, or still less in purgatory. And although such heresy and error were later rejected by all men of Christian belief, and although those who live and remain in such error were considered, recognized, and proclaimed by the holy councils as cut off from the mother of Christian churches, still one now finds those who stir up these things anew, and strive to bring into doubt that which many years ago was recognized and decided upon as untrue and erroneous by pope and bishop. They try to drive us from old customs, which have endured and stood in honor these seven hundred years, planning to overturn and upset all things. For first they went at the pope, cardinals, and bishops; then they turned all cloisters topsy-turvy; after that they fell upon purgatory. And when they had left the earth, they at last ascended to heaven and went at the saints and great servants of God. Saint Peter with his keys, indeed our dear Lady, the Mother of God, could not escape their disgraceful attacks. And I know some places where they had gone so far as even to Christ himself. . . .

Shall not all that which the pious, holy fathers assembled in the Holy Spirit of God have made and unanimously decided be nothing and count as nothing? It must have grown up to the great injury and disgrace of all Christendom. For the holy fathers and all our ancestors must have erred, and for fourteen hundred years now, Christianity must have been misled and ruled in error, which, I do not need to say, would be unchristian to believe. Now if the intercession of the dear saints has ever been ratified as necessary and useful by popes, bishops, fathers, and councils, and if since the time of the holy Pope Gregory it has continued in use among all Christianity, it seems strange to me that now for the first time, people desire to consider this wrong and erroneous. . . .

Truly, dear sirs, it would be well to consider beforehand what dangers and dissensions might arise for Christianity if one were not in harmony and agreement with the whole community in these matters. . . . It seems to me not to be sufficient that one apply or bring forward Scripture, but it is also important that one understand Scripture correctly. With that in view, perhaps one should attend to such matters at the universities, as I said before. . . .

ZWINGLI: We well know that many things were decided upon in times past by the fathers in council assembled, which were afterward repealed and revoked by others who thought they assembled in the spirit of God, as is plainly found in the Nicene Council and that of Gangra,[4] in the first of which the clergy were allowed to marry, and all those who spoke against it were cursed, while the second decided upon the opposite. It is also a fact that many times ordinances have been issued and ordered by the fathers in council to which their successors paid no heed.... Also many ordinances or rules of the fathers are found which were changed afterwards, especially in our times, and otherwise not kept or given up by the influence of money, so that such things are allowed which were formerly forbidden by the fathers. From this we can see that councils have not always acted in the spirit of the Holy Ghost, but sometimes according to human will and judgment, which is, of course, forbidden by divine Scripture. For the Holy Ghost does not say this today and that tomorrow, but its ordinances and regulations must remain everlasting and changeless....

We know from the Old and New Testaments of God that our only comforter, redeemer, savior, and mediator with God is Jesus Christ, in whom and through whom alone we can obtain grace, help, and salvation, and from no other being in heaven or on earth.

FABRI: I well know that Jesus Christ alone is the comfort, redemption, and salvation of all, and an intercessor and mediator between us and God, his heavenly Father, the highest round by which alone is an approach to the throne of divine grace and charity, according to Hebrews 4:16. Nevertheless, one may perhaps attain the highest round by means of the lower. It seems to me the dear saints and the Virgin Mary are not to be despised, since there are few who have not felt the intercession of the Virgin and the saints. I do not care what everyone says or believes. I have placed a ladder against heaven; I believe firmly in the intercession of the much-praised Queen of Heaven, the Mother of God, and another may believe or hold what he pleases....

[*The decision of the Zurich council*]

NARRATOR: After all had eaten, they were told to appear again in the city hall to hear the decision made by the wise council of Zurich. After all had gathered, there was publicly read before the council as is written hereafter:

... Since Master Ulrich Zwingli, canon and preacher of the Great Minster in the city of Zurich, has been formerly much talked against and blamed for his teachings, yet no one, upon his declaring and explaining his articles, has arisen against him or attempted to overcome him by means of the Scriptures, and when he has several times also called upon those who have accused him of being a heretic to step forward, and no one showed the least heresy in his doctrines, thereupon the aforesaid mayor, council, and great council of this city of Zurich, in order to quell disturbance and dispute, upon

---

4 The Council of Nicaea was the first ecumenical council and met in 325 CE. The date of the Council of Gangra is unclear, but it took place sometime in the mid-fourth century.

due deliberation and consultation have decided, resolved, and it is their earnest opinion, that Master Ulrich Zwingli continue and keep on as before to proclaim the holy Gospel and the correct divine Scriptures with the spirit of God in accordance with his capabilities so long and so frequently until something better is made known to him.

Furthermore, all your secular clergy, spiritual guides and preachers in your cities and counties and estates, shall undertake and preach nothing except what they can defend by the Gospels and other right divine Scriptures; furthermore, they shall in no way in the future slander, call each other "heretic," or insult in such manner.

XIV. THE COLLOQUY OF MARBURG

Zurich's decision to turn Protestant left it vulnerable to attack by the Catholic cantons of Switzerland and the Habsburgs.[5] Fears grew after the 1529 Diet of Speyer, where Emperor Charles V declared his intention to enforce the Edict of Worms outlawing Lutheranism in Germany. In light of this threat, the German Protestant leader Philip of Hesse thought the time was ripe for a German-Swiss Protestant military alliance. As a step toward such an alliance, Philip brought Luther and Zwingli together, along with several of their followers, at a meeting called a *colloquy* in the city of Marburg. The crucial doctrinal issue to confront was the difference of opinion on the Eucharist. From early in his career, Zwingli adopted a theology of the Eucharist that differed sharply from Luther's. Although Luther denied the Catholic doctrine of transubstantiation, he still believed that the true, corporeal body and blood of Christ were present together with the bread and wine in the sacrament. Zwingli, by contrast, taught that the bread and wine were merely symbolic of Christ's body and blood.

 The document below contains a hybrid account of the Marburg Colloquy. Several eyewitness accounts were recorded at the time, but they

---

[5] The Habsburg dynasty included both Emperor Charles V and Archduke Ferdinand of Austria at the time (see also below, §XXVIII).

all reflected their own doctrinal interests. In 1929, the historian Walther Köhler pieced together several of these accounts to try to come up with an accurate, unbiased version of the events.[6] The English translation used here is based on Köhler's German version.

Apart from Zwingli and Luther, the other main speaker during the colloquy was Johannes Oecolampadius (1482–1531), pastor in Basel and the second most important Reformed leader at the time after Zwingli. In the end, the two sides could not come to a theological agreement on the Eucharist, and the proposed alliance failed.

Focus Questions

1. How does each side justify its position on the Eucharist?
2. What accusations does each side cast at the other?
3. Explain the argument over the location of Christ's body.
4. Identify what you believe was the fundamental disagreement separating the two sides.
5. Why do you think failure to agree on a theological issue such as the Eucharist led the two sides to abandon the idea of a military alliance?

28. The Debate at the Colloquy of Marburg, 1529[7]

Zwingli: [L]et us now discuss the Lord's Supper, and at the end of our discussion we shall be most happy to talk about any and all other points of dispute.

Luther: ... Your basic contentions are these: In the last analysis you wish to prove that a body cannot be in two places at once, and you produce arguments about the unlimited body which are

---

[6] Walther Köhler, "Das Marburger Religionsgespräch 1529: Versuch einer Rekonstruction," *Schriften des Vereins für Reformationsgeschichte* 48 (1929): 7–38.

[7] Source: Donald J. Ziegler, ed., *Great Debates of the Reformation* (New York: Random House 1969), 74–77, 80, 82–86, 93, 97–98, 104–5.

based on natural reason. I do not question how Christ can be God and man and how the two natures can be joined. For God is more powerful than all our ideas, and we must submit to his word.

Prove that Christ's body is not there where the Scripture says, "This is my body"! Rational proofs I will not listen to. Corporeal proofs, arguments based on geometrical principles I repudiate absolutely.... God is beyond all mathematics, and the words of God are to be revered and carried out in awe. It is God who commands, "Take, eat, this is my body." I request, therefore, valid scriptural proof to the contrary.

(Luther writes on the table in chalk, "This is my body," and covers the words with a velvet cloth.)

Oecolampadius: The sixth chapter of John clarifies the other scriptural passages. Christ is not speaking there about a local presence. "The flesh is of no avail," he says [John 6:63]. It is not my intention to employ rational, or geometrical, arguments—neither am I denying the power of God—but as long as I have the complete faith I will speak from that. For Christ is risen; he sits at the right hand of God; and so he cannot be present in the bread. Our view is neither new nor sacrilegious, but is based on faith and Scripture.

It is from a physical to a spiritual repast that one must proceed. The Holy Scripture employs figurative language, metaphors, metonyms, and comparable terms, where the words mean something other than what they say. And so even the words "This is my body" may contain language that is figurative, like those that read, "John is Elijah" [Matt. 11:14], "The rock was Christ" [1 Cor.

10:4], "I am the true vine" [John 15:1], "The seed is the word of God" [Luke 8:11].

LUTHER:... I do not deny figurative speech, but you must prove that this is what we have here. It is not enough to say that these words— "This is my body"—could be interpreted in this way. You must prove that they must be so interpreted in a figurative sense.... Just because Christ speaks in the sixth chapter of John about a spiritual repast, you conclude that there is no physical repast whatsoever. You want me to place my trust in this, which is no proof at all. And so my faith is strong because you have not proved your words. My text is priceless and full of authority. Agree with it!

This is what I find so annoying—that you don't prove what you are supposed to prove.

Oecolampadius: Well then! I shall prove that the words—"This is my body"—must be taken figuratively. Listen to John 6. (*He reads John 6:48–63*). Christ is speaking here to the Jews and also to his disciples about the eating of his body and the drinking of his blood, and when they took him to mean a physical eating and shuddered at the thought, he replied: "It is the spirit that gives life; the flesh is of no avail" [verse 63]. From this, one ought to understand that he repudiated once for all the physical eating of his flesh; and it ought to follow that he neither could nor would maintain this repudiated view thereafter.

LUTHER:... I reply that he [Christ] wanted to teach the Jews of Capernaum that he should not be eaten like bread and meat in a bowl, like roast pork. When I partake of Christ in the bread, it is not in the vulgar sense, but as a gift of the Holy

Spirit. Hence, it is not a repast that is petty and repulsive, but one that is most holy. Man can still believe those words; the body of Christ is there. . . .

ZWINGLI: It is a prejudice, a preconception, which keeps Doctor Luther from yielding his point. He refuses to yield until a passage is quoted that proves that the body in the Lord's Supper is figurative. It is the prejudice of a heretic somewhat reminiscent of Helvidius, who denied that Jesus was the only son of Mary because it was clearly stated, "So his brothers said to him" [John 7:3]. One cannot reason thus from Scripture! Comparison of scriptural passages is always necessary. Although we have no scriptural passage that says, "This is the sign of the body," we still have proof that Christ dismissed the idea of a physical repast. Since it is our task here to investigate scriptural passages, and since the passage in John 6 moves away from the physical repast, we must therefore take it into account. From this it follows that Christ did not give himself in the Lord's Supper in a physical sense. . . .

LUTHER: [W]heresoever the word of God is, there we find a spiritual repast. When God speaks to us, then faith is required. This is what is meant by "eating." If he appends a physical sense to its meaning, then we must obey. We eat in faith this body, which is given for us. The mouth receives the body of Christ, the soul believes the words as it eats the body. . . .

ZWINGLI: That the body is eaten in the mouth is a statement that utterly amazes me. If Christ is present, then he is there to sustain the soul, not the body. How can he reconcile opposites? . . . I speak therefore from an under-standing of the spiritual sense of the Scriptures, and when Luther interprets them differently, and ambiguously, then he does violence to the Scriptures. . . .

LUTHER: Faith, in short, means this: It is not for us to comment on the loving word of God, only when faith or the articles of faith are contradicted by an absurdity. . . .

If you interpret the Lord's Supper figuratively, why not do the same with these words—"He was taken up into heaven" [Mark 16:19]?

I call upon you as before: your basic contentions are shaky. Give way, and give glory to God!

ZWINGLI: And we call upon you to give glory to God and to quit begging the question! The issue at stake it this: Where is the proof of your position? I am willing to consider your words carefully—no harm meant! You're trying to outwit me. I stand by this passage in the sixth chapter of John [verse 63] and shall not be shaken from it. You'll have to sing another tune!

LUTHER: You're being obnoxious! . . .

It is your point which must be proved, not mine. But let us stop this sort of thing. It serves no purpose.

ZWINGLI: It certainly does! It is for you to prove that the passage in John 6 speaks of a physical repast.

LUTHER: You express yourself poorly and make about as much progress as a cane standing in a corner. You're going nowhere.

ZWINGLI: No, no, no! This is the passage that will break your neck!

LUTHER: Don't be so sure of yourself. Necks don't break this way. You're in Hesse, not Switzerland. . . .

OECOLAMPADIUS: Everybody can only be in one place, confined within limits.

LUTHER: Mathematical hairsplitting I will not listen to. God—this even the Aristotelians grant—can make a body be in one place alone or in several places at the same time or in no place at all; and he can make several be in one place at the same time.... It is not arguments of this nature, based upon reason, but scriptural passages of clarity and certainty, that are called for....

OECOLAMPADIUS: In Matthew 26[:11], it says: "You will always have the poor with you, [but you will not always have me]." From this it follows that Christ is always and everywhere present in his divinity, grace, and power. When, however, he says that he would be absent, it must be his human nature that is absent. But if his human nature were absent, then he cannot be present in the Lord's Supper in a bodily sense. Christ resembled us in all respects. As he is of the same nature as the Father in his divinity, so he is of the same nature as ourselves in his humanity....

LUTHER: God is beyond all mathematics! Christ can make his body be nowhere, as he can make it be in one place. He is in the Lord's Supper, not in the sense of being in one place....

ZWINGLI: I have proved that Christ was in one place. You prove in return that he is nowhere at all or in many places....

LUTHER (raising the tablecloth): "This is my body"! Right here is our Scripture. You haven't torn it away from us yet like you promised to do. We need none other. My esteemed lords, as long as the text of my Lord Jesus Christ is there—*Hoc est corpus meum*[8]—then truly I cannot pass over it, but must confess and believe that Christ's body is there....

OECOLAMPADIUS (or Zwingli): We can neither comprehend nor believe that Christ's body is there.

LUTHER: I commend you to God and to his judgment. My thanks to you, Herr Oecolampadius, for presenting your case, not in a spirit of bitterness, but with friendliness. Also to you, Herr Zwingli, I express my thanks despite your expressions of bitterness. Please forgive me if I have spoken harshly to you. I am after all only flesh and blood. I should like to have had the matter settled to our mutual satisfaction.

OECOLAMPADIUS: I call upon the will of God to protect the poor church.

ZWINGLI: I call upon you, Doctor Luther, to forgive my bitterness. I have always desired your friendship a great deal, and I want it still. (*With tears in his eyes.*) There are no others in Italy and France whom I would rather see.

LUTHER: Call upon God, that you may receive understanding.

OECOLAMPADIUS: Call upon him yourself, for you need it just as much as we!

---

[8] "This is my body."

XV. ZWINGLI AND THE ANABAPTISTS

Soon after Zwingli started his reform in Zurich, some of his followers, notably Conrad Grebel, Felix Manz, and George Blaurock, started to push for more radical reform. They focused primarily on two things. First, they believed that Zwingli's willingness to wait for the Zurich city council to abolish the Mass constituted an unacceptable inclination to obey man rather than God. Second, they believed that there was no scriptural justification for infant baptism and insisted that baptism had to follow belief. On January 21, 1525, Blaurock and Grebel baptized each other and other adult believers. Because they had all been baptized as infants, most of their opponents labeled them "Anabaptists," which means "rebaptizers." Zwingli refers to them instead as "Catabaptists," which means "those who are opposed to baptism."

Anabaptism spread quickly in the Swiss Confederation, despite the great risk it posed to its adherents. Nearly all authorities in the area, both Catholic and Protestant, soon made Anabaptism a capital crime. Although Grebel died a natural death in 1526 (after his imprisonment), Manz and Blaurock both became Anabaptist martyrs. Thus, from the very beginning, the Anabaptists saw themselves as the closest heirs to the martyrs of the early church. Another prominent Anabaptist martyr was Michael Sattler, who had joined the Swiss Brethren (as the Swiss Anabaptists called themselves) in Zurich. In 1527, Sattler presided over a meeting at Schleitheim (in canton Schaffhausen, on the Swiss/German border), where Anabaptist leaders drew up the Schleitheim Confession of Faith (doc. 29). Sattler was arrested and executed soon afterwards. Anabaptist groups varied widely in their specific beliefs, but the Schleitheim Confession represents foundational Anabaptist beliefs as well as any single document can. The confession circulated widely, prompting Zwingli to respond to it point by point in *Refutation of the Tricks of the Catabaptists* (doc. 30).

Focus Questions

1. What are the basic positions taken in each of the seven articles of the Schleitheim Confession?

2. What are Zwingli's arguments against each of the articles?
3. What position does the Confession take with regard to "the world"? How does this compare to the position taken by Catholic monastics?
4. How would you characterize the fundamental, overarching difference between the worldview of the Anabaptists and that of Zwingli?

29. *The Schleitheim Confession of Faith*, 1527[9]

The articles which we discussed and on which we were of one mind are these 1. Baptism; 2. The Ban [Excommunication]; 3. Breaking of Bread; 4. Separation from the Abomination; 5. Pastors in the Church; 6. The Sword; and 7. The Oath.

First. Observe concerning baptism: Baptism shall be given to all those who have learned repentance and amendment of life, and who believe truly that their sins are taken away by Christ, and to all those who walk in the resurrection of Jesus Christ, and wish to be buried with Him in death, so that they may be resurrected with Him, and to all those who with this significance request it [baptism] of us and demand it for themselves. This excludes all infant baptism, the highest and chief abomination of the pope. In this you have the foundation and testimony of the apostles. Matt. 28, Mark 16, Acts 2, 8, 16, 19. This we wish to hold simply, yet firmly and with assurance.

Second. We are agreed as follows on the ban: The ban shall be employed with all those who have given themselves to the Lord, to walk in His commandments, and with all those who are baptized into the one body of Christ and who are called brethren or sisters, and yet who slip sometimes and fall into error and sin, being inadvertently overtaken. The same shall be admonished twice in secret and the third time openly disciplined or banned according to the command of Christ. Matt. 18. But this shall be done according to the regulation of the Spirit (Matt. 5) before the breaking of bread, so that we may break and eat one bread, with one mind and in one love, and may drink of one cup.

Third. In the breaking of bread we are of one mind and are agreed [as follows]: All those who wish to break one bread in remembrance of the broken body of Christ, and all who wish to drink of one drink as a remembrance of the shed blood of Christ, shall be united beforehand by baptism in one body of Christ which is the church of God and whose Head is Christ. For as Paul points out we cannot at the same time be partakers of the Lord's table and the table of devils; we cannot

---

[9] Source: John C. Wenger, "The Schleitheim Confession of Faith," *Mennonite Quarterly Review* 19 (1945): 243–53.

at the same time drink the cup of the Lord and the cup of the devil. That is, all those who have fellowship with the dead works of darkness have no part in the light. Therefore all who follow the devil and the world have no part with those who are called unto God out of the world. All who lie in evil have no part in the good.

Therefore it is and must be [thus]: Whoever has not been called by one God to one faith, to one baptism, to one Spirit, to one body, with all the children of God's church, cannot be made [into] one bread with them, as indeed must be done if one is truly to break bread according to the command of Christ.

Fourth. We are agreed [as follows] on separation: A separation shall be made from the evil and from the wickedness which the devil planted in the world; in this manner, simply that we shall not have fellowship with them [the wicked] and not run with them in the multitude of their abominations.... For truly all creatures are in but two classes, good and bad, believing and unbelieving, darkness and light, the world and those who [have come] out of the world, God's temple and idols, Christ and Belial; and none can have part with the other....

To us then the command of the Lord is clear when He calls upon us to be separate from the evil and thus He will be our God and we shall be His sons and daughters.

He further admonishes us to withdraw from Babylon and the earthly Egypt that we may not be partakers of the pain and suffering which the Lord will bring upon them.

From this we should learn that everything which is not united with our God and Christ cannot be other than an abomination which we should shun and flee from. By this is meant all popish and antipopish works and church services, meetings and church attendance, drinking houses, civic affairs, the commitments [made in] unbelief and other things of that kind, which are highly regarded by the world and yet are carried on in flat contradiction to the command of God, in accordance with all the unrighteousness which is in the world. From all these things we shall be separated and have no part with them for they are nothing but an abomination, and they are the cause of our being hated before our Christ Jesus, Who has set us free from the slavery of the flesh and fitted us for the service of God through the Spirit Whom He has given us....

Fifth. We are agreed as follows on pastors in the church of God: The pastor in the church of God shall, as Paul has prescribed, be one who out-and-out has a good report of those who are outside the faith. This office shall be to read, to admonish and teach, to warn, to discipline, to ban in the church, to lead out in prayer for the advancement of all the brethren and sisters, to lift up the bread when it is to be broken, and in all things to see to the care of the body of Christ, in order that it may be built up and developed, and the mouth of the slanderer be stopped....

Sixth. We are agreed as follows concerning the sword: The sword is ordained of God outside the perfection of Christ. It punishes and puts to death the wicked, and guards and protects the good. In the Law the sword was ordained for the punishment of the wicked and for their death, and the same [sword] is [now] ordained to be used by the worldly magistrates.

In the perfection of Christ, however, only the ban is used for a warning and for the excommunication of the one who has sinned, without putting the flesh to death—simply the warning and the command to sin no more.

Now it will be asked by many who do not recognize [this as] the will of Christ for us, whether a Christian may or should employ the sword against the wicked for the defense and protection of the good, or for the sake of love.

Our reply is unanimously as follows: Christ teaches and commands us to learn of Him, for He is meek and lowly in heart and so shall we find rest to our souls. Also Christ says to the heathenish woman who was taken in adultery, not that one should stone her... but in mercy and forgiveness and warning, to sin no more. Such [an attitude] we also ought to take completely according to the rule of the ban....

Thirdly, it will be asked concerning the sword: Shall one be a magistrate if one should be chosen as such? The answer is as follows: They wished to make Christ king, but He fled and did not view it as the arrangement of His Father. Thus shall we do as He did....

Finally it will be observed that it is not appropriate for a Christian to serve as a magistrate because of these points: The government magistracy is according to the flesh, but the Christians' is according to the Spirit; their houses and dwelling remain in this world, but the Christians' are in heaven; their citizenship is in this world, but the Christians' citizenship is in heaven; the weapons of their conflict and war are carnal and against the flesh only, but the Christians' weapons are spiritual, against the fortification of the devil....

Seventh. We are agreed as follows concerning the oath:... Christ, who teaches the perfection of the Law, prohibits all swearing to His [followers], whether true or false—neither by heaven, nor by the earth, nor by Jerusalem, nor by our head—and that for the reason which He shortly thereafter gives, For you are not able to make one hair white or black [Mt 5:34–36]. So you see it is for this reason that all swearing is forbidden: we cannot fulfill that which we promise when we swear, for we cannot change [even] the very least thing on us....

[T]herefore we shall not swear at all.

30. Zwingli, *Refutation of the Tricks of the Catabaptists*, 1527[10]

CATABAPTISTS: "Baptism should be administered to all who have been taught penitence and change of life, and who believe really that their sins are done away with through Christ...."

REPLY: Who does not know that baptism should be administered to all in Christ, both penitents and those confessing that remission of sins is found? There is no contest here, except

[10] Source: Jackson, *Selected Works of Huldreich Zwingli*, 178–85, 188–92, 196–98, 202–03, 206, 208–13, text modernized.

about whether it may be given to those alone and not also to their infant children. Second, they conceal justification by works, and though they admit remission of sins through Christ here, they clearly deny it elsewhere. For they who trust in works make Christ of no effect. For if justification is by the works of the law, Christ has died in vain [Gal. 2:21].... Fourth, where in the Scripture do you read that baptism is to be given to none except to one who can make a confession and demand baptism? You assert this by yourselves, for circumcision was most often given to those who could neither make confession nor demand. But you reject the whole Old Testament. This is what you clearly betray in the former confutation.... Sixth, where do you find this custom of the apostles to baptize no one who had not made this confession of yours and forthwith demanded baptism?...

CATABAPTISTS: "Second, this is our opinion regarding the ban or excommunication: All ought to be excommunicated who after they have given themselves to the Lord... either slip or fall into sin and imprudently are thrown headlong...."

REPLY:... If an adulterer or drunkard, or one addicted to any other crime, defile the church he ought to be warned according to the command of Christ, and if he refuse to confess after the testimony of witnesses before the church, he ought to be shunned or to be excluded from the church, but only if contumacious. But if only rumor travels around, or he who is under suspicion can rightly ward it off, so that he appears to carry himself honestly, then he ought not rashly to be excommunicated, unless the thing is absolutely certain for which he is excommunicated.

This I say not of myself, but after comparing carefully and weighing the words of Jesus on this subject. For when he says to Peter that one is to be forgiven seventy-seven times, and in another place orders the tares to be permitted to grow until harvest, he evidently shows that there are some things at which fraternal love may wink. But when, on the other hand, he commands to expel straightway after the reproof of the church has been despised, he surely means in those matters which are manifest and may defile the church....

CATABAPTISTS: "Third. In the breaking of bread we thus agree and unitedly determine that they who wish to break one bread in commemoration of the broken body of Christ, and to drink of one cup in commemoration of his shed blood, shall first come together into one body of Christ.... "

REPLY: Doubtless, all this superstition tends to this, that the untaught people who rise to every novelty be led away into catabaptism and to an evil church. You admit no one to the Lord's Supper unless he has first been united by baptism into the one body of Christ. So by baptism as by a cement each one is united to this body. Why, then, do you strive so mightily that no one be baptized unless he first believe and confess with his own mouth? See how consistent you are! But you would not speak here of the Church's baptism, but of heretical baptism, i.e., your sect's, and this, as it is born outside the Church, is justly called *pseudo-* or *catabaptism* (some prefer *anabaptism*).... And while your words appear as though you were unwilling to admit anyone to the table of the Lord unless he has been baptized, what you really mean is that no one in your evil church should hope to be a participant at the table of the Lord unless he has been rebaptized....

They carry around a long document in their church, in which they show from the decrees of the pontiffs that infant baptism was begun under popish rule—wicked men that they are, since I showed them before that in Origen's time, who lived about 150 years after Christ's ascension, baptism was in common use, and afterwards in Augustine's time, who flourished about 400 years after. For both testify that infant baptism had remained to their own times from the custom of the apostles. But in those times the name of pope, and also monarchy or tyranny, had not come into the churches.

And I refuted their statement that the baptism of the pope is not Christ's but a demon's in the following way: If baptism were of the pope alone, I would not object to their calling the pope's baptism either "not Christ's" or a demon's. But the baptism of Christ is not the pope's, even if the pope were the archdemon himself and used Christ's baptism.... So when the pope baptized not in his own name, but in that of the Father and Son and Holy Ghost, it could in no way be vitiated so as not to be the baptism of Christ's church....

CATABAPTISTS: "Fourth. We thus decide about the revolt, separation and avoidance, which ought to be manifested as to that evil planted by the devil—that we have no commerce with those nor agree with them in the communication or their abominations...."

REPLY: We who stand by the Gospel are assailed here. The reason is that we alone show up and shun catabaptism and their wholesale sedition. By the papists we are called "heretics," by the catabaptists "secundopapists," because we preserve in the Church infant baptism and some other things which they will have nothing of. So are we exercised in the Lord's glory that we may bring to him a victory the more excellent the more numerous those are by whom we are assailed.

I will show in a few words the deceit they conceal in the words of this article. What they allege from Scripture about separation is not said in the sense to which they wrest it.... We ought, therefore, first to be separated from ourselves, of which Christ also speaks. He who hates his own life in this world, he says, saves it for life eternal [John 12:25]. This separation results when we daily set forth a desire for betterment, and with our might exhort the brethren to this by example and prayer. But according to this we do not seek to be separate from those who have infirmities in common with us....

Second, we are separated not from those who are weak, but from those who are evil, a thing that both piety and love will teach. For Christ himself also taught that the contumacious and impudently wicked man ought to be shunned only when he had reached in obstinacy the point of not respecting the Church.

But I know the goal of this scornful avoidance. As soon as they have lured one to their faction, above all they forbid him to go for at least a month, if they cannot get it for all time or for longer, to any assembly where one teaches who is opposed to their sect. And this order is at the beginning strongly suspected by those who are not yet wholly demented. Indeed, many who return to a good mind testify to this....

And it is strange that they have omitted here what elsewhere they have urged as a prime objection. In the assemblies of the city, they allege, murders often take place—as if this did not happen more frequently in the marketplace and the country. According to that, we must not assemble in the country or the marketplace.... They prefer those where many meet in some wood by night rather than by day, when the way home has to be felt out through the dense darkness by the more comely girls and matrons, and they consummate spiritual marriage with carnal copulation; or where two or three meet at the house of a man who is a little better off, and eat and chat, lead astray the women, and in a word do many things you would hardly dare imagine. By this hunting they find much greater booty than if their listeners should hear in the assembly of the churches what is against their doctrines....

Now they condemn the state also, not seeing that Paul preserved himself from violence by this one means. Is it not clear now that they have come to the point of obscuring all things, of dissolving all friendship and all union? Who ever forbade one to be a citizen?...

CATABAPTISTS: "Sixth. The sword is an ordinance of God outside of the perfection of Christ, by which the evil man is punished and slain and the good man defended. In the law, the sword is ordained against the evil for punishment and death, and for this the magistracy of the world is constituted. But in the perfection of Christ we use only excommunication...."

REPLY: I strive with all my powers against the proposition that Christians need no magistracy. For I grant this, that it is easy for them to say that a real Christian needs no magistracy, for of faith he omits none of those things that ought to be done and does none of the deeds that are not right. But it is our misfortune that among men we do not find such absolute perfection and may not hope to find that all who confess Christ are wholly happy, as long as we bear about this domicile of the body....

They mean ... that the heretical church of the rebaptized needs no sword, for it is within the perfection of Christ. For the foolish men assume what the monks used to assume, namely, that they are in a state of perfection....

These most seditious men, therefore, would take away the sword so that they may the more freely throw all into confusion.... In their evil church, they would have the sword removed, so that they might more freely associate with harlots, defile matrons, seduce the women with their flattery, confuse all settled conditions, even overthrow cities and men's dwelling places. For in this way a little band of robbers will be able to compel to make common the goods of those who are unwilling to put them to common use. So that the more the sword ought to be preserved even on their own account, since they assail with so many stratagems the public peace, the more they deny that it can be employed among Christians....

[Christ] came not to be tended and ministered to as tyrants are, but to minister.... Yet he never forbade a Christian and one worthy of empire to become a king even.... Peter also baptized Cornelius the centurion [Acts 10]. The high functionary of the Ethiopian Candace was baptized by Philip [Acts 8:26–39]. But if, according to your opinion, a Christian may not exercise the magistracy, and penitence and confession of faith are required before being baptized, then Peter and Philip did wrong in baptizing these before they had resigned office.... The kingdom of Christ is not divided when a Christian exercises the magistracy; it is built up and united.

CATABAPTISTS: "Seventh. We thus decide and determine concerning the oath:... Christ, who teaches the perfection of the law, forbids all oaths.... So notice! All swearing is prohibited...."

REPLY: Take away the oath and you have dissolved all order.... An oath is an appeal to God in deciding or vouching for something. This is not our definition, but his through whom we swear. Exodus 22:10[–11] thus commands: "When someone delivers to another a donkey, ox, sheep, or any other animal for safekeeping, and it dies or is injured or is carried off, without anyone seeing it, an oath before the Lord shall decide between the two of them that the one has not laid hands on the property of the other; the owner shall accept the oath, and no restitution shall be made."... An oath is, therefore, a divine thing, a sacred anchor to which we flee when human wisdom can go no further....

But the whole source of the error arises from their not seeing the opinion of Christ in Matt. 5:33; indeed, they do not know the very words.... So the Latin has three words, *jurare, dejerare,* and *perjerare;* the first means a sacred obligation, the second to swear off-hand to anything either falsely or truly, the third to swear falsely. Christ would not forbid us to swear [*jurare*], but to swear lightly or off-hand [*dejerare*]. But as these men do not, or will not, see this (I have often set it forth to them), they willingly and wittingly stumble.... Christ [indicated] that they ought not swear off-hand [*dejerare*] either to the true or false in ordinary discourse; everything was to be said and done so truly that if one said, "Yes," the neighbor should know that what the other had said was true, or if he said, "No," the neighbor should know that for truth. About the official oath nothing is said here....

What follows establishes this. He says: "Either by heaven, for it is the throne of God, or by the earth, for it is his footstool, or by Jerusalem, for it is the city of the great King. And do not swear by your head, for you cannot make one hair white or black" [Matt. 5:34–36]. These examples show that Christ did not refer to the oath required by magistrates. For which of the Hebrews ever took an oath by heaven, earth, Jerusalem, or his head? On the other hand, who does not swear off-hand by these? One man promises something by the cross of Christ, another declares solemnly by heaven and earth. This then is what Christ forbade....

FURTHER READING

Estep, William. *The Anabaptist Story: An Introduction to Sixteenth-Century Anabaptism.* Grand Rapids, MI: Eerdmans, 1996.

Gäbler, Ulrich. *Huldrych Zwingli: His Life and Work.* Translated by Ruth C.L. Gritsch. Philadelphia: Fortress Press, 1986.

Gordon, Bruce. *The Swiss Reformation*. Manchester: Manchester University Press, 2002.

Locher, Gottfried. *Zwingli's Thought: New Perspectives*. Leiden: Brill, 1981.

Potter, G.R. *Zwingli*. Cambridge: Cambridge University Press, 1976. http://dx.doi.org/10.1017/CBO9780511561290.

Roth, John D., and James M. Stayer, eds. *A Companion to Anabaptism and Spiritualism, 1521–1700*. Leiden: Brill, 2007.

Stayer, James M. *Anabaptists and the Sword*. Lawrence, KS: Coronado, 1972.

Stephens, W. P. *The Theology of Huldrych Zwingli*. Oxford: Clarendon Press, 1986.

Wandel, Lee-Palmer. *The Eucharist in the Reformation: Incarnation and Liturgy*. Cambridge: Cambridge University Press, 2006.

V

French Reform and Calvinism

The ideas of the Reformation soon spread out from German-speaking Europe. In France, they combined with Renaissance humanist ideas in the reform circle at Meaux (§XVI), where Bishop Guillaume Briçonnet (c. 1470–1532) gathered several reform-minded individuals around him, including, most importantly, Jacques Lefèvre d'Etaples (c. 1460–1536). The Meaux group instituted evangelical preaching in the diocese and began translating the Bible into French. Despite fierce opposition from the Paris Faculty of Theology (commonly referred to as the Sorbonne), which effectively shut down the Meaux experiment, French evangelicals made reasonable headway into the 1530s, but then the "Affair of the Placards" took place (§XVII), which forced King Francis I to take a stronger position against Protestant ideas. In the following years, hundreds of suspected heretics were executed in France, and many others were driven into exile. France would remain overwhelmingly Catholic, but a substantial Protestant minority would remain, later giving rise to the French Wars of Religion (see below, chapter 8).

The suppression of Protestantism in France following the Affair of the Placards led many French evangelicals either to go underground or to flee the country. One evangelical who had already fled the country a year earlier was John Calvin (1509–64), who would assume leadership of the French Protestant movement from Geneva. Calvin had a difficult start in Geneva, for he and Guillaume Farel, an early member of the Meaux group who had initiated Protestant reform in Geneva, tried to institute too many changes too quickly, particularly by trying to force all citizens of Geneva to subscribe to their confession of faith (based on Calvin's *Instruction and Confession*. See §XVIII). The council banished Calvin and Farel from the city. A key prelude to Calvin's return would be his response to a letter from Jacopo Sadoleto, cardinal-bishop of the French city of Carpentras (§XIX), to the people of Geneva, encouraging them to return to the Catholic Church. Once re-established in Geneva, Calvin would give shape to the Reformation movement there. In the process, he became the chief spokesman and theologian for the French evangelical movement. His monumental work, the *Institutes of the Christian Religion*, would be the most important handbook of Reformed theology for centuries. Calvin also placed a great deal of emphasis on moral discipline, for he believed that the church was the body of Christ and as such must be kept free of pollution brought about by immoral behavior. Thus, he encouraged the city council to pass laws on morality, and he instituted the consistory, a body of church elders who watched over the moral life of the city (§XX).

XVI. THE REFORM GROUP OF MEAUX

At the start of the Reformation, Jacques Lefèvre d'Etaples was a retired professor from the University of Paris. He had spent most of his career studying Aristotle but had also been heavily influenced by the Italian Renaissance. In his later years, he turned to theology and humanist studies of the Bible. His *Fivefold Psalter* was a typically humanist, philological examination of several translations of the Psalms, with a new translation of his own. In 1521, his former student Bishop Guillaume Briçonnet invited him to Meaux (28 miles east of Paris) to help with a program of reform. Briçonnet and Lefèvre hoped to bring the "word of God" directly to the people, through both an aggressive preaching program and the translation of the New Testament into French. Both endeavors were influenced by the ideas Luther was developing in neighboring Germany. At virtually the same time that Luther was translating the Bible into German, Lefèvre was hard at work on a French translation. In 1523, he completed his translation of the Gospels, and his preface to the edition is below (doc. 31).

While the Meaux group gravitated toward the new teachings from Germany, the Sorbonne grew increasingly hostile to them. In 1521, it condemned Luther's theology and then focused on perceived threats from within France. Central to its investigations was the Meaux group. First, a few individuals associated with Meaux were condemned, and then the Faculty issued a broad condemnation of the teachings of the entire group (doc. 32). The condemnations follow a formula whereby a statement or proposition by the accused is quoted first, followed by the Faculty's censure of that proposition. Soon after the condemnation by the Sorbonne, Bishop Briçonnet turned against evangelical reform, the Meaux group was disbanded, and Lefèvre and his associates were forced to find refuge elsewhere, many of them with Marguerite of Navarre, the sister of King Francis I and an important supporter of evangelical reform.

Focus Questions

1. Why does Lefèvre d'Etaples believe that the Bible should be translated into French?
2. Does it sound like he has been influenced by Luther and/or Erasmus? Based on the text, would you call him a Protestant? Why or why not?
3. According to the Sorbonne's censures, what other heretical teachings did the Meaux group embrace?
4. Why did the Sorbonne view these teachings as threats?

31. Jacques Lefèvre d'Etaples, Preface to the French Translation of the Gospels, 1523[1]

When St. Paul was on the earth, preaching and announcing the word of God with the other apostles and disciples, he said, "Behold, now is the acceptable time; behold, now is the day of salvation" (2 Cor. 6[:2]). So also now in our day the time has come when our Lord Jesus Christ—sole salvation, truth, and life—wants his Gospel to be purely announced through all the world, so that people no longer wander off by other doctrines of men who think they are something but (as St. Paul says) are really nothing, since they deceive themselves (Gal. 6[:3]). Therefore, now we can say, as he said: "Behold, now is the acceptable time; behold, now is the day of salvation."

And so that everyone who knows the French language but not Latin may be better disposed to receive this present grace—which God by his goodness, pity, and mercy presents to us in this time by the sweet and loving regard of Jesus Christ, our only Savior—the Gospels are given to you, by his grace, in the common tongue, translated from the Latin which is commonly read everywhere, without adding or taking away anything. In this way, the simple members of the body of Jesus Christ, having this in their language, can be as certain of the evangelical truth as those who have it in Latin. And afterwards they will have... the remainder of the New Testament, which is the book of life, and the sole rule of Christians, as is now the case in various regions and in various languages across most of Europe among Christians, since the spirit of our Lord Jesus Christ, our salvation, our glory, and our life, has moved their hearts towards this endeavor.

And his infinite goodness again shows us that it is necessary in this time for both great and small to know the holy Gospel. For he threatens to send us the Turks, enemies of our faith, just as the Babylonians were in ancient times the enemies of the Israelites' faith. And this is in order to correct the faults in Christendom, which are very great, if we do not return to him soon, leaving behind all other foolish trust in any created thing and in all other human traditions, which cannot save us. Instead, we must follow the only word of God, who is spirit and life....

Let us all strive, therefore, to know his will through the holy Gospel, so that in the time of temptation which is at our door, we will not be left behind with the reprobate. Let us receive the sweet visitation of Jesus Christ, our only help, in the heavenly, evangelical light, which... is the rule of Christians, the rule of life, and the rule of salvation. And whoever wants to institute or

---

[1] Source: Amié-Louis Herminjard, *Correspondance des Réformateurs dans les pays de langue française*, 9 vols. (Geneva: H. Georg, 1866–97), 1:133–38, translated by the editor.

uphold a different rule from the one God has established,... they are like those about whom St. Paul by the spirit of Jesus Christ speaks to Timothy, saying, "The aim of our charge is love that issues from a pure heart and a good conscience and a sincere faith. Certain persons by swerving from these have wandered away into vain discussion, desiring to be teachers of the law, without understanding either what they are saying or the things about which they make assertions" (1 Tim. 1[:5–6]). Let us follow, therefore, the wisdom of God, where there can be neither vanity, nor lack of intelligence, nor anything affirmed which is not the truth....

Therefore, my brothers and sisters, let us travel in the light of the day, in the light of the holy Gospel, holding all our trust in the true sun, and let us never offend God.... Let us not go, therefore, to any other than to the heavenly Father through Jesus Christ, and in Jesus Christ, as his word commands, and we will be children of God in him and by him, children of grace and of light, children of spirit and of life....

Let us know that men and their doctrines are nothing unless they are corroborated and confirmed by the word of God. But Jesus Christ is all: He is wholly man and wholly divine, and every human is nothing except in him. And no word of man is anything except in the word of God....

And if any want to stop the people of Jesus Christ from reading in their own language the Gospel, which is the true doctrine of God, they should know that Jesus Christ speaks against them, saying through St. Luke, "Woe to you, teachers of the law, for you have taken away the key of knowledge; you did not enter yourselves, and you hindered those who were entering" (Luke 11:52). And does he not say this again by St. Mark: "Go into all the world and preach the Gospel to the whole creation" (Mark 16:15)? And by St. Matthew: "teaching them to observe all that I have commanded you" (Matt. 28:20). And how can they preach the Gospel to the whole creation, how can they teach them to observe all that Jesus Christ commanded, if they do not want the simple people to see and read the Gospel of God in their own language?

32. Paris Faculty of Theology, Condemnation of the Meaux Reforms, 1523[2]

Some in this stormy time have dared to pour out the poison of their impiety in pestilential books or by dangerous preaching. For these impious men assert that it does no good to pray to the saints or honor them except by love and imitation. They forbid our prayers or sacrifices to be directed

---

[2] Source: Charles du Plessis d'Argentré, *Collectio Judiciorum de Novis Erroribus* (Paris: André Cailleau, 1728), 2:xiv–xviii, translated by the editor.

toward them. They ridicule and disparage the relics, miracles, images, and deeds of the saints.... They do not consider that such pestilential dogmas were rejected and condemned many years ago. Thus, anyone who dares to consent to such things can in no way be counted among the number of Catholics.... By their work, they have also given free rein to the simple folk to interpret the Scriptures, to argue about the faith, to call together meetings, and to gather in conventicles....

[*Specific propositions condemned:*]

... *First proposition of the heretics:* "The saints are not our mediators to God."

Censure: This proposition is like the aforementioned errors about the Virgin Mary and wrongly draws the faithful away from the veneration owed to the saints.

Second proposition: "The saints can do nothing to help us."

Censure: This proposition is false and detracts from the dignity of the saints, and it consents with the erroneous opinion of the aforementioned heretics [Lutherans, Wycliffites, etc.]....

On relics of the saints. The first proposition: "It is not appropriate that the bones of the saints be adorned with gems, gold, and other precious things, because in this way more honor is given to them than to God."

Censure: This proposition impiously revives the heresy of Eunomius and Vigilantius,[3] nor do those who show honor to the bodies of the saints detract in any way from the honor to the divine....

On the images of the saints. First proposition: "One should not genuflect before the images of the saints of God, but only before God."

Censure: This proposition is erroneous and impious, and taken from the error of those who reject icons or images of the saints....

On the license given to simple folk. First proposition: "All Christians and especially clerics must be led to the study of Holy Scripture, because other things are human doctrines and of little use."

Censure: This proposition, according to the first part, which gives approval for all the laity and also the clergy to study Holy Scriptures and the difficult passages therein, is taken from the error of the Poor Men of Lyon.[4] As for the second part, which states that all doctrine apart from the bare literal biblical teaching is human and useless, it is rashly and arrogantly asserted in conformity with the errors of the aforementioned heretics.

Second proposition: "It is licit for the simple people to gather on feast days and other days to confer about the Bible and its difficult passages."

Third proposition: "It is licit for simple people to argue about the Catholic faith and to interpret Holy Scripture since they are Christians."

Censure: Both of these propositions are rashly and falsely asserted and establish the errors of the Waldensians and Bohemians [i.e., Hussites]. Conventicles of the simple folk must not be allowed, nor disputations about the difficult

---

3 Fourth-century heretics.

4 The Waldensians were a medieval sect founded by Peter Waldo in Lyon that was deemed heretical; they were among the first to attempt to translate the New Testament into French.

matters of the faith, since they are condemned by law....

On favor shown towards Luther. Sole proposition: "What Luther has said well, no one has said better."

Censure: This proposition is false, injurious to the holy Doctors, and impudently and mendaciously supports the execrable teaching of Luther.

XVII. THE AFFAIR OF THE PLACARDS

After the breakup of the Meaux group, several French evangelicals found their way to French-speaking Switzerland, where the city council of Bern was helping to implement Protestant ideas among its allies and in territories under its control. The city of Neuchâtel adopted the Reformation in 1530 and established the first openly Protestant printing press in French-speaking Europe. In 1534, a pastor in Neuchâtel named Antoine Marcourt (ca. 1485–1561) aggressively sought to quicken the pace of reform back in France through an event known as the "Affair of the Placards." Marcourt published in poster or "placard" form the treatise below (doc. 33), which harshly condemned the Catholic Mass. His associates back in France posted his placards all over Paris and the surrounding area during a single night. On Sunday morning, 18 October 1534, people walking to church saw this poster all over the city.

The general reaction in France was outrage, and King Francis I was forced to crack down on Protestants in the realm. The second text (doc. 34) is from a journal kept by an ordinary citizen of Paris. It describes the processions and executions that were held after the Affair of the Placards. Note that the term "Lutheran" was used in France to describe any Protestant, whether or not they agreed wholeheartedly with Luther.

Focus Questions

1. Explain in your own words Marcourt's four main articles against the Mass.

2. Does Marcourt seem to be closer to Luther or to Zwingli in his understanding of the Eucharist (see above, doc. 28)?

3. Undoubtedly, Marcourt knew that there would be a largely negative reaction to his posting of his placard. Why, then, do you think he did it?

4. In the description of the procession in the second document, which people played the most prominent roles? What items seem to have been most important to carry through the town? Why would that have been the case?

5. Compare the description of the Paris procession to our public rituals today. What forms do ours take? What is their purpose? What objects seem most important? Which people take part?

33. Antoine Marcourt, the Placards of 1534[5]

Trustworthy Articles on the Horrible, Great, & Unbearable Abuses of the Papal Mass: devised directly against the Holy Supper of Jesus Christ.

I invoke heaven and earth in witness of the truth, against this pompous and proud papal Mass, by which the world (if God does not soon provide a remedy) is and will be totally desolated, ruined, lost, and laid low: for in the Mass our Lord is so outrageously blasphemed, and the people seduced and blinded—something which we ought no longer to suffer or endure. But, in order that the case may be more easily understood by each one, it is appropriate to proceed by articles.

First, it is and must be very certain to every faithful Christian that our Lord and Savior Jesus Christ, as the Great Bishop and Pastor eternally ordained by God, has offered up his body, his soul, his life, and his blood for our sanctification in a most perfect sacrifice: which cannot and must never be repeated by any visible sacrifice. For this would be to renounce him as if he were ineffective, insufficient, and imperfect.... The earth has been and still at present is in several places loaded and filled with miserable sacrificers,[6] who as if they were our redeemers put themselves in place of Jesus Christ, or make themselves of him, saying that they offer to God

---

[5] Source: John Calvin, *Institutes of the Christian Religion, 1536 Edition*, trans. Ford Lewis Battles (Grand Rapids, MI: Eerdmans, 1975), 339–42.

[6] Here meaning Catholic priests.

a sacrifice as agreeable and pleasing as that of Abraham, Isaac and Jacob, for the salvation both of the living and of sinners. This thing they do openly against the whole truth of Holy Scripture. For by the great and wonderful sacrifice of Jesus Christ all outward and visible sacrifice is abolished and voided, and never is another to remain....

Secondly, in this unhappy Mass one has provoked as it were the whole world to public idolatry, when one falsely gives to understand that under the species of bread and wine, Jesus Christ bodily, really, and actually, entirely and personally is flesh and bones, as great and perfect as at present he is living, is contained and hidden. This, Holy Scripture and our faith do not teach us, but completely to the contrary. For Jesus Christ after the resurrection ascended into heaven, seated at the right hand of God the Almighty Father, and will come to judge the living and the dead. Also, St. Paul in Colossians 3[:1] writes thus: "If you are raised up with Christ, seek the things that are above, where Christ is seated at the right hand of God." He does not say, "Seek Christ who is in the Mass, or at the altar," but in heaven. For this reason it may be rightly sensed: if his body is in heaven, during the same time he is not on earth, and if he were on the earth, he would not be in heaven, for certainly a true body is ever only in one place at one time....

Thirdly, these poor sacrificers, to heap error upon error, have in their madness said and taught that after having breathed or spoken over this bread that they take in their fingers and upon this wine that they put in the cup, that it does not remain either bread or wine, but as they speak in great and wonderful words,

by Transubstantiation Jesus Christ is hidden and covered under the accidents of bread and wine, which is a doctrine of devils, against all truth, and manifestly against all Scripture.... See how St. Paul writes: "Let a man examine himself" [1 Cor. 11:28]. He does not say, Look to a tonsured one to examine you, but he says, let a man examine himself: then taste and eat of this bread; he does not say that the body of Jesus Christ is under the substance, under the species or appearance of bread, but only and purely he says, "Eat of this bread" [1 Cor. 11]. Now it is certain that Scripture uses no deception: and that in this there is no fantasy, since he senses very well that it is bread. Similarly in another place it is written as follows: "On the Sabbath day when we are gathered together to break bread" [Acts 20]. In these very clear passages Holy Scripture expressly says and declares it to be bread, not species, appearance, or semblance of bread. Who will be able to sustain, bear and endure such mockers, such plagues, false antichrists? They, as presumptuous and arrogant men, according to their ordinary custom, have been so rash and stubborn as to conclude and decide to the contrary. For this reason, as enemies of God and of his Holy word, rightly one ought to reject and greatly detest them.

Fourthly, the fruit of the Mass is quite contrary to the fruit of the Holy Supper of Jesus Christ, which is not surprising, for between Christ and Belial there is nothing in common [2 Cor. 6:15]. The fruit of the Holy Supper of Jesus Christ is publicly to make declaration of faith in him, and in certain assurance of salvation to have actual remembrance of the death and passion of Jesus Christ, by which we are redeemed from damnation and perdition.... And this clearly restores the faithful soul, filling it with divine consolation, in complete humility increasing in faith from day to day, exercising itself in all goodness, most gentle and lovable charity. But the fruit of the Mass is quite different, just as experience shows us, for by it all knowledge of Jesus Christ is wiped out, and preaching of the Gospel rejected and hindered, time occupied in bell-ringing, cries, chantings, ceremonies, candlelightings, censings, disguises, and such sorts of buffooneries, by which the poor world is like a flock of sheep miserably deceived, and by these ravening wolves eaten, gnawed and devoured. And who could not ponder the thefts of these fornicators? By this Mass they have laid hold of all, destroyed all, engulfed all, they have disinherited princes and kings, merchants, lords, and all that one can say, whether dead or alive. By it they live in care-freeness, they need do nothing, strive still less; what more do you wish? One must not wonder that they maintain it so strongly: they kill, they burn, they destroy, they murder as brigands all those who have contradicted them, for anything else than force they do not have. Truth fails them; truth threatens them; truth pursues and catches them. Truth overcomes them. In short, by it they will be destroyed. So be it. So be it. Amen.

34. Paris Processions in Response to the Placards, 1534–1535[7]

In 1534, heretics put up placards against the holy sacrament of the altar and against the honor of the saints. When the court heard this, it was proclaimed with trumpets that if anyone could prove who had put up the placards, he would be rewarded with a hundred *écus*.[8] Moreover, the guilty would be burned. Because of this, as God willed, the matter came to light in such a way that soon after, several people were imprisoned in Châtelet.

The following Thursday and Sunday, general processions were held in which the body of Christ [i.e., the consecrated communion bread] was carried through the streets. There were rumors that the placards had even been put up in the Château of Amboise, where the king was, and that the king ordered the court of the parlement[9] and the attorney general to exact rigorous justice. It was also rumored that

---

[7] Source: Ludovic Lalanne, ed., *Journal d'un bourgeois de Paris sous le règne de François premier* (Paris: Jules Renouard, 1854), 441–42, translated by the editor.

[8] This was a substantial sum of money. An *écu* was worth 45 *sous*, and a farm laborer earned about 3 *sous* a day. Thus, a hundred *écus* would be approximately the equivalent of over four years' wages for a peasant. Wage information from Emmanuel Le Roy Ladurie, *Peasants of Languedoc*, trans. John Day (Urbana: University of Illinois Press, 1974), 107.

[9] The French parlements were judicial bodies, not representative and legislative ones like the English Parliament. There were also several of them across the country, not just one in the capital.

the king gave the attorney general a bonus of six hundred francs[10] per year above his ordinary wages for the rest of his life.

On Thursday, January 21, 1535, there was a beautiful general procession in Paris, called for by the king, who was there in person together with the entire nobility, and the queen and all the ladies were there on horseback. And in order to know the order, all the parochial churches went to Notre Dame, with their crosses and banners, in great honor. Then came all the clergy, namely all the canons accompanied by all the processions, carrying with them relics that had never been carried, namely the head of St. Philip and the reliquary of St. Sebastian, the reliquary of St. Marcel, and a very large silver image from Notre Dame, and other relics.

There was also the clergy of the Sainte-Chapelle of the palace carrying the true cross, the head of St. Louis, and other relics, and the canons vested in copes.

Also, St. Genevieve and its abbot, and the goldsmiths of Paris carried the reliquary.

Also, the monks of St. Germain-des-Près and St. Martin-des-Champs with their relics.

Also, the abbot and monks of St. Magloire, and generally all the relics and churches of Paris,

in good order and procession, who went to the church of St. Germain-l'Auxerrois, because the king was there.

Afterwards, all the processions returned to Notre Dame in good order, and there the body of the Lord, which had left the church of St. Germain, was under the beautiful sky, and the four who carried the canopy of the holy sacrament were the children of the king, namely the Dauphin and the Dukes of Orléans and of Angoulême, and a young prince, the son of Count Louis from Germany, who was at the king's court at that time…. And the king was there in person, holding a torch of burning wax in his hand, on foot with his head bare, in great honor, after the body of the Lord, and the Cardinal of Lorraine was there with him, holding a wax candle in his hand, along with all the nobility. And the streets were decorated wherever they went. Several cardinals and a great many prelates were there as well. After the service was over, the king and queen went to dine at the home of the Bishop of Paris.

The same day, six Lutherans were burned, namely three at the Croix du Tirouer and three at Les Halles, and several others followed in the next weeks, which I leave out for the sake of brevity.

XVIII. JOHN CALVIN'S THOUGHT

In 1536, John Calvin published the first edition of his best-known work, *Institutes of the Christian Religion.* When he arrived in Geneva that year, he summarized the main points of his teaching in the *Instruction and*

---

[10] The French franc, also called the *livre tournois*, was worth about a third of an *écu*, that is, about 15 *sous*, five days' wages for a farm laborer, or about three days' work for a stone mason.

Confession of Faith used in the Church of Geneva, the text below. This is one of the most succinct statements of Calvin's theology, and he wanted it to serve as a common confession of faith to which all the citizens of Geneva would subscribe. Highlighted here are three of the distinctive features of Calvin's thought, namely his views on predestination, the sacraments, and excommunication. In order to compare Calvin's thought to that of Luther and Zwingli, review Luther's *Bondage of the Will* (doc. 19) and the account of the Marburg Colloquy (doc. 28).

Focus Questions

1. How does Calvin's theology as expressed in this text compare to that of Luther and Zwingli?
2. Where would Calvin stand in the controversy between Luther and Zwingli over the Eucharist?
3. Why does Calvin believe excommunication is a necessary tool of the church?

35. John Calvin, *Instruction and Confession of Faith Used in the Church of Geneva*, 1537[11]

On election and predestination. The seed of the word of God takes root and bears fruit only in those whom the Lord by his eternal election has predestined as his children and heirs of the heavenly kingdom. To all others, who by the same counsel of God before the creation of the world are rejected, the clear and evident preaching of the truth cannot be anything other than the stench of death in death. Now, why does the Lord show his mercy to some and exercise the rigor of his judgment against others? We must allow that the reason is known to him alone, and he wanted it sealed from all of us, and not without good cause. For the ignorance of our spirit could not bear such great clarity, and our smallness could not comprehend so great a

---

[11] Source: John Calvin, *Instruction et Confession de Foy dont on use en l'Eglise de Genève*, in *Ioannis Calvini Opera quae supersunt omnia*, edited by J.-W. Baum, E. Cunitz, and E.W.E. Reuss (Braunschweig: C. A. Schwetschke and Sons, 1863–1900), 22:46–47, 68–69, 72–73, translated by the editor.

wisdom. And in fact, all those who try to raise themselves to that point and do not want to tame the rashness of their spirit will learn that it is true what Solomon says, that he who would like to seek the majesty will be overcome by the glory (Prov. 25). Let us simply be resolved that this dispensation of the Lord, although it is hidden from us, nevertheless is holy and just, for if he wanted to destroy the entire human race, he has the right to do so, and in those whom he withdraws from perdition, one cannot contemplate anything other than his sovereign goodness. Therefore, let us recognize that the elect are vessels of his mercy (as truly they are) and the reprobate are vessels of his wrath, which nevertheless is only just....

On the sacraments. The sacraments are instituted for this purpose: that they might be exercises of our faith towards both God and man.... The promise always precedes what is included in the word; the sign is added, which confirms and seals that promise....

What a sacrament is. A sacrament, therefore, is an outward sign by which the Lord represents and testifies to us his good will towards us in order to sustain the weakness of our faith, or (to speak more briefly and clearly) it is a witness of the grace of God declared by an outward sign. The Christian Church uses only two sacraments, namely baptism and the Lord's Supper.

Baptism. Baptism was given to us by God, first, to support our faith toward him, and second, as our confession toward men.... Baptism particularly represents two things: The first is the purgation which we obtain in the blood of Christ; the other is the mortification of our flesh, which we have from his death.... The water is not the cause or the instrument of purgation and regeneration, but only the knowledge that such gifts are received in this sacrament.... It serves equally as our confession towards humans, for it is a mark by which we publicly make profession that we want to be numbered among the people of God, so that we can serve and honor him in the same religion with all the faithful....

On the Lord's Supper. The promise which is added to the mystery of the Lord's Supper declares clearly to what end it was instituted and what its purpose is, that is to say, that it confirms for us that the body of the Lord was given once for us in such a way that it is ours now and also will be forever, that his blood was once poured out for us in such a way that it will be ours forever. The signs are the bread and the wine, under which the Lord presents to us the true, spiritual communication of his body and blood, which... does not require an enclosed presence, or of flesh under the bread or of blood under the wine. For although Christ, raised to heaven, left the habitation of the earth on which we are still pilgrims, nevertheless, no distance can dissolve his power [*vertu*] which he feeds to his people from himself....

On excommunication. Excommunication is the means by which open lechers, adulterers, thieves, murderers, etc., if they do not mend their ways after being warned, are according to the commandment of God rejected from the company of the faithful. It is not that the Church throws them down into perpetual ruin and hopelessness, but it condemns their life and their morals, and if they do not improve, it makes them already certain of their damnation. Now, this discipline is necessary among the faithful, since the Church is the body of Christ and it should not be polluted and contaminated by such depraved members who bring dishonor to the head. Moreover, it prevents the saints from being (as commonly happens) corrupted and ruined by the conversation of the wicked. It is also profitable to those being chastised for their malice, for otherwise, if they were tolerated, they would become more obstinate; by this means, being shamed, they learn to mend their ways.

XIX. CALVIN'S DEBATE WITH SADOLETO

The Geneva city council was hesitant to require the city's citizens to subscribe to Calvin's confession of faith. In April 1538, after an additional conflict over whether to adopt the religious ceremonies used in Bern, Calvin and Farel refused to administer the Eucharist on Easter, and the council banished the reformers from the city. Calvin would spend the next three years chiefly in Strasbourg, and the Genevan church struggled in his absence. Attempting to take advantage of the confusion in the city, Jacopo Sadoleto (1477–1547), bishop of Carpentras, wrote an open letter to Geneva in which he encouraged the city to return to Catholicism (doc. 36). Sadoleto was a cardinal, a humanist, a friend of Erasmus, and an advocate of reform from within the Catholic Church. The Genevans asked the Bernese for advice, and they suggested asking Calvin to respond. He did so in the second text below (doc. 37).

Focus Questions

1. How do Sadoleto and Calvin address the problem of corruption in the church?
2. What motives does Sadoleto ascribe to the Protestant reformers? How does Calvin explain their motives?
3. Compare the fictional speeches of the commoner before the judgment seat created by both Sadoleto and Calvin. What are the chief arguments on both sides? Based on your knowledge of the Reformation thus far, do you think they fairly represent the actual beliefs of people during the Reformation?

36. Jacopo Sadoleto, Letter to Geneva, 1539[12]

After it was brought to my ears that certain crafty men, enemies of Christian unity and peace, had ... cast among you ... the wicked seeds of discord, had turned the faithful people of Christ aside from the way of their fathers and ancestors, and from the perpetual sentiments of the Catholic Church, and filled all places with strife and sedition, ... I declare before Almighty God ... that I was exceedingly grieved. ...

We all, therefore, believe in Christ in order that we may find salvation for our souls. ... Moreover, we obtain this blessing of complete and perpetual salvation by faith alone in God and in Jesus Christ. When I say "by faith alone," I do not mean, as those inventors of novelties do, a mere credulity and confidence in God, by which, to the exclusion of charity and the other duties of a Christian mind, I am persuaded that in the cross and blood of Christ all my faults are unknown; this, indeed, is necessary and forms the first access which we have to God, but it is not enough. For we must also bring a mind full of piety towards Almighty God and desirous of performing whatever is agreeable to him; in this, especially, the power of the Holy Spirit resides. ...

The point in dispute is whether is it more expedient for your salvation, and whether you think you will do what is more pleasing to God, by believing and following what the Catholic Church throughout the whole world now for more than fifteen hundred years ... approves with general consent, or innovations introduced within these twenty-five years by crafty, or, as they think themselves, clever men, but men certainly who are not themselves the Catholic Church? ...

On this discrimination and choice, the salvation of every person's soul, the pledges of future life, are at stake: whether our lot is to be one of eternal felicity or of infinite misery. What, then, shall we say? Let us here suppose two persons, one of each class, that is, from each road, let them be placed before the dread tribunal of the Sovereign Judge, and there let their case be examined and weighed, in order to ascertain whether a condemnatory or a saving sentence can justly be pronounced. They will be interrogated whether they were Christians. Both will say that they were. Did they properly believe in Christ? Both will, in like manner, answer yes. But when they will be examined as to what they believed, and how they believed, ... he who was educated in the lap and discipline of the Catholic Church will say:

"Having been instructed by my parents, who had learned it from their fathers and forefathers, that I should, in all things, be obedient to the Catholic Church, and revere and observe its laws, admonitions, and decrees, as if you yourself, O Lord, had made them, ... I strove to make myself acceptable to you by the same faith which the Catholic Church keeps and inculcates. And

---

[12] Source: John Calvin, *Tracts Relating to the Reformation*, trans. Henry Beveridge (Edinburgh: Calvin Translation Society, 1844), 1:4–5, 8–9, 14, 16–19, 21–22, text modernized.

though new men had come with the Scripture much in their mouths and hands, who attempted to stir some novelties, to pull down what was ancient, to argue against the Church, to snatch away and wrest from us the obedience which we all yielded to it, I was still desirous to adhere firmly to that which had been delivered to me by my parents, and observed from antiquity, with the consent of most holy and most learned Fathers. And although the actual manners of many prelates and ecclesiastics were such as might move my indignation, I did not, therefore, abandon my sentiments. For I concluded that it was my duty to obey their precepts, which were certainly holy, as you, God, had commanded in your Gospel, while you thought right to be the only judge of their life and actions; and especially since I was myself stained by the many sins which were manifest to you on my forehead, I could not be a fit judge of others. For these sins, I now stand before your tribunal, imploring not strict justice, O Lord, but rather your mercy and readiness to forgive."

Thus will this one plead his cause.

The other will be summoned, and will appear. He will be commanded to speak. Supposing him to be one of those who are, or have been, the authors of dissension, he will thus begin his oration:

"Almighty God, when I beheld the manners of ecclesiastics almost everywhere corrupt, and saw the priests, nevertheless, from a regard to religion, universally honored, I was offended at their wealth, and a just indignation ... inflamed my mind, and made me their opponent; and when I beheld myself, after having devoted so many years to literature and theology, without that place in the Church which my labors

had merited, while I saw many unworthy persons exalted to honors and priestly offices, I betook myself to the assailing of those who I thought were by no means pleasing and acceptable to you. And because I could not destroy their power without first trampling on the laws enacted by the Church, I induced a great part of the people to disregard those rights of the Church which had long before been ratified and inviolate. If these had been decreed in general councils, I said we were not to yield to the authority of councils; if they had been instituted by ancient Fathers and Doctors, I accused the old Fathers as unskillful and devoid of sound understanding; if by the Roman Pontiff, I affirmed that they had raised up a tyranny for themselves and falsely assumed the name of Vicars of Christ. By all means, in short, I contended that all of us, your worshippers, should shake off the tyrannical yoke of the Church, which sometimes forbids meats, which observes days, which will have us to confess our sins to priests, which orders vows to be performed, and which binds with so many chains of bondage men made free, O Christ, in you; and that we should trust to faith alone, and not also to good works (which are particularly extolled and proclaimed in the Church) to procure us righteousness and salvation—seeing, especially, that you had paid the penalty for us, and by your sacred blood wiped away all faults and crimes, in order that we, trusting to this our faith in you, might thereafter be able to do, with greater freedom, whatever we liked...."

After he has thus spoken, and spoken truly (for there is no room to lie before that heavenly Judge, though he has kept back much concerning his ambition, avarice, love of popular applause, inward fraud and malice, of which he is perfectly conscious, and which will appear inscribed on his very forehead), I ask you, my Genevan brethren, whom I long to have of one mind with me in Christ, and in the Church of Christ, what judgment do you think will be passed on these two men and their associates and followers? Is it not certain that he who followed the Catholic Church will not be judged guilty of any error in this respect? First, because the Church errs not, and even cannot err, since the Holy Spirit constantly guides her public and universal decrees and councils. Secondly, even if she did err, or could have erred, . . . no such error would be condemned in him who should, with a mind sincere and humble towards God, have followed the faith and authority of his ancestors. But the other one, trusting to his own head, having none among the ancient Fathers, and not even general assemblies of the whole bishops, whom he deems worthy of honor, and to whom he can bring his mind to yield and submit, arrogating all things to himself, more prepared to slander than to speak or teach, after revolting from the common Church, to what does he look as the haven of his fortunes? . . .

But if all other things might in the same way be tolerated and overlooked, how will this be borne (for this, I think, there cannot be with God any place for mercy and pardon), that they attempted to tear the spouse of Christ in pieces, that the garment of the Lord, which heathen soldiers were unwilling to divide, they attempted not only to divide, but to rend? For already, since these men began, how many sects have torn the Church? Sects not agreeing with them, and yet disagreeing with each other—a manifest indication of falsehood, as all doctrine declares. Truth is always one, while falsehood is varied and multiform. . . .

And I beg and exhort you, my Genevan brethren, after the mists of error have at length cleared away from the eyes of your mind, and the light been displayed, that you would raise your eyes to that heaven which God has set before you as your everlasting country, that you would be pleased to return to concord with us, yield faithful homage to the Church, our mother, and worship God with us in one spirit. . . .

Carpentras, March 18, 1539

37. Calvin, Reply to Sadoleto, 1539[13]

You lately addressed a letter to the Senate and People of Geneva, in which you sounded their inclination as to whether, after having once shaken off the yoke of the Roman Pontiff, they would submit to have it again imposed upon them. . . . And here (so help you) you bear down

---

[13] Source: Calvin, *Tracts Relating to the Reformation*, 1:25–26, 29, 35, 37, 41–43, 55–58, 61–64, 68, text modernized.

full sail upon those who, under pretense of the Gospel, have by wicked arts urged on the city to what you deplore as the subversion of religion and of the Church. I, however, Sadoleto, profess to be one of those whom with so much enmity you assail and stigmatize....

Although your letter has many windings, its whole purport substantially is to recover the Genevans to the power of the Roman Pontiff.... In order that you may claim it for your party, you assume that the most certain rule of worship is that which is prescribed by the Church.... But here you bring a charge against us. For you teach that all which has been approved for fifteen hundred years or more, by the uniform consent of the faithful, is, by our headstrong rashness, torn up and destroyed.... You know, Sadoleto, ... not only that our agreement with antiquity is far closer than yours, but that all we have attempted has been to renew that ancient form of the Church, which, at first sullied and distorted by illiterate men of indifferent character, was afterwards flagrantly mangled and almost destroyed by the Roman Pontiff and his faction....

You, in the first place, touch upon justification by faith, the first and keenest subject of controversy between us.... Wherever the knowledge of it is taken away, the glory of Christ is extinguished, religion abolished, the Church destroyed, and the hope of salvation utterly overthrown. That doctrine, then, though of the highest moment, we maintain that you have nefariously effaced from the memory of men.... But you very maliciously stir up prejudice against us, alleging that, by attributing everything to faith, we leave no room for works....

What have you here, Sadoleto, to bite or carp at? Is it that we leave no room for works? Assuredly, we do deny that in justifying a man, they are worth one single straw. For Scripture everywhere cries aloud that all are lost.... We deny that good works have any share in justification, but we claim full authority for them in the lives of the righteous. For, if he who has obtained justification possesses Christ, and, at the same time, Christ never is where his Spirit is not, it is obvious that gratuitous righteousness is necessarily connected with regeneration. Therefore, if you would duly understand how inseparable faith and works are, look to Christ, who, as the Apostle teaches (1 Cor. 1:30), has been given to us for justification and for sanctification. Wherever, therefore, that righteousness of faith is, which we maintain to be gratuitous, there too Christ is, and where Christ is, there too is the Spirit of holiness, who regenerates the soul to newness of life. On the contrary, where zeal for integrity and holiness is not in vigor, there neither is the Spirit of Christ nor Christ himself; and wherever Christ is not, there is no righteousness, no, there is no faith; for faith cannot apprehend Christ for righteousness without the Spirit of sanctification....

But since, towards the end [of your letter], a person has been introduced to plead our cause, and you have cited us as defenders to the tribunal of God, I have no hesitation in calling upon you there to meet me. For such is our consciousness of the truth of our doctrine that it has no dread of the heavenly Judge, from whom, we doubt not, that it proceeded. But it dwells not on those frivolities with which it has pleased you to amuse yourself.... In so far as our ministry is concerned, there is none of us who will not be able to speak like this:

"O Lord, I have, indeed, experienced how difficult and grievous it was to bear the invidious accusations with which I was harassed on the earth.... They charged me with two of the worst of crimes: heresy and schism. And the heresy was that I dared to protest against dogmas which they received. But what could I have done? I heard from your mouth that there was no other light of truth which could direct our souls into the way of life than that which was kindled by your word. I heard that whatever human minds of themselves conceive concerning your Majesty, the worship of your divinity, and the mysteries of your religion, was vanity. I heard that they were introducing into the Church, instead of your word, doctrines sprung from the human brain, which was sacrilegious presumption. But when I turned my eyes towards men, I saw very different principles prevailing. Those who were regarded as the leaders of faith neither understood your word, nor greatly cared for it. They only drove unhappy people to and fro with strange doctrines and deluded them with I know not what follies....

"The true meaning of baptism and the Lord's Supper, also, were corrupted by numerous falsehoods. And then, when all, with no small insult to your mercy, put confidence in good works, when by good works they strove to merit your favor, to procure justification, to expiate their sins, and make satisfaction to you (each of these things obliterating and making void the virtue of Christ's cross), they were yet altogether ignorant wherein good works consisted...."

Such, Sadoleto, is our pleading, not the fictitious one which you, in order to aggravate our case, were pleased to devise, but that the perfect truth of which is known to the good even now, and will be made manifest to all creatures on that day.

Nor will those who, instructed by our preaching, have adhered to our cause, be at a loss what to say for themselves, since each will be ready with this defense:

"I, O Lord, as I had been educated from a boy, always professed the Christian faith. But at first I had no other reason for my faith than that which then everywhere prevailed. Your word, which ought to have shined on all your people like a lamp, was taken away, or at least suppressed as to us. And lest anyone should long for greater light, an idea had been instilled into the minds of all that the investigation of that hidden celestial philosophy was better delegated to a few, whom the others might consult as oracles—that the highest knowledge befitting plebeian minds was to subdue themselves into obedience to the Church....

"I had learned, indeed, to worship you only as my God, but as the true method of worshiping was altogether unknown to me, I stumbled at the very threshold. I believed, as I had been taught, that I was redeemed by the death of your Son from liability to eternal death, but the redemption I thought of was one whose virtue could never reach me. I anticipated a future resurrection but hated to think of it, as being an event most dreadful. And this feeling not only had dominion over me in private, but was derived from the doctrine which was then uniformly delivered to the people by their Christian teachers. They, indeed, preached of your clemency towards men, but confined it to those who should show themselves deserving of it. They, moreover, placed this desert in the righteousness of works, so that he only was received into your favor who reconciled himself to you by works.... Then, because you were a stern judge and strict avenger of iniquity, they showed how dreadful your presence must be. Hence, they bade us flee first to the saints, that by their intercession you might be rendered malleable and propitious to us.

"When, however, I had performed all these things, though I had some intervals of quiet, I was still far off from true peace of conscience, for whenever I descended into myself or raised my mind to you, extreme terror seized me—terror which no expiations nor satisfactions could cure....

"Still, as nothing better offered, I continued the course which I had begun, when, lo, a very different form of doctrine started up, not one which led us away from the Christian profession, but one which brought it back to its fountainhead and, as it were, clearing away the dross, restored it to its original purity. Offended by the novelty, I lent an unwilling ear, and at first, I confess, strenuously and passionately resisted.... One thing, in particular, made me averse to those new teachers, namely, reverence for the Church.

"But when I opened my ears, and allowed myself to be taught, I perceived that this fear of taking away from the majesty of the Church was groundless. For they reminded me how great the difference is between schism from the Church and studying to correct the faults by which the Church herself was contaminated. They spoke

nobly of the Church and showed the greatest desire to cultivate unity....

"On the whole, they made it clear and palpable, to learned and unlearned, that the true order of the Church had then perished; that the keys under which the discipline of the Church is comprehended had been altered very much for the worse; that Christian liberty had fallen; in short, that the kingdom of Christ was prostrated when this [papal] primacy was reared up.... My mind being now prepared for serious attention, I at length perceived, as if light had broken in upon me, in what a sty of error I had wallowed, and how much pollution and impurity I had thereby contracted.... And now, O Lord, what remains to a wretch like me, but, instead of defense, earnestly to supplicate you not to judge that fearful abandonment of your word as it deserves, from which, in your wondrous goodness, you have at last delivered me."

Now, Sadoleto, if you please, compare this pleading with that which you have put into the mouth of your plebeian. It will be strange if you hesitate which of the two you ought to prefer. For the safety of that man hangs by a thread whose defense turns wholly on this: namely, that he has constantly adhered to the religion handed down to him from his forefathers. At this rate, Jews and Turks and Saracens would escape the judgment of God. Away, then, with this vain quibbling at a tribunal which will be erected not to approve the authority of man, but to condemn all flesh of vanity and falsehood, and vindicate the truth of God only....

The Lord grant, Sadoleto, that you and all your party may at length perceive that the only true bond of ecclesiastical unity would exist if

Christ the Lord, who has reconciled us to God the Father, were to gather us out of our present dispersion into the fellowship of his body, that so, through his one word and Spirit, we might join together with one heart and one soul.

Basel, September 1, 1539

XX. MORAL DISCIPLINE IN GENEVA

One feature of Calvin's reformation that distinguishes it from those led by Luther and Zwingli is its strong insistence on moral discipline enforced by the church. While both Luther and Zwingli encouraged moral behavior and good works, Luther believed that enforcing rigorous rules for moral behavior could encourage people once again to believe that they would be justified by their works, and Zwingli believed that moral discipline should be enforced chiefly by the city council, not the church. Calvin, on the other hand, believed that discipline belonged properly to the church and was necessary in order to prevent unfaithful members of the body of Christ from polluting the head, namely Christ. The following documents contain, first, some of the laws on morality and marriage established in Geneva, and second, records from the consistory. The consistory was conceived by Calvin as the body of church elders, including both the pastors of the city and several lay members, usually drawn from the city council. The two documents allow us to compare what was prescribed by law with what was actually practiced with regard to moral discipline in Geneva.

Note that the consistory records are essentially meeting minutes, and as such, can be somewhat difficult to read. The secretary often wrote in short phrases rather than full sentences, the same person's name might be spelled differently each time it is used, and so on. For example, the phrase, "Jean because of the word of God" means that Jean was summoned to the consistory because there were doubts about his religious life and faithfulness to the word of God.

Focus Questions

1. Compare the ordinances with the consistory records. What are they chiefly concerned with? Are they both concerned with the same kinds of things?

2. Marriage clearly is a concern in both the ordinances and the consistory records. Why do you think this was?

3. The consistory is often characterized as a kind of "morals police." Do the excerpts below justify that characterization? Why or why not?

4. What can we learn about "popular religion" (i.e., the religious beliefs and practices of the common people) of Geneva from these records? What about their moral lives?

5. What steps did the consistory take with offenders to try to turn Geneva into a "godly city"?

38. Geneva Ordinances

A. Ordinances for the Regulation of the Churches Dependent upon the Seigniory of Geneva, 1547[14]

Concerning the Times of Assembling at Church. That the temples [i.e., churches] be closed for the rest of the time [other than during church services], in order that no one shall enter therein out of hours, impelled thereto by superstition; and if anyone be found engaged in any special act of devotion therein or nearby he shall be admonished for it; if it be found to be of a superstitious nature for which simple correction is inadequate then he shall be chastised.

Blasphemy. Whoever shall have blasphemed, swearing by the body or by the blood of our Lord,

or in similar manner, he shall be made to kiss the earth for the first offence; for the second to pay 5 *sous*,[15] and for the third 6 *sous*, and for the last offence be put in the pillory for one hour.

Drunkenness. 1) That no one shall invite another to drink under penalty of 3 *sous*. 2) That taverns shall be closed during the sermon, under penalty that the tavern-keeper shall pay 3 *sous*, and whoever may be found therein shall pay the same amount. 3) If anyone be found intoxicated he shall pay for the first offence 3 *sous* and shall be remanded to the consistory; for the second offence he shall be held to pay the sum of 6 *sous*, and for the third 10 *sous* and be put in prison....

Songs and Dances. If anyone sings immoral, dissolute, or outrageous songs, or dances the *virollet* or

---

[14] Source: *Translations and Reprints from the Original Sources of European History*, Reformation Number (Philadelphia: Department of History of the University of Pennsylvania, 1897), 3:10–11.

[15] With regard to the monetary values noted in this document, around 1530, a stonemason in the Languedoc region of France earned about five *sous* a day, a farm laborer just over three *sous* a day. A single *sou* would also buy about a day's worth of bread for a manual laborer. Ladurie, *Peasants of Languedoc*, 107.

other dance, he shall be put in prison for three days and then sent to the consistory.

Usury. That no one shall take upon interest or profit more than 5%, upon penalty of confiscation of the principal and of being condemned to make restitution as the case may demand.

Games. That no one shall play at any dissolute game or at any game whatsoever it may be, neither for gold nor silver nor for any excessive stake, upon penalty of 5 *sous* and forfeiture of stake played for.

B. The Ecclesiastical Ordinances of 1561[16]

How soon marriage must be consummated after the promise is made. After the promise is made, the marriage shall not be deferred more than six weeks; otherwise, the parties shall be called before the consistory, in order that they may be admonished. If they do not obey, they shall be remanded to the council and be constrained to celebrate the marriage.

Banns and Conditions. That the banns [i.e., marriage announcements] shall be published three Sundays in the church prior to the marriage, having first received the signature of the chief syndic as a certificate of recognition of the parties, in such a way, however, that the marriage may take place at the third publication, and if one of the parties be resident in another parish there shall be also a certificate from the said place.

Concerning the Celebration of the Marriage. That the parties at the time when they are to be married shall go modestly to the church, without drummers and minstrels, preserving an order and gravity becoming to Christians; and this before the last stroke of the bell, in order that the marriage blessing may be given before the sermon. If they are negligent and come too late they shall be sent away.

Of the Common Residence of Husband and Wife. That the husband shall have his wife with him and they shall live in the same house, maintaining a common household, and if it should happen that one should leave the other to live apart they shall be summoned in order that they may be remonstrated with and constrained to return, the one to the other.

39. Geneva Consistory Records[17]

[*Preface: Charge to the neighboring village overseers*] *Thursday, October 12, 1542.*

Pierre Bezanson of Choully, Pierre Gallatin of Peney... etc. Summoned to the Consistory to establish order in the church by watching over those who live badly in their villages and to conserve the holy church, to show a good example to those others who wish to err in

---

[16] Source: *Translations and Reprints*, 3:11.

[17] Source: Thomas A. Lambert and Isabella M. Watt, eds., *Registers of the Consistory of Geneva in the Time of Calvin*, trans. M. Wallace McDonald (Grand Rapids, MI: Eerdmans, 2000), 29–30, 33, 37–38, 40–41, 67, 103–4, 111, 178.

the church, for the sake of the Word of God, which should be well heard. And it being known that they are honest and peaceable and a good example to others, that they should admonish them with the minister about the Word of God and see that others do their duty. And not to spare anyone, neither their families, wives, children, servants or maids, at instruction after dinner. And that they should remand those in error to the Consistory, and those who retain papal superstitions from the former times. Also give good admonitions [to] tavern-goers, blasphemers and other evil livers, also those with anger and hatred for each other and those who rebel against the Word of God and the honor of justice, as far as they can.

[The Case of Mermete Jappaz]

Thursday, March 30, 1542. Mermeta Jappaz. Said she is pregnant by the son of Berthelomier Fouson, named Bezanson, and she already felt the child at Christmas, and this was at the said Fouson's house. And she did not say her Pater[18] well, and she goes to sermons on Monday and other days not. And she wants to give it to its father, and her mother knows nothing, and she has had another child. And the other child was put to nurse and died.... The Consistory advises that she abstain from taking Communion because of her serious fornication. Remanded to Thursday....

Thursday, April 6, 1542. Besanson Fouson. About his foolish acts throughout the city, also about the woman he has made pregnant, called Mermetaz. Answers that he knew her about St. John's Day and said that Furbi's boy and Foy's valet have also been with her; therefore he says the child is not by him....

The Consistory advises that he be forbidden to receive Holy Communion because of his fornication and remanded to Thursday until it is evident that he has improved, and that he frequent the sermons. Yesterday he named Jaques Furbi's son and Thibaut Tissot, Nantermetaz's son, and Foy's valet for Thursday, who knew the said Mermete as well as he....

Thursday, April 13, 1542. Jaques, son of Furby. Asked about his bad behavior concerning the pregnant woman Mermete. And once about a year ago, being with Fouson's son, the said Besanson opened the door to him and said to the said Furbi: "Stay a little." And meanwhile she entered, as though he had consented to what he did to the said Mermete.

Thibault Tissot because of the said Mermete. Answers that he knew the said Mermete about a year ago in the clock-tower of the Corraterie.

The Consistory advises that all three be held, that they not be released, because of the child of the said Mermete, and that they be remanded before the Council in order that young people not ruin themselves thus; and that they be admonished that fornication is forbidden by the commandment of God. And that it would be good to drive such fornicators from the city to avoid such scandals and so they would not abuse themselves with fornication....

[The case of Jacques Symond]

Thursday, May 11, 1542. Monsieur Jaques Symond. Touching the Word of God and the Holy

---

[18] Pater Noster = "Our Father," i.e., the Lord's Prayer.

Gospel and frequenting of sermons. Answers the exhortations made to him; answers that he does not despise the Word of God. Said the Pater and confession.[19] Also said that it was proper to pray to God and the Virgin Mary, because he was in great danger from brigands when he called on Our Lord and the Virgin Mary. And is still in this error and asks advice about it and still believes that it is good because of the angelic salutation[20] that descended from heaven. And he does not understand that it is idolatry, and has received Holy Communion. And he did not understand that it was idolatry to invoke the Virgin Mary, and he was in this error a long time. And he considers the Mass not good, and abominable. Asked if he is certain about the holy sacrament of Holy Communion. Answers that he believes as is now believed among us, as is announced to us among us, and the custom of the city. The Consistory gave him proper admonitions....

[The case of Pernete Aubrier and Pierre Mamburier]

Thursday, August 10, 1542. Matrimonial case of Pierre Mamburier of Bons.... Pernete, daughter of the late Jaque Aubrier, from Sallanche, *habitant*[21] of Geneva, said [that] the said Pierre had promised himself to another wife and published the banns twice.... And the said Pernete said that he swore faith at the house of Master Pierre Vallet, carpenter, and his son named Tuppin. And the said Pierre gave them to drink together, when she said and understood that it was in the name of marriage. And the said Pierre denies it and says that it is not so. Pernete: the said Pernete was asked whether she had his company. Answers yes, twice, and that it was not at night. Claude, son of Pierre de Vallet, carpenter, called Tupin, his master, Françoyse his wife, the mother of the wife of the said Tuppin, the wife of Gervex were present when they drank together.

The said Pierre was asked why he does not want to complete this marriage. Answers that he has never had her company, and denied it vehemently. Asked about the said promise of marriage, denies the said marriage; denies everything repeatedly.

Confronted with each other, the said Pernete said that she had his company once or twice, and it was at the house of his master Pierre Vallet at night and that he promised her that he would never have another wife than her. And she would prove it, and how they drank together, by his master and others when it was necessary. The Consistory advises that she be asked if she was induced to say what she did and when and at what time it was. The said Pernete answers that the lieutenant urged her to go to the Consistory and that no one advised her to say such words, except God who advised her. And that the said Tuppin told her she should complain, and it was over a year ago. And that the said Pierre was a servant and earned wages in a carpenter's shop. And says he gave her nothing, the said Pierre, in the name of marriage. The Consistory advises that both be remanded to Monday before the Council and that the said Pernete bring her witnesses before the council.

---

[19] This is referring to the confession of faith, probably the Apostles' Creed.

[20] Meaning the Ave Maria.

[21] A habitant was a resident but not a citizen of Geneva.

Note:... the Council determined that they had drunk in the name of marriage, and because of the oath taken by Pernette the Council ordered "that the said marriage should go into effect."

[The cases of Mamad and Claudaz Buctin and of Claude and Martina Soutiez]

August 17, 1542. Mama Buctin, Claudaz his wife, and the wife of Claude Soutiez, named Martinaz, because of the word of God. The said Mamad answers that he cannot come because he has work to do, and that he goes to the sermon, and his wife, when they can. And he has such a thick head that he can retain nothing of the preaching. And he was there Sunday and Master Calvin preached. His wife answers that she was at the sermon Tuesday and retained nothing. Said the prayer and the confession. The said Mamad said the prayer and the confession, the confession poorly.

The said Martinaz, wife of Claude Soutiez, butcher, was asked when she got a bad eye and who did it. Answers that fully four months ago her husband beat her so much that she lost an eye and can see nothing with it, that the barber who treated it cut off a thread, and she was struck with a broom, and the blow was struck thus. And she asks for mercy, and did not dare to say it because of her husband who, if anyone opposed him at all, would go away and leave behind his wife and children and her mother. Then she said she was wrong and asks that he might be pardoned so he will not go, because he will leave great misery in his household.

The Consistory advises that he be given remonstrances and correction, and at his wife's request that nothing be done to him and that he be remanded to Monday before the Council and that he promise not to get angry or beat his said wife, have any anger between him and his wife.

Touching the said Mamad and his wife, the Consistory advises that he be made to learn his creed and appear on Thursday before the next Holy Communion to give an account of his faith, and go to catechism on Sundays and frequent the sermons when he can.

Touching Martinaz, the Consistory is of the advice and opinion that she always be obedient to her husband, and let them live in peace with each other....

[The case of Roland Marquerex]

Thursday, January 11, 1543. Roland the baker, bourgeois. Because of the games he holds in his house and whether it is a long time since there was gambling at [his] house. Answers that there was playing last Sunday after dinner at skillets and cards, at "triumph," for drinks, and he does not know who it was. And they did not play at vespers, and he puts himself at the mercy of the Seigneurie if anyone played at night at his house, that no one could say it in truth and that no one shelters at his house. And he was at the first and second sermons on Sunday, and he did not recognize the preacher. The Consistory advises, because he has lied to the Council, that he be admonished and remanded before the lieutenant, and that he shelter no one and follow the sermons. The said Roland admitted that he had played "malcontent" and does not remember about it.

Note: On January 19, 1543, Roland Marquereux is found in prison because he "sold as in a tavern and permitted gambling. On which resolved that he be forbidden the tavern for two years and that he be commanded to go to the sermon."

134

FURTHER READING

Benedict, Philip. *Christ's Churches Purely Reformed: A Social History of Calvinism*. New Haven, CT: Yale University Press, 2002.

de Greef, Wulfert. *The Writings of John Calvin: An Introductory Guide*. Translated by Lyle Bierma. Louisville, KY: Westminster John Knox, 2008.

Gordon, Bruce. *Calvin*. New Haven, CT: Yale University Press, 2009.

Hughes, Philip Edgecumbe. *Lefèvre: Pioneer of Ecclesiastical Renewal in France*. Grand Rapids, MI: Eerdmans, 1984.

Monter, E. William. *Calvin's Geneva*. New York: Wiley, 1967.

Naphy, William. *Calvin and the Consolidation of the Genevan Reformation*. Manchester: Manchester University Press, 1994.

Olin, John C. *A Reformation Debate: Sadoleto's Letter to the Genevans and Calvin's Reply*. New York: Fordham University Press, 2000. http://dx.doi.org/10.5422/fso/9780823219902.001.0001.

Reid, Jonathan. *King's Sister—Queen of Dissent: Marguerite of Navarre (1492–1549) and Her Evangelical Network*. Leiden: Brill, 2009. http://dx.doi.org/10.1163/ej.9789004174979.i-810.

Selderhuis, Herman J. *The Calvin Handbook*. Grand Rapids, MI: Eerdmans, 2009.

Wendel, François. *Calvin: Origins and Development of His Religious Thought*. Translated by Philip Mairet. Grand Rapids, MI: Baker Books, 1997.

Witte, John, Jr., and Robert M. Kingdon. *Sex, Marriage, and Family in Calvin's Geneva*. Grand Rapids, MI: Eerdmans, 2005.

VI

The English Reformation

On its surface, the English Reformation was an act of state. In Germany, Switzerland, and France, evangelical ideas were pushed, at least initially, by priests, scholars, and the people. England, by contrast, broke from Rome for one main reason: King Henry VIII needed to divorce Catherine of Aragon so that he could sire a male heir.

Of course, the whole story of the English Reformation is far more complicated than that, and generations of scholars have debated whether religious events in England were driven from the top down, from the bottom up, or from the middle. Scholars have also analyzed in detail how people in different parts of the country reacted to the break from Rome and to the subsequent changes in religion ordered by Henry's children and successors: the strongly Protestant Edward VI, the Catholic Queen Mary I, and the moderately Protestant Queen Elizabeth I.

Few clear answers have emerged from these studies of the English Reformation, save one: the English people of the sixteenth century were divided in their religious views. Some seem to have embraced the Reformation wholeheartedly; others remained steadfast Catholics; many others simply accepted what the state mandated from one monarch to the next. This chapter will explore some of the key debates about and official changes in religion during the reigns of Henry VIII, Edward VI, Mary I, and Elizabeth I.

XXI. THOMAS MORE AND WILLIAM TYNDALE ON THE ENGLISH BIBLE

Even before Henry VIII's break from Rome, Protestant ideas found their way into England. As Luther had done in Germany and Jacques Lefèvre d'Etaples had in France (see above, §XVI), William Tyndale (c. 1494–1536) in England translated the Bible into the vernacular. Although John Wyclif and the Lollards had already produced an English translation of the Bible (see above, introduction to §II), Tyndale's was the first to be based on the original Hebrew and Greek texts and the first to be printed.

After studies at Oxford and possibly Cambridge, Tyndale moved to the continent and studied in Wittenberg, where he probably worked on his translation of the New Testament. He completed it in 1525, and it was published the following year in Worms, Germany, and soon after in Antwerp as well. Thus, copies had to be smuggled back to England, and many were. The English ecclesiastical authorities denounced the translation and burned copies of it publicly. Tyndale later produced an English translation of the Old Testament.

Thomas More (1478–1535) provided the most in-depth denunciation of Tyndale's translation. We first encountered More among the possible true authors of *Defense of the Seven Sacraments* (doc. 15), officially attributed to Henry VIII. As a humanist, More was by no means a knee-jerk reactionary who automatically rejected anything other than the Vulgate.[1] He supported Erasmus's publication of the Greek New Testament with his new Latin translation, and he was not in principle opposed to vernacular translations. He thought Tyndale's translation, however, was misleading and heretical for the reasons he lays out below in his *Dialogue Concerning Heresies* (doc. 40). Two years later, Tyndale defended his translation with *An Answer to Sir Thomas More's Dialogue* (doc. 41).

---

[1] The Vulgate was St. Jerome's Latin translation of the Bible that was commonly used at the time, hence the name *Biblia vulgata*, or "commonly known Bible." Its use would be officially sanctioned at the Council of Trent (see below, doc. 48).

Both Tyndale and More met untimely ends. In 1536, Tyndale was captured in the Low Countries, tried for heresy, and executed. Ironically, shortly thereafter, Henry VIII required all English parishes to have a copy of the Great Bible, an English translation largely based on Tyndale's. His translation was also extensively copied in the later King James Bible; scholars estimate about 83 per cent of the KJV's New Testament came straight from Tyndale's translation.

You will read about Thomas More's trial and execution in the next section.

Focus Questions

1. Does Thomas More believe the order to burn Tyndale's New Testament was justified? Why or why not?
2. What three words does More highlight as pernicious translations and for what reason?
3. How does Tyndale defend his translation choices?
4. Can you think of other situations when a translation has caused controversy? To what extent is translation a question of substituting words and to what extent does it entail interpretation of the text?

40. Thomas More, *Dialogue Concerning Heresies*, 1529[2]

Book III, chapter 8. Characters: The Messenger and Thomas More

MESSENGER: But now I pray you, let me know your mind concerning the burning of the New Testament in English which Tyndale recently translated, and, as men rightly say, makes them greatly wonder at the burning.

MORE: To me, it is a great wonder that any good Christian man who has a drop of wit in his head would wonder or complain at all about the burning of that book if he knew the matter. Whoever calls it the "New Testament" calls it by a wrong name. It should be called "Tyndale's Testament" or "Luther's Testament." For Tyndale, following Luther's counsel, had so corrupted and changed it from the good and wholesome doctrine of Christ to the devilish heresies of their own, that it was an entirely different thing.

---

[2] Source: *The Workes of Sir Thomas More Knyght* (London: John Cawood et al., 1557), 220–23, text modernized.

MESSENGER: It is a wonder that it should be so entirely different, for it seemed quite similar to some who read it.

MORE: It is, nevertheless, different, and all the more perilous. A copper coin covered in silver looks like a true silver coin but is so much the more false by virtue of being counterfeited to look like the true coin. In the same way, the translation was all the more contrary in how much it was craftily devised to be similar, and so much more perilous in how hard it was for the unlearned folk to discern the difference.

MESSENGER: Why? What faults were there in it?

MORE: To tell you all that would require rehearsing to you the whole book, in which there were found and noted more than a thousand texts falsely translated.

MESSENGER: I would like to hear some.... What words are these?

MORE: One is this word *priests*. Another, the *Church*. The third, *charity*. For wherever he speaks of the priests of Christ's Church, he never calls them priests but always "seniors." The Church he always calls the "congregation," and charity he calls "love." Now these words in our English tongue do not express the things that are meant by them, and it also appears (considering the circumstances) that he had a mischievous mind in the change. For first, as for priests and priesthood, in the old days they commonly used to choose quite elderly men to be priests, and therefore, in the Greek tongue priests were called *presbiteri*, or as we might say *elders*. Yet, neither all priests were old, as appears by St. Paul writing to Timothy, "Let no one despise your youth" [1 Tim. 4:12], nor is every old man a priest....

Now, for what reason does he always call the Church the *congregation*? For everyone sees clearly that although the Church is indeed a congregation, yet not every congregation is the Church. But a congregation of Christian people has in England always been called and known by the name of the Church. What good cause or pretense could he find to turn this word into *congregation*, a word common to a company of Christians or a company of Turks.

There was similar wisdom in changing the word *charity* into *love*. For although charity is always love, yet as you know well, love is not always charity.... Since *charity* signifies in English men's cares—not every common love, but a good, virtuous, and well-ordered love—he who wishes will eagerly flee from the name of good love and always speak just of *love*, leaving out the *good*....

Now it is to be considered that at the time of this translation, Tyndale was with Luther in Wittenberg and set certain glosses in the margin, framed for promoting that ungracious sect.

MESSENGER: By Saint John! If it is true that Tyndale was at that time with Luther, it is a plain token that he worked somewhat with his counsel and was willing to help promote his cause here....

MORE: But now the reason why he changed the name of charity, and of Church, and of priesthood is not very difficult to perceive. For since Luther and his fellows among their other damnable heresies have one that says our entire salvation stands on faith alone and that toward our salvation good works have no force, therefore, it seems that Tyndale purposely worked to diminish the reverent mind that men bear to charity. Therefore, he changed the name of holy, virtuous affection into the bare name of "love."...

And because Luther utterly denies the true Catholic Church on earth and says that the

Church of Christ is an unknown congregation of some folks, here two and there three,... therefore, Tyndale in the New Testament cannot abide the name of the Church but turns it into the name "congregation."...

Now, regarding the reason why he changed the name of priest into "senior," you must understand that Luther and his adherents hold the heresy that all holy order is nothing. And that a priest is nothing else but a man chosen among the people to preach, and that by that selection to that office, he is priest by and by without further ado, and he becomes not a priest again whenever the people choose another in his place, and that a priest's office is nothing but to preach. For as for saying Mass and hearing confession and giving absolution, he says that every man, woman, and child may do all this as well as any priest. Now Tyndale, therefore, to set forth this opinion after his master's heresy, puts away the name of *priest* in his translation, as though priesthood were nothing....

I tell you this much only for this reason, that you may perceive that he has thus employed himself in his translation to the intent that he would set forth Luther's heresies and his own with it. For first, he would make the people believe that we should believe nothing but plain Scripture, in which point he teaches a plain and pestilent heresy. And then he would with his false translation make the people believe further that such articles of our faith as he works to destroy, which are well proved by Holy Scripture, are not spoken of at all in Holy Scripture, but that for fifteen hundred years all the preachers have misreported the Gospel and translated the Scripture wrong in order to lead the people purposely out of the right way.

....

41. William Tyndale, *An Answer to Sir Thomas More's Dialogue*, 1531[3]

Why Tyndale uses this word congregation, *rather than* Church, *in the translation of the New Testament.*

Insofar as the clergy had appropriated to themselves the term that should be common to the whole congregation of those who believe in Christ, and with their false and subtle wiles had beguiled and mocked the people and brought them into the ignorance of the word, making them understand by this word *Church* nothing but the shaved flock of those who sheared the whole world, therefore, in the translation of the New Testament, where I found this word *ecclesia*, I interpreted it by this word *congregation*. So I did it, and not from any mischievous mind or purpose to establish heresy, as Master

---

[3] Source: William Tyndale, *An Answer to Sir Thomas More's Dialogue, the Supper of the Lord after the True Meaning of John VI. and 1 Cor. XI.*, ed. Henry Walter (Cambridge: Cambridge University Press, 1801), 13–21, text modernized.

More untruly reports of me in his dialogue, where he rails against the translation of the New Testament.

And when Mr. More says that this word *Church* is known well enough, I ask the consciences of all the land whether he speaks truth or otherwise; or whether the lay people understand by *Church* the whole multitude of all who profess Christ, or the juggling spirits [i.e., the clergy] only. And when he says that *congregation* is a more general term, if it were, it does not matter, for the circumstance always tells which congregation is meant. Nevertheless, he does not speak the truth. For wherever I may say a *congregation*, there I may also say a *church*, as the church of the devil, the church of Satan, the church of wretches, the church of wicked men, the church of liars, and a church of Turks also. For Mr. More must grant (if he will have *ecclesia* translated throughout all the New Testament by this word *church*) that *church* is as common as *ecclesia*. Now *ecclesia* is a Greek word and was in use before the time of the Apostles, and taken for a congregation among the heathen, where there was no congregation of God or Christ. Luke himself uses *ecclesia* for a church or congregation of heathen people three times in one chapter, in the nineteenth chapter of Acts....

Another thing which he rebukes is that I interpret this Greek word *presbyteros* by this word *senior*. Truly, *senior* is not very good English, though *senior* and *junior* are used in the universities, but no better word came to my mind at the time. Nevertheless, I spied my fault since then, long before Mr. More told me, and I have mended it in all the works which I have made since and call it an *elder*. Since he makes it a heresy to call *presbyteros* an *elder*, he condemns their own old Latin text of heresy, which they still use daily in the church and have used, I suppose, for fourteen hundred years. For that text calls it an *elder* likewise. In 1 Peter 5, the Latin text says, *Seniores ergo qui in vobis sunt obsecro consenior, pascite qui in vobis est gregem Christi:* "Now as an elder myself... I exhort the elders among you to tend the flock of God that is in your charge" [1 Pet. 5:1–2]. There, *presbyteros* is called an *elder*.... Here you see that I have erred no more than their own text, which they have used since the Scripture was first in the Latin tongue, and that their own text understands by *presbyteros* nothing other than *elder*.... And all who were called *elders* (or *priests*, if they so will) were also called *bishops*, though they have divided the names now....

He rebukes me also that I translate the Greek word *agape* into *love*, and not rather into *charity*, so holy and so known a term. Truly, *charity* is not good English, in the sense which *agape* requires.... When we say, "God help you; I have done my charity for today," do we not take it for alms? And, "The man is ever chiding and out of charity,"... there we take it for patience. And when I say, "A charitable man," it is taken for merciful.... Also we do not say, "This man has a great charity to God," but "a great love." Therefore, I had to use this general term *love*, often in spite of my heart. And *agape* and *caritas* were words used among the heathen before Christ came, and signified for them more than a *godly love*.... And finally, I do not say, "Charity God," or "Charity your neighbor," but "Love God," and "Love your neighbor."

XXII. HENRY VIII'S BREAK FROM ROME

By the time of the More/Tyndale debate, King Henry VIII (r. 1509–47) was obsessed with one problem: How to divorce Catherine of Aragon (1485–1536), a problem which became known as the "King's Great Matter." Catherine had been married to Henry's older brother, Arthur, but when Arthur died just months into their marriage, it was arranged that Henry, the new heir to the throne, would marry his brother's widow to preserve the marital alliance with Spain. Catherine became pregnant by Henry several times, but all of the children were either miscarried or died in infancy, save one, a daughter named Mary (the future Queen Mary I). England had not had a queen since the controversial Empress Mathilda in the twelfth century, and the country had only just recovered from the War of the Roses, a long struggle over the succession to the throne. To avoid becoming the king who launched England back into chaos and civil war, Henry needed a male heir.

By the late 1520s, Catherine was reaching the end of her child-bearing years, and Henry was convinced that her failure to provide him with a son was the result of divine punishment for having married his brother's widow. He initially sought the divorce the traditional way, by appealing to the pope for an annulment. When that failed, he jumped on the Reformation bandwagon, creating his own church and thus guaranteeing his right to divorce Catherine.

To legitimize his decision, however, he did two things: First, he sought approval for his divorce case from the chief university theology faculties in Europe and received enough supportive responses to defend his decision. Second, rather than break from Rome by royal decree, he did so through the English Parliament. From 1529 to 1534, the so-called Reformation Parliament passed a series of laws that gradually separated England from obedience to the pope. One of the last of these laws, the Act of Supremacy (doc. 42), is included below.

With his break from Rome, Henry was free to divorce Catherine and marry Anne Boleyn, but he also needed an act of Parliament to change the rules of the succession, so that his children by Anne Boleyn would be his legitimate heirs rather than his daughter Mary. With the Act of

Succession, Henry made all of his chief councilors agree to exactly that, and he demanded their acceptance of the Act of Supremacy as well.

Not everyone would agree to Henry's conditions. One of the most famous hold-outs was Sir Thomas More (see above, §XXI). More had served King Henry faithfully, most notably as Lord Chancellor of England. But when it became clear that More would not support Henry's divorce of Catherine, Henry replaced him as right-hand man with Thomas Cromwell (not to be confused with the later Lord Protector Oliver Cromwell). More refused to acknowledge the legitimacy of Henry's divorce, and he refused to take the oath upholding the Act of Supremacy. For this steadfast opposition, he was imprisoned, tried for treason, and executed. An account of his trial is included below (doc. 43).

Focus Questions

1. What authority and powers does the Act of Supremacy give the monarch of England?
2. Why do you think Henry worked through Parliament to adopt the Reformation rather than simply issue a royal decree?
3. What charges were brought against More, and what defense does he make to them?
4. How does his response shift after he hears the verdict?

42. Henry VIII's Reformation Parliament, Act of Supremacy, 1534 (26 Henry VIII c. 1)[4]

Although the King's Majesty justly and rightfully is and ought to be the Supreme Head of the Church of England, and so is recognized by the clergy of this realm in their convocations, yet nevertheless for the corroboration and confirmation thereof, and for increase of virtue in

---

[4] Source: *The Statutes of the Realm*, reprint (London: Dawsons, 1817), 3:492, text modernized. The designation "26 Henry VIII c. 1" is the standard way of describing Parliamentary laws. "26 Henry VIII" means that it was done in the twenty-sixth year of the reign of Henry VIII, and "c. 1" indicates that it was the first law passed during that year.

Christ's religion within this realm of England, and to repress and extirpate all errors, heresies, and other enormities and abuses heretofore used in the same: Be it enacted by authority of this present Parliament that the King our Sovereign Lord, his heirs and successors, kings of this realm, shall be taken, accepted, and reputed the only Supreme Head on earth of the Church of England called the Anglican Church, and shall have and enjoy annexed and united to the imperial crown of this realm both the title and style thereof, and all honors, dignities, pre-eminences, jurisdictions, privileges, authorities, immunities, profits, and commodities belonging and appertaining to the said dignity of the Supreme Head of the same Church. And that our said Sovereign Lord, his heirs and successors, kings of this realm, shall have full power and authority from time to time to visit, repress, redress, reform, order, correct, restrain, and amend all such errors, heresies, abuses, offenses, contempts, and enormities whatsoever they be, which by any manner spiritual authority or jurisdiction ought or may lawfully be reformed, repressed, ordered, redressed, corrected, restrained, or amended, most to the pleasure of Almighty God, the increase of virtue in Christ's religion, and for the conservancy of the peace, unity, and tranquility of this realm, notwithstanding any usage, custom, foreign laws, foreign authority, prescription, or any other thing or things to the contrary hereof.

43. Trial of Sir Thomas More, 1535[5]

Sir Thomas, having continued a prisoner in the Tower of London somewhat more than a year, for he was committed about the middle of April 1534, was brought to his trial on May 7, 1535. He went into the court leaning on his staff because he was much weakened by his imprisonment, but appeared with a cheerful and composed countenance....

Presently after the indictment was read, the Lord Chancellor [Thomas Cromwell] and the Duke of Norfolk [Thomas Howard] spoke to him to this effect: "You see now how grievously you have offended his Majesty, yet he is so very merciful that if you will lay aside your obstinacy and change your opinion, we hope you may obtain pardon and favor in his sight."

But Sir Thomas stoutly replied, "Most noble lords, I have great reason to return thanks to your honors for this your great civility, but I beseech Almighty God that I may continue in the mind I am in, through his grace, unto death....

"As to the first crime objected against me, that I have been an enemy out of stubbornness of mind to the king's second marriage, I confess, I always told his Majesty my opinion, according to the dictates of my conscience, which I neither ever would, nor ought to have concealed, for

---

[5] Source: *Cobbett's Complete Collection of State Trials and Proceedings for High Treason and Other Crimes and Misdemeanors* (London: T. C. Hansard, 1809), 1:387–94, text modernized.

which I am so far from thinking myself guilty of high treason, that, on the contrary, being required to give my opinion by so great a prince in an affair of so much importance upon which the peace of the kingdom depended, I should have basely flattered him and my own conscience had not I spoken the truth as I thought. Then indeed I might justly have been esteemed a most wicked subject, and a perfidious traitor to God....

"The second charge against me is that I have violated the Act made in the last Parliament, that is, being a prisoner, and twice examined, I would not, out of a malignant, perfidious, obstinate, and traitorous mind, tell them my opinion whether the king was Supreme Head of the Church or not, but confessed then that I had nothing to do with that Act, as to the justice or injustice of it, because I had no benefice in the Church. Yet then I protested that I had never said nor done anything against it; neither can any one word or action of mine be alleged or produced to make me culpable. No, this I acknowledge was then my answer to their honors, that I would think of nothing else hereafter but of the bitter passion of our blessed Savior, and of my exit out of this miserable world. I wish nobody any harm, and if this does not keep me alive, I desire not to live; by all which I know, I would not transgress any law, or become guilty of any treasonable crime, for neither this statute nor any other law in the world can punish any man for his silence, seeing they can do no more than punish words or deeds; it is God alone who is the judge of the secrets of our hearts."

Attorney. "Sir Thomas, though we have not one word or deed of yours to object against you, yet we have your silence, which is an evident sign of the malice of your heart, because no dutiful subject, being lawfully asked this question, will refuse to answer."

More. "Sir, my silence is no sign of any malice in my heart, which the king himself must acknowledge by my conduct upon various occasions; neither does it convince any man of the breach of the law, for it is a maxim among experts in both civil and canon law, *Qui tacet consentire videtur*, 'he who holds his peace seems to give his consent.... '"

Now the jury, having withdrawn, were out scarcely a quarter of an hour before they returned with their verdict, by which they found the prisoner guilty, upon which the Lord Chancellor, as chief in the commission for this trial, immediately began to proceed to judgment.

Sir Thomas, observing this, said to him, "My lord, when I was practicing law, the procedure in such cases was to ask the prisoner before sentence whether he had anything to offer why judgment should not be pronounced against him."

The Lord Chancellor hereupon stopping his sentence, wherein he had already proceeded in part, asked Sir Thomas what he was able to say to the contrary.

More presently answered in these words: "For as much as, my lords, this indictment is grounded upon an Act of Parliament directly repugnant to the laws of God and his Holy Church, the supreme government of which, or of any part thereof, no temporal person may by any law presume to take upon him, being that which rightfully belongs to the See of Rome, which by special prerogative was granted by the mouth of our Savior Christ himself to St. Peter—and the Bishops of Rome his successors only—while he lived, and was personally present here on earth. It is, therefore, among Catholic Christians, insufficient in law, to charge any Christian to obey it."...

The Lord Chancellor then presently proceeded to give sentence to this effect: "That he should be carried back to the Tower of London... and from thence drawn on a hurdle through the city of London to Tyburn, there to be hanged till he should be half dead, that then he should be cut down alive, his privy parts cut off, his belly ripped, his bowels burnt, his four quarters set up over four gates of the city, and his head upon London Bridge."

XXIII. PROTESTANTISM UNDER EDWARD VI AND CATHOLICISM UNDER MARY I

Henry VIII removed England from Roman obedience, but he was by no means an ardent Protestant. The Six Articles issued in 1539 proclaimed as the law of the land the traditionally Catholic doctrines and practices of transubstantiation, communion in one kind, private confession, private masses, clerical celibacy, and the validity of monastic vows (even though Henry was already in the process of shutting down the monasteries and taking their land and wealth).

King Edward VI (r. 1547–53), Henry's long-awaited son by his third wife Jane Seymour, held strongly Protestant views. With the help of his regents and the archbishop of Canterbury, Thomas Cranmer, Edward began to turn England into a solidly Protestant state. Cranmer (1489–1556) had been the first to suggest to Henry VIII that he end his quest for a papal annulment and ask the university faculties for their opinions about his divorce case instead. As a reward to him and as a favor to Anne Boleyn, Henry elevated him to the position of archbishop of Canterbury. As archbishop under Henry, Cranmer was careful not to speak too boldly of sweeping Protestant reform, but he began to develop relationships with several prominent Protestant theologians on the continent. He also published the first edition of his most famous work, a new vernacular liturgy for the Church of England called *The Book of Common Prayer*.

When Edward VI took the throne in 1547 at the age of nine, Cranmer was able to push his reform efforts much further. He revised *The Book of Common Prayer* to be more Protestant, while Edward's Parliament issued the Act of Uniformity requiring its use in all English churches. Cranmer also contributed to *The Homilies*, a book of sermons that was required to be read in English churches in order to teach the people (and, no doubt, many priests) the new Reformed faith. The selection below (doc. 44) is one of Cranmer's contributions to this sermon collection.

King Edward was a sickly child and died in 1553 without producing an heir. After an ill-fated attempt to place a Protestant cousin, Lady Jane Grey, on the throne, Edward's half-sister Mary (r. 1553–58), daughter of Catherine of Aragon, took the throne. Mary was a stalwart Catholic. She repealed all the Protestant Parliamentary acts passed during the reigns of her father and brother and returned England to Roman obedience. To assist her in her efforts, she brought back to England Cardinal Reginald Pole (1500–58). Pole was English but had lived in exile on the continent since his break with Henry VIII over the divorce. In 1536, Pope Paul III made him a cardinal in the Catholic Church, and he became deeply involved in the theological debates of the Reformation. When Mary took the throne, the pope named him papal legate to England, and Mary herself made him the new archbishop of Canterbury after having Cranmer executed for treason. Pole became Mary's most important advisor and led the effort to return the people of England to the Catholic fold through, for example, speeches like the one below (doc. 45).

Focus Questions

1. What attitudes do Cranmer and Pole take with regard to ceremonies and traditions, and what is their reasoning?
2. What are their positions on reading the Bible?
3. What does each one think is most important in Christianity?
4. How does each one view the past religious changes that have taken place in England?

44. Thomas Cranmer, *Homily or Sermon of Good Works Annexed unto Faith*, 1547[6]

You have heard how much the world, from the beginning until Christ's time, was ever ready to fall from the commandments of God and to seek other means to honor and serve him, after a devotion imagined of their own heads, and how they extolled their own traditions as high or above God's commandments, which has happened also in our times.... What man having any judgment or learning, joined with a true seal unto God, does not see and lament to have entered into Christ's religion such false doctrine, superstitious idolatry, hypocrisy, and other enormities and abuses, so that little by little, through the sour leaven of these things, the sweet bread of God's holy word has been much hindered and laid apart? In their worst blindness, the Jews never had so many pilgrimages to images, nor used so much kneeling, kissing, and censing of them as has been used in our time. The Jews did not have a fraction of the sects and feigned religions, nor were they more superstitiously and ungodly abused as they have been recently among us; these sects and religions had so many hypocritical works in their state of religion, as they arrogantly named it, that their lamps, as they said, always ran over, able to satisfy not only for their own sins, but also for all their other benefactors, brothers, and sisters of their religion, as they had most ungodly and craftily persuaded the multitude of ignorant people, keeping in various places, as it were, marts or markets of merits, being full of their holy relics, images, shrines, and works of supererogation ready to be sold. And everything they had was called "holy": holy cowls, holy girdles, holy pardoned beads, holy shoes, holy rules, and all full of holiness....

And so, through their traditions and rules, the laws of God could bear no rule with them. And therefore, what Christ said to the Pharisees might be most truly said of them: "You break the commandment of God for the sake of your tradition; you honor God with your lips, but your hearts are far from him" [Matt. 15:3, 8]....

Honor be to God, who put light in the heart of his faithful and true minister of most famous memory, King Henry VIII, and gave him the knowledge of His word, and an earnest affection to seek His glory, and to put away all such superstitious and pharisaical sects invented by Antichrist, and to set up instead the true word of God and the glory of his most blessed name, as he gave the like spirit to the most noble and famous princes Jehoshaphat, Josiah, and Hezekiah. God grant all of us, the King's Highness's faithful and true subjects, to feed on the sweet and savory bread of God's own word, and, as

---

6 Source: Thomas Cranmer, *Miscellaneous Writings and Letters*, ed. John Edmond Cox (Cambridge: Cambridge University Press, 1846), 146–48, text modernized.

Christ commanded, to eschew all our pharisaical and papistical leaven of man's feigned religion. Although this feigned religion is most abominable before God and contrary to his commandments and to Christ's pure religion, yet it was extolled to be a most godly life and the highest state of perfection, as though a man might be more godly and more perfect by keeping the rules, traditions, and professions of men, than by keeping the holy commandments of God....

Vain inventions, unfruitful ceremonies, and ungodly laws, decrees, and councils of Rome were advanced in such a way that nothing was thought comparable in authority, wisdom, learning, and godliness, so that the laws of Rome, as they said, were to be received by all men just as the four evangelists, and all princes must give place to these laws. And the laws of God were also partly omitted and less esteemed, so that the said laws, decrees, and councils, with their traditions and ceremonies, might be more duly observed and held in greater reverence. Thus were the people, through ignorance, so blinded with the goodly show and appearance of those things, that they thought that observing them held more holiness and was a more perfect service and honoring of God, and more pleasing to God, than keeping God's commandments.

45. Cardinal Reginald Pole, Speech to the Citizens of London, c. 1555[7]

I am constrained for your welfare to warn you of this, exhorting you to extend your hand more to the aid of the poor, who are so dear to Christ that he says whatever is given to them in his name, he takes it as given to himself.... This is the very thing that, the less it is used, the more you ought to remember in this realm, especially in comparison to what I have seen in other realms and countries where I have been.... In just two cities in Italy, more alms are given to monasteries and poor people in one month than in this realm in a whole year. I wish you would strive to surpass those cities; by doing so, you should surpass them in grace and in all wealth and knowledge of God, which follows doing all of these works of mercy....

And here is another fruit that you must show worthy of a repentant mind, that whereas you have sorely offended God by giving favor to heretics, you should now temper your favor in such a way that if you can convert them in any way into the unity of the Church, then do it, for it is a great work of mercy. But if you cannot and if you permit and favor them, know that there cannot be a greater work of cruelty against the commonwealth than to nourish or favor them. For be assured, there are no men more pernicious to the commonwealth than they are; there

---

[7] Source: John Strype, *Ecclesiastical Memorials Relating Chiefly to Religion and the Reformation of It...* (Oxford: Clarendon Press, 1822), 3.2:483–505, text modernized.

are no thieves, no murderers, no adulterers, nor any kind of treason compared to theirs. They, as it were, undermine the chief foundation of the entire commonwealth, which is religion; they give entry to all kinds of vices in the most heinous manner, as we have often experienced since the religion was changed. After that time, what kinds of vices are there that did not take place here and had their supporters? This would have been to the utter undoing of the realm if our return to our ancient religion had been deferred any longer....

And now with this I shall make an end, showing you how you may see and follow Christ, no less at this present time than if he were bodily walking before you: which is to follow his commandments and to follow the commandments of the Church, his spouse, which does not move a foot without Christ going before her, having the Spirit of Christ for her perpetual guide and mover. And this you shall do, following her discipline,... which for a long time has been despised, and especially the discipline of ceremonies, which have been utterly cast out, all the sooner the older they were. And because man cannot live without ceremonies, nor was religion ever utterly devoid of them, they preferred in those days to use none than to accept the old, since they despised the discipline of their mother so much, and delighted in their new inventions.... From the observation of ceremonies begins the very education of the children of God, as the old law shows, which was full of ceremonies and which St. Paul called the "pedagogue to Christ" [Gal. 3:24]. And among all the privileges and graces that God gave the people he took to his own governance, this is reckoned the first grace: that they had such cer-

emonies with their law as no other nation had. And as God makes this the beginning of the good education of his children with appropriate ceremonies, so the heretics make this the first point of their schism and heresy, to destroy the unity of the Church by contempt or change of ceremonies, which seems nothing at the beginning. As it seemed nothing here among you to take away holy water, holy bread, candles, ashes, and palms; but what it came to, you saw and all felt. Therefore, take good heed how you break these small things, lest you lose the fruit of the great and the small and yourself in addition.

For there is nothing so little commanded or ordered by the Church but that breaching or disordering it makes a great offense.... Disobedience is a true poison to man's soul and body, as obedience saves both. This begins to show itself, first, by the observation and keeping of ceremonies, and there Christ began to declare his obedience, by which we were saved. And whoever wants to be saved, there he must begin his work; it's not that those ceremonies give salvation, but that their contempt brings damnation; not that they give us that light by which we seek to see Christ and his benefits in the Church, but they blind those eyes by which Eve saw the apple of her damnation, which were her bodily eyes and the eyes of her natural discourse and understanding. And this is counted a happy blindness, which is the very way to light. But the Spirit of God gives the true light, not the ceremonies which the heretics reject, nor yet the Scripture to which they cleave so, as though reading it were the only way to come to the knowledge of Christ; no doubt, it brings great knowledge if it is well understood. But I dare say this, and Scripture also agrees, that the observation of ceremonies for the sake of obedience will give more light than all the reading of Scripture can do if the reader does not have the knowledge to understand what he reads, even though he puts as much diligence in reading as he can, with the contempt of ceremonies. Neither ceremonies nor the Scripture gives us the true light, but they are most apt to receive light who are more obedient to follow ceremonies than to read....

But what gives the true light and what shows the very way to come to it—which all heretics pretend they seek and pretend they have more than others, because they say they stick more to Scripture than those who reprove them— I will now show you, as I have been taught of

the Church.... The right and principal way to come to the light of the knowledge of God and his ways, as the prophet calls them, is not gotten by reading; the prophet Isaiah expresses what it is, speaking not a word of reading the law, and the first lesson he gives to all who have this desire of that light, is to take away the impediment of that light, which is our sins [cf. Isa. 58:1–2], which are taken away by the sacrament of penance....

Here now you have heard the true way to come to the light, not by reading Scriptures, which you who break the unity of the Church speak of so much; and the prophet says nothing about any other way that can be imagined if works and mercy are absent.

XXIV. ELIZABETHAN (UN)SETTLEMENT: PURITANS AND ANGLICANS

Mary I died of cancer after ruling for only five years. She was succeeded by her half-sister Elizabeth I (r. 1558–1603), daughter of Henry VIII's second wife, Anne Boleyn. Elizabeth's personal religious beliefs have been the subject of much discussion and disagreement. Publicly, however, she encouraged compromise, an approach often called the *via media* ("middle way") that would please Protestants without completely dismantling traditional religion or the episcopal hierarchy in England. Elizabeth restored the Acts of Supremacy and Uniformity, once again severing England from the pope and restoring the use of Cranmer's *Book of Common Prayer.* In 1563, the Thirty-Nine Articles, which unlike Henry's Six Articles were firmly Protestant, were adopted and became the official statement of religious belief in England.

Not everyone was happy with the Elizabethan Settlement, as it is sometimes called. Puritans believed she had kept far too much from the Catholic Church, and they demanded that the Church be "purified" of such "papist idolatry." Their program was outlined in a manifesto presented to Parliament written by London clergymen John Field and Thomas Wilcox (doc. 46). The chief defender of Elizabeth's moderate position was Richard Hooker (1554–1600), whose *Laws of Ecclesiastical Polity* (doc. 47) offered the most important theory in defense of Anglicanism with all of the ceremonies, ornaments, and bishops that the Puritans wanted to do away with.

Focus Questions

1. What do Field and Wilcox want to see changed in the church?
2. According to them, what should be the basis of all religious belief and practice?
3. How does Hooker counter their arguments? How does he think religious belief and practice should be determined?
4. How does Hooker defend the retention of bishops?
5. Why do Field and Wilcox find the things they criticize so threatening, and why does Hooker find the Puritans so dangerous?

46. John Field and Thomas Wilcox, *Admonition to Parliament*, 1572[8]

Seeing that nothing in this mortal life is more diligently to be sought for and carefully to be looked unto than the restitution of true religion and reformation of God's Church, it shall be your parts (dearly beloved) in this present Parliament assembled, as much as lies in you to promote the same, and to employ your whole labor and effort not only in abandoning all popish remnants both in ceremonies and regiment, but also in bringing in and placing in God's Church only those things which the Lord himself in his word commands. Because it is not enough to take pains in taking away evil, but also to be occupied in placing good in the stead thereof....

May it therefore please your wisdoms to understand that we in England are so far off from having a Church rightly reformed, according to the prescript of God's word, that as yet we are not come to the outward face of the same. For to speak of that wherein all consent, and whereupon

---

[8] Source: W.H. Frere and C.E. Douglas, eds., *Puritan Manifestoes: A Study of the Origin of the Puritan Revolt* (London: SPCK, 1907), 8–19, text modernized.

all writers agree, the outward marks whereby a true Christian Church is known are preaching of the word purely, ministering of the sacraments sincerely, and ecclesiastical discipline, which consists in admonition and correction of faults severely.

Touching the first, namely the ministry of the word, although it must be confessed that the substance of doctrine by many delivered is sound and good, yet here it fails: that the ministers are not proved, elected, called, or ordained according to God's word.... In those days [of the ancient church] no idolatrous sacrificers or heathen priests were appointed to be preachers of the Gospel, but we allow and like well popish mass-mongers, men for all seasons, King Henry's priests, King Edward's priests, Queen Mary's priests, who in truth (if God's word were precisely followed) should be utterly removed.... Titles, livings, and offices devised by Antichrist are given to them, such as Metropolitan, Archbishop, Lord's Grace, Lord Bishop, Suffragan, Dean, Archdeacon, Prelate of the Garter, Earl, County Palatine, Honor, High Commissioners, Justices of Peace and Quorum, etc. All which, together with their offices, as they are strange and unheard of in Christ's Church, nay plainly are forbidden in God's word, so are they utterly with speed to be removed out of the same.

In the early Church, ministers were not tied to any form of prayers invented by man but as the Spirit moved them, so they poured forth hearty supplications to the Lord. Now they are bound of necessity to a prescribed order of service and *Book of Common Prayer* in which a great number of things contrary to God's word are contained, such as baptism by women, private communions, Jewish purifyings, observing of holydays, etc., patched (if not altogether, yet the greatest piece) out of the pope's Mass book....

These, and a great many other abuses are remaining in the ministry, which unless they be removed and the truth brought in, not only God's justice shall be poured forth, but also God's Church in this realm shall never be built....

The way, therefore, to avoid these inconveniences, and to reform these deformities is this: Your wisdoms have to remove advowsons, patronages, impropriations,[9] and bishops' authority, claiming to themselves thereby the right to ordain ministers, and instead to bring in that old and true election, which was accustomed to be made by the congregation. You must displace those ignorant and unable ministers already placed, and appoint in their places such men as both can and will by God's assistance feed the flock.... Appoint to every congregation a learned and diligent preacher. Remove [prescribed] homilies, articles, injunctions, a prescript order of service made out of the Mass book. Take away the lordship, the loitering, the pomp, the idleness, and livings of bishops, but employ them to such ends as they were in the old

---

[9] Advowson and patronage were the rights traditionally belonging to various noblemen and ecclesiastical officials to nominate individuals for clerical positions. Impropriations entailed bestowing ecclesiastical property and revenue from tithes to certain individuals.

Church appointed for. Let a lawful and a godly council of elders see that they preach, not quarterly or monthly, but continually, not for filthy lucre's sake, but of a ready mind. . . .

Now to the second point, which concerns the administration of the sacraments. . . . To redress the abuses surrounding the sacraments, your wisdoms have to remove (as before) ignorant ministers, to take away private communions and baptisms, to enjoin deacons and midwives not to meddle in ministers' matters; if they do, to see them sharply punished. . . . That people be instructed to receive the sacrament sitting, for avoiding of superstition, rather than kneeling, which has in it the outward show of evil, from which we must abstain. That excommunication be restored to its old former force. That papists nor other, neither constrainedly nor customably, communicate in the mysteries of salvation. That both the sacrament of the Lord's Supper and baptism also may be administered according to the ancient purity and simplicity. That the parties to be baptized may make rehearsal of their faith, if they be of the years of discretion by themselves and in their own persons, or if they be infants, by their parents, . . . and also if their faith be sound and agreeable to Holy Scriptures and they desire to be baptized. And finally, that nothing be done in this or any other thing, but that which you have the express warrant of God's word for.

Let us come now to the third part, which concerns ecclesiastical discipline. . . . Now then, if you will restore the church to its ancient officers, you must do this: Instead of an Archbishop or Lord Bishop, you must make equality of ministers. Instead of Chancellors, Archdeacons, Officials, Commissaries, Proctors, Doctors, Summoners, Churchwardens, and such like, you have to plant in every congregation a lawful and godly council of elders. The deaconship must not be confused with the ministry; the collectors for the poor may not usurp the deacon's office; but he that has an office must look to his office, and every man must keep himself within the bounds and limits of his own vocation. And to these three jointly, that is, the ministers, elders, and deacons, is the whole regiment of the church to be committed.

This regiment consists especially in ecclesiastical discipline, which is an order left by God unto his Church, whereby men learn to frame their wills and doings according to the law of God, by instructing and admonishing one another, yea and by correcting and punishing all willful persons, and contemners of the same. . . . The final end of this discipline is the reforming of the disordered, and to bring them to repentance, and to bridle such as would offend. The chief part and last punishment of this discipline is excommunication, determined by the consent of the church, if the offender be obstinate. . . .

Amend, therefore, these horrible abuses, and reform God's Church, and the Lord is on your right hand; you shall not be removed forever. For he will deliver and defend you from all your enemies, either at home or abroad, as he did faithfully Jacob and good Jehoshaphat. Leave these things alone, and God is a righteous judge; he will one day call you to your reckoning. . . .

You may not do as heretofore you have done, patch and piece, nay rather go backward, and never labor or contend to perfection. But altogether remove whole Antichrist, both head, body, and branch, and perfectly plant that purity of the word, that simplicity of the sacraments, and severity of discipline, which Christ has commanded and commended to his Church.

47. Richard Hooker, *The Laws of Ecclesiastical Polity*, 1594[10]

II.8. Two opinions there are concerning the sufficiency of Holy Scripture, each extremely opposite unto the other, and both repugnant unto truth. The schools of Rome teach Scripture to be insufficient, as if, unless traditions were added, it did not contain all revealed and supernatural truth which absolutely is necessary for the children of men in this life to know, so that they may in the next be saved. Others, justly condemning this opinion, grow likewise unto a dangerous extremity, as if Scripture did not only contain all things in that kind necessary, but all things period, and in such sort that to do anything according to any other law is not only unnecessary but even opposite unto salvation, unlawful, and sinful.... Just as incredible praises given to men often abate and impair the credit of their deserved commendation, so we must likewise take great heed, lest in attributing to Scripture more than it can have, the incredibility of that causes even those things which indeed it has most abundantly to be less reverently esteemed....

III.5. They who first put forth that "Nothing ought to be established in the Church which is not commanded by the word of God," thought this principle plainly warranted by the manifest words of the law: "You must neither add anything to what I command you nor take away anything from it, but keep the commandments of the Lord your God with which I am charging you" [Deut. 4:2]. Wherefore, having an eye to a number of rites and orders in the Church of England, such as marrying with a ring, making the sign of the cross in the one sacrament [baptism], kneeling at the other [Eucharist], observing festival days other than that which is called the Lord's day, enjoining abstinence at certain times from some kinds of meat, churching of women after childbirth, degrees taken by divines in universities, various church offices, dignities, and callings, for which they found no commandment in the Holy Scripture, they thought by the single stroke of that axiom to have cut them off. But that which they took for an oracle, being sifted, was repelled....

III.8. No man in justice and reason can be reproved for those actions which are framed according to that known will of God, whereby we are to be judged. And no sound theologian in the world ever denied that the will of God by which we are to judge our actions to be in part made manifest even by the light of Nature

---

[10] Source: Richard Hooker, *The Laws of Ecclesiastical Polity, Books I–IV*, ed. Henry Morley (London: George Routledge and Sons, 1888), 167, 184, 188–189, 228–29, 234, 236–37, 285–87, text modernized.

and not by Scripture alone. If the Church, being directed by the former (which God who gave the latter has also given so that man might in different sort be guided by them both), if the Church, I say, approves and establishes that which thereby it judges appropriate and finds not repugnant to any word or syllable of Holy Scripture, who shall warrant our presumptuous boldness, controlling herein the Church of Christ? But so it is that the name of the light of Nature is made hateful to men; the star of reason and learning, and all other similar aids, begins to be thought of no differently than if it were an unlucky comet or as if God had so cursed it that it should never shine or give light in things concerning our duty towards him in any way.... By these and similar disputes an opinion has spread very far in the world as if the way to be ripe in faith is to be raw in wit and judgment, as if reason were an enemy to religion....

III.11. The matters in which Church polity is concerned are the public religious duties of the Church, as well as the administration of the word and sacraments, prayers, spiritual censures, and the like.... Hereupon we hold that God's clergy are a state which has been and will be—as long as there is a Church upon earth—necessary by the plain word of God himself, a state to which the rest of God's people must be subject regarding things that pertain to their souls' health. For where polity is, it cannot but appoint some to be leaders of others, and some to be led by others. "If one blind person guides another, both will fall into a pit" [Matt. 15:14].... Again, insofar as where the clergy are any great multitude, order necessarily requires that they be distinguished by degrees; we hold that there have ever been

and ever ought to be in such case, at least two sorts of ecclesiastical persons, the one subordinate to the other, as other ministers of the word and sacraments have been to the apostles in the beginning, and to the bishops ever since, as we find plainly both in Scripture and in all ecclesiastical records....

IV.2. The first thing blamed about our rites and ceremonies is that in many things we have departed from the ancient simplicity of Christ and his apostles, that we have embraced more outward stateliness, and that we have orders in the exercise of religion which those who best pleased God and served him most devoutly never had.... Our end ought always to be the same, our ways and means thereto not so. The glory of God and the good of his Church was the thing which the apostles aimed at, and therefore ought to be our goal as well. But seeing that those rites and order may be at one time more available to that purpose which at another time are less, what season is there in these things to urge the state of only one age as a pattern for all to follow?...

IV.3. "Yes, but," [they say], "we have framed ourselves to the customs of the Church of Rome; our orders and ceremonies are papistical. It is seen that our Church founders were not as careful as they should have been in this matter but contented themselves with such discipline as they took from the Church of Rome. We ought to reform their error by abolishing all popish orders. There must be no communion, nor fellowship with papists, neither in doctrine, ceremonies, nor government. It is not enough that we are divided from the Church of Rome by the single wall of doctrine, retaining as we do part of their ceremonies and almost their whole government, but government or ceremonies or whatsoever it is which is popish; away with it." This is the thing they require of us, the utter relinquishment of all things popish....

IV.14. Surely, it must have been odious for one Christian Church to abolish that which all had received and held for the space of many ages without any detriment to religion.... For the Church of England, in casting out papal tyranny and superstition, to have... left not so much as the names which the Church of Rome gives to innocent things; to have rejected whatever that Church makes account of,... without any other crime to charge it with, other than that it happened to be used by the Church of Rome and not commanded in the word of God: This kind of proceeding might happily have pleased a few men.... But the Almighty, who gives wisdom and inspires with right understanding whomever it pleases him, foresaw that which man's wit had never been able to reach, namely what tragedies the

attempt of such an extreme alteration would raise in some parts of the Christian world, and for the endless good of his Church, he used the bridle of his provident restraining hand to stay those eager affections in some and to settle their resolution upon a calmer and more moderate course....

To the singular good of the Church, it cannot but serve as a profitable direction to teach men what is most likely to prove available when they shall quietly consider the trial that has taken place so far of both kinds of reformation: this moderate kind which the Church of England has taken, and that other more extreme and rigorous which certain churches elsewhere have preferred. In the meantime, it may be that suspending judgment and exercising charity is safer and more appropriate for Christian men than the hot pursuit of these controversies, in which those who are more eager to dispute are not always the most able to determine. But who are on God's side and who are against him, our Lord in his good time shall reveal.

FURTHER READING

Campbell, W.E. *Erasmus, Tyndale, and More.* London: Eyre and Spottiswoode, 1949.

Collinson, Patrick. *The Religion of Protestants: The Church in English Society, 1559–1625.* Oxford: Clarendon, 1982.

Daniell, David. *William Tyndale: A Biography.* New Haven, CT: Yale University Press, 1994.

Dickens, A.G. *The English Reformation*, 2nd ed. University Park: Pennsylvania State University Press, 1989.

Duffy, Eamon. *Fires of Faith: Catholic England under Mary Tudor.* New Haven, CT: Yale University Press, 2009.

Elton, G.R. *Reform and Reformation: England, 1509–1558.* Cambridge, MA: Harvard University Press, 1977.

Guy, John. *Thomas More*. New York: Oxford University Press, 2000.

Haigh, Christopher. *English Reformations: Religion, Politics, and Society under the Tudors*. Oxford: Clarendon, 1993.

Logan, George M., ed. *The Cambridge Companion to Thomas More*. Cambridge: Cambridge University Press, 2011. http://dx.doi.org/10.1017/CCOL9780521888622.

MacCulloch, Diarmaid. *Thomas Cranmer: A Life*. New Haven, CT: Yale University Press, 1996.

Mayer, Thomas F. *Reginald Pole: Prince and Prophet*. Cambridge: Cambridge University Press, 2000.

Shagan, Ethan H. *Popular Politics and the English Reformation*. Cambridge: Cambridge University Press, 2003.

VII

The Catholic/Counter-Reformation

Traditionally, the reforms made by the Catholic Church in the sixteenth century have been labeled the Counter-Reformation. Yet, well before Luther posted his Ninety-Five Theses in 1517, there was widespread agreement that the Catholic Church needed reform. We saw some of these efforts in previous chapters; the Council of Constance, humanists such as Erasmus, and individual bishops such as Guillaume Briçonnet all pushed for reform from within the church. Since these Catholic reform efforts preceded Luther, they cannot have been "counter" to Protestant reform. Increasingly, therefore, many historians refer instead to the "Catholic Reformation." Nevertheless, mid-sixteenth-century Catholic developments were necessarily responses, at least in part, to the Protestant Reformation; thus, some scholars still use the term "Counter-Reformation" to describe those later efforts. Regardless of the nomenclature, dramatic developments took place within the Catholic Church during the fifteenth and sixteenth centuries that changed the face of Catholicism for hundreds of years.

This chapter explores three important developments in the Catholic Church. First, the Council of Trent (§XXV) met with a twofold purpose: to clarify Catholic doctrine and reform abuses. Its canons and decrees shaped Catholicism for the next 400 years until the Second Vatican

Council issued its major reforms in the 1960s. Second, mysticism and monasticism were given new life through such figures as Teresa of Ávila, but mystics in particular came under increasing scrutiny as the Inquisition cracked down on suspected heresy and unorthodox behavior (§XXVI). And third, Ignatius of Loyola founded the Society of Jesus, better known as the Jesuits, which became one of the most important educational and missionary religious orders of the early modern and modern worlds (§XXVII).

XXV. THE COUNCIL OF TRENT, 1545–1563

Despite widespread agreement within the Catholic Church on the necessity for a general council to respond to the Protestant Reformation, several factors delayed its convocation. First, the threat of conciliarism (see above, §I) still hung in the air. Successive popes feared that a new council could reassert its authority over the papacy. Second, one of the lessons of the Western Schism had been that a council's effectiveness depended in part on the support of Europe's monarchs, yet the leading Catholic monarchs of Europe during the Reformation, King Francis I of France and Emperor Charles V, were almost constantly at war with one another. Despite these obstacles, Pope Paul III (r. 1534–49) was determined to call a council.

After a few false starts, Pope Paul III's long-awaited council finally opened in Trent (Trento, Italy) in December 1545. The council would meet over three periods with several years separating them. The first period was from December 1545 to September 1547; the second from May 1551 to April 1552; and the third from January 1562 to December 1563. The Council of Trent was charged with clarifying Catholic doctrine and reforming abuses in the church. The council (referred to primarily as a "synod" in the text below) took both charges seriously, and the result was a much clearer set of doctrines, an ambitious program for reform, and a Catholic Church more firmly controlled by Rome. Far from resurrecting conciliarist ideas, the council put power over the church squarely in the hands of the papacy. Together with the unifying Roman Catechism and Tridentine[1] Mass that were published soon afterwards, the Council of Trent, in effect, created *Roman* Catholicism, a faith thoroughly centered on Rome, the pope, a single body of doctrine, and a single prescribed form of worship. The council's decisions set the standards for Catholic belief and practice for the next several hundred years.

Protestants kept a close watch on the Council of Trent and eagerly shared news and rumors about what the council was doing. Several individuals wrote refutations of the council's decrees. John Calvin was one of the first to do so with his *Antidote* to the Council of Trent. Written following the first period of the council, the text thus addresses only the first few decrees of the council.

Focus Questions

1. Why do you think the Council of Trent addressed the questions of Scripture/tradition and justification first?
2. How would you characterize the doctrinal decisions made at Trent? Liberal? Conservative? Moderate? Why?
3. What reforms did the Council of Trent enact to ensure that priests would be better trained?
4. What did the council decide about saints, relics, and images?
5. Having read substantial excerpts from the Council of Trent, do you believe the term "Counter-Reformation" or "Catholic Reformation" more appropriate for its canons and decrees? Why?
6. What are Calvin's chief arguments against the council?
7. At the beginning of the Reformation, Luther hoped to reform the church from within. Does the council or Calvin seem to think that is still possible at this point?

---

[1] "Tridentine" is the adjective referring to things having been done at Trent, from the Latin name of the city, *Tridentinum.*

48. Canons and Decrees of the Council of Trent[2]

Decree concerning the Canonical Scriptures

The sacred and holy, ecumenical, and general Synod of Trent... keeping this always in view that with errors having been removed, the purity of the Gospel should be preserved in the Church. Our Lord Jesus Christ, the Son of God, first announced this Gospel, which had been promised through the prophets in the Holy Scriptures, with his own mouth. He then commanded it to be preached by his apostles to every creature, as the source of both saving truth and moral discipline. This truth and discipline are contained both in the written books and in the unwritten traditions which have come down to us, having been received by the apostles from the mouth of Christ himself, or from the apostles themselves with the Holy Ghost dictating, and transmitted as it were from hand to hand. Seeing this clearly, the Synod, following the examples of the orthodox Fathers, receives and venerates with an equal affection of piety and reverence, all the books both of the Old and of the New Testament—seeing that one God is the author of both—as also the said traditions, those pertaining to faith as well as to morals, as having been dictated either by Christ's own word of mouth, or by the Holy Ghost, and preserved in the Catholic Church by a continuous succession....

Decree concerning the Edition and the Use of the Sacred Books

Moreover, the same sacred and holy Synod... ordains and declares that the old and Vulgate edition [of the Bible], which by the lengthened usage of so many years has been approved of in the Church, be in public lectures, disputations, sermons and expositions, held as authentic, and that no one is to dare or presume to reject it under any pretext whatever.

Furthermore, in order to restrain petulant spirits, it decrees that no one... presume to interpret the said sacred Scripture contrary to that sense which Holy Mother Church—whose duty it is to judge of the true sense and interpretation of the Holy Scriptures—has held and holds; or even contrary to the unanimous consent of the Fathers....

Canons on Justification

Canon I. If anyone says that man may be justified before God by his own works, whether done through the teaching of human nature or that of the law, without the grace of God through Jesus Christ, let him be anathema....

Canon III. If anyone says that without the prevenient inspiration of the Holy Ghost, and without his help, man can believe, hope, love, or be penitent as he ought, so that the grace of

---

2 Source: *The Canons and Decrees of the Sacred and Ecumenical Council of Trent*, trans. J. Waterworth (London: Dolman, 1848), 17–20, 44–45, 54, 76, 78, 153–55, 157–58, 187–88, 232–36, 277–78, text modernized.

justification may be bestowed upon him, let him be anathema.

Canon IV. If anyone says that man's free will, moved and excited by God, by assenting to God who excites and calls him, in no way cooperates towards disposing and preparing itself for obtaining the grace of justification, that it cannot refuse its consent if it would, but that, as something inanimate, it does nothing whatever and is merely passive, let him be anathema....

Canon IX. If anyone says that by faith alone the impious person is justified, in such a way as to mean that nothing else is required to cooperate in order to obtain the grace of justification, and that it is not in any way necessary that he be prepared and disposed by the movement of his own will, let him be anathema....

On the Sacraments in General

Canon I. If anyone says that the sacraments of the New Law were not all instituted by Jesus Christ our Lord, or that they are more or less than seven, namely, baptism, confirmation, the Eucharist, penance, extreme unction, holy orders, and matrimony, or even that any one of these seven is not truly and properly a sacrament, let him be anathema....

Decree concerning the Most Holy Sacrament of the Eucharist

Chapter I. On the Real Presence of our Lord Jesus Christ in the Most Holy Sacrament of the Eucharist.

In the first place, the holy Synod teaches and openly and simply professes that in the august sacrament of the holy Eucharist, after the consecration of the bread and wine, our Lord Jesus Christ, true God and man, is truly, really, and substantially contained under the species of those sensible things. For these things are not mutually exclusive, namely, that our Savior himself always sits at the right hand of the Father in heaven according to the natural mode of existing and that, nevertheless, he may be in many other places sacramentally present to us in his own substance....

Chapter IV. On Transubstantiation.

And because Christ, our Redeemer, declared that which he offered under the species of bread to be truly his own body, therefore has it ever been a firm belief in the Church of God, and this holy Synod now declares it anew, that by the consecration of the bread and of the wine, a conversion is made of the whole substance of the bread into the substance of the body of Christ our Lord, and of the whole substance of the wine into the substance of his blood. This conversion is suitably and properly called *transubstantiation* by the holy Catholic Church....

Doctrine on the Sacrifice of the Mass

Chapter I. On the Institution of the most Holy Sacrifice of the Mass.

Our Lord Jesus Christ,... so that his priesthood would not be extinguished by his death... and so that he might leave to his own beloved spouse the Church a visible sacrifice,... whereby that bloody sacrifice... on the cross might be represented and the memory of it remain until the end of the world, and its salutary virtue be applied to the remission of those sins which we daily commit,... in the Last Supper on the night in which he was betrayed, he offered up to God the Father his own body and blood under the species of bread and wine; and, under the symbols of those same things, he delivered his own body and blood to be received by his apostles, whom he then constituted priests of the New Testament. And by those words, "Do this in memory of me," he commanded them and their successors in the priesthood, to offer them, even as the Catholic Church has always understood and taught....

Chapter II. That the Sacrifice of the Mass is Propitiatory both for the Living and the Dead.

And forasmuch as in this divine sacrifice which is celebrated in the Mass, that same Christ is contained and sacrificed in an unbloody manner who once offered himself in a bloody manner on the altar of the cross, the holy Synod teaches that this sacrifice is truly propitiatory and that by means thereof this is effected: that we obtain mercy and find grace in seasonable aid if we draw nigh unto God, contrite and penitent, with a sincere heart and upright faith, with fear and reverence.... Wherefore, not only for the sins, punishments, satisfactions, and other necessities of the faithful who are living, but also for those who are departed in Christ, and who are not as yet fully purified, is it rightly offered, agreeably to a tradition of the apostles....

Chapter VIII. On not celebrating the Mass everywhere in the vernacular; the Mysteries of the Mass to be Explained to the People.

Although the Mass contains great instruction for the faithful people, nevertheless, it has not seemed expedient to the Fathers that it should be everywhere celebrated in the vernacular. Wherefore, the ancient usage of each Church, and the rite approved by the holy Roman Church, the mother and mistress of all churches, being in each place retained, and that the sheep of Christ

may not suffer hunger, nor the little ones ask for bread and there be none to break it unto them, the holy Synod charges pastors and all who have the cure of souls that they frequently during the celebration of Mass expound either by themselves or others some portion of those things which are read at Mass, and that, amongst the rest, they explain some mystery of this most holy sacrifice, especially on the Lord's days and festivals....

Method of Establishing Seminaries for Clerics

Since the age of youth, unless it be rightly trained, is prone to follow after the pleasures of the world, and unless it be formed from its tender years unto piety and religion,... the holy Synod ordains that all cathedral, metropolitan, and other churches greater than these shall be bound... to maintain, to educate religiously, and to train in ecclesiastical discipline, a certain number of youths of their city and diocese.... Into this college shall be received those who are at least twelve years old, born in lawful wedlock, and who know how to read and write competently, and whose character and inclination afford a hope that they will always serve in the ecclesiastical ministry. And it wishes that the children of the poor be principally selected, though it does not, however, exclude those of the more wealthy, provided they be maintained at their own expense and show a desire of serving God and the Church. The bishop... shall, when it seems to him expedient, assign some of them to the ministry of the churches; the others he shall keep in the college to be instructed and shall supply the place of those who have been withdrawn by others, so that this college may be a perpetual seminary of ministers of God. And that the youths may be the more advantageously trained in the aforesaid ecclesiastical discipline, they shall always at once wear the tonsure and the clerical dress; they shall learn grammar, singing, ecclesiastical computation, and the other liberal arts; they shall be instructed in sacred Scripture, ecclesiastical works, the homilies of the saints, the manner of administering the sacraments, especially those things which shall seem adapted to enable them to hear confessions, and the forms of the rites and ceremonies. The bishop shall take care that they be present every day at the sacrifice of the Mass and that they confess their sins at least once a month and receive the body of our Lord Jesus Christ as the judgment of their confessor shall direct, and on festivals serve in the cathedral and other churches of the place....

Decree concerning Purgatory

Whereas the Catholic Church, instructed by the Holy Ghost, has, from the sacred writings and the ancient tradition of the Fathers, taught in sacred councils and very recently in this ecumenical Synod that there is a purgatory, and that the souls there detained are helped by the suffrages of the faithful, but principally by the acceptable sacrifice of the altar, the holy Synod enjoins on bishops that they diligently endeavor that the sound doctrine concerning purgatory, transmitted by the holy Fathers and sacred councils, be believed, maintained, taught, and everywhere proclaimed by the faithful of Christ....

On the Invocation, Veneration, and Relics of Saints, and on Sacred Images

The holy Synod enjoins on all bishops, and others who sustain the office and charge of teaching that ... they especially instruct the faithful diligently concerning the intercession and invocation of saints, the honor paid to relics, and the legitimate use of images, teaching them that the saints, who reign together with Christ, offer up their own prayers to God for humans, that it is good and useful suppliantly to invoke them and to have recourse to their prayers, aid, and help for obtaining benefits from God, through his Son, Jesus Christ our Lord, who alone is our Redeemer and Savior. And let them teach that those think impiously who deny that the saints ... are to be invoked, or who assert either that they do not pray for men or that the invocation of them to pray for each of us even in particular is idolatry, or that it is repugnant to the word of God and is opposed to the honor of the one mediator of God and men, Christ Jesus, or that it is foolish to supplicate, vocally or mentally, those who reign in heaven. Also, let them teach that the holy bodies of holy martyrs and of others now living with Christ ... are to be venerated by the faithful, through which bodies many benefits are bestowed by God on men, so that they who affirm that veneration and honor are not due to the relics of saints, or that these and other sacred monuments are uselessly honored by the faithful and that the places dedicated to the memories of the saints are in vain visited with the view of obtaining their aid, are wholly to be condemned, as the Church has already long since condemned and now also condemns them.

Moreover, that the images of Christ, of the Virgin Mother of God, and of the other saints, are to be had and retained particularly in temples, and that due honor and veneration are to be given them, not that any divinity or virtue is believed to be in them, on account of which they are to be worshipped, or that anything is to be asked of them, or that trust is to be reposed in images, as was done of old by the Gentiles who placed their hope in idols, but because the honor which is shown them is referred to the prototypes which those images represent, in such a way that by the images which we kiss and before which we uncover the head and prostrate ourselves, we adore Christ, and we venerate the saints whose similitude they bear....

Moreover, in the invocation of saints, the veneration of relics, and the sacred use of images, every superstition shall be removed, all filthy lucre be abolished; finally, all lasciviousness is to be avoided, in such a way that figures shall not be painted or adorned with a beauty exciting to lust; nor are the celebration of the saints and the visitation of relics to be perverted by any into reveling and drunkenness, as if festivals are celebrated to the honor of the saints by luxury and wantonness.

Decree concerning Indulgences

Whereas the power of conferring indulgences was granted by Christ to the Church, and she has even in the most ancient times used the said power, delivered unto her of God, the sacred holy Synod teaches and enjoins that the use of indulgences... is to be retained in the Church. And it condemns with anathema those who either assert that they are useless or who deny that there is in the Church the power of granting them. In granting them, however, it desires that, in accordance with the ancient and approved custom in the Church, moderation be observed, lest by excessive facility, ecclesiastical discipline be enervated. And being desirous that the abuses which have crept therein—and by occasion of which this honorable name of indulgences is blasphemed by heretics—be amended and corrected, it ordains generally by this decree that all evil gains for the obtaining thereof... be wholly abolished.

49. Calvin, *Antidote to the Council of Trent*, 1547[3]

[*On the council's decrees on Scripture*] There is an old proverb: The Romans conquer by sitting. Trusting to this, those degenerate and bastard sons of the Roman See, i.e., the great harlot, sat down to conquer when they appointed the third session. For what hinders them from raising a trophy, and coming off victorious to their hearts' content, if we concede to them what they have comprehended in one decree?...

First, they ordain that in doctrine we are not to stand on Scripture alone, but also on things handed down by tradition.... Thirdly,

---

[3] Source: John Calvin, *Tracts Relating to the Reformation*, trans. Henry Beveridge (Edinburgh: Calvin Translation Society, 1844), 3:67–71, 74, 108, 116, 171–72, text modernized.

repudiating all other versions whatsoever, they retain the Vulgate only and order it to be authentic. Lastly, in all passages either dark or doubtful, they claim the right of interpretation without challenge. These things being established, who can deny that the war is ended?... For whatever they produce, if supported by no authority of Scripture, will be classed among traditions, which they insist should have the same authority as the Law and the Prophets. What, then, will it be permitted to disapprove?...

But as the Hebrew or Greek original often serves to expose their ignorance in quoting Scripture, to check their presumption, and so keep down their boasting, they ingeniously meet this difficulty also by determining that the Vulgate translation only is to be held authentic. Farewell, then, to those who have spent much time and labor in the study of languages, that they might search for the genuine sense of Scripture at the fountainhead!

In regard to traditions, I am aware that not infrequent mention of them is made by ancient writers, though not with the intention of carrying our faith beyond the Scriptures, to which they always confine it. They only say that certain customs were received from the apostles. Some of them appear to have that origin, but others are unworthy of it. These touch only upon a few points, and such as might be tolerated. But now we are called to believe that whatever the Romanists are pleased to obtrude upon us flowed by tradition from the apostles; and so shameless are they that without observing any distinction, they bring into this class things which crept in not long ago, during the darkness of ignorance.

Therefore, though we grant that the apostles of the Lord handed down to posterity some customs which they never committed to writing, still, first, this has nothing to do with the doctrine of faith (as to it, we cannot extract one iota from them), but only with external rites subservient to decency or discipline; and secondly, it is still necessary for them to prove that everything to which they give the name is truly an apostolic tradition.... We must ever adhere to Augustine's rule, "Faith is conceived from the Scriptures."...

I come to the right of interpreting, which they arrogate to themselves whenever the meaning is doubtful. It is theirs, they say, to give the meaning of Scripture, and we must acquiesce. For everything which they bestow upon the Church they bestow upon themselves.... They wish by their tyrannical edict to deprive the Church of all liberty and arrogate to themselves a boundless license, for whatever the meaning which they affix to Scripture may be, it must be immediately embraced....

[*On the council's canons and decrees on justification*] The doctrine of man's justification would be easily explained, did not the false opinions by which the minds of men are preoccupied spread darkness over the clear light.... Their definition of justification at length contains nothing else than the trite dogma of the schools: that men are justified partly by the grace of God and partly by their own works, thus showing themselves only somewhat more modest than Pelagius was....

[*On the council's canons and decrees on the sacraments*] They insist that seven sacraments were instituted by Christ. Why, then, did they not order him to institute them? The number *seven*, which they place under the sanction of an anathema, has not only no support from Scripture, but none even from any approved author. This is little. Of the sacraments which they enumerate we show that some were temporary, such as the anointing of the sick, and others called so falsely, such as matrimony. The arguments by which we evince this are plain and strong.... If a sacrament consists of spiritual grace and an external sign, where will they find anything of the kind in penance? For giving marriage this name they have no other rea-son than the gross ignorance of the monks, who reading in the Epistle to the Ephesians (Eph. 5:32) the word *sacrament* used instead of *mystery*, and that concerning the secret union between Christ and his Church, transferred it to marriage. Of all these things our writings contain clear and copious demonstrations, which the good Fathers refute by shouting out, "Anathema!" This is to conquer without a contest, or rather to triumph without a victory!

XXVI. WOMEN, MYSTICISM, AND INQUISITION

Monastic renewal constituted an important part of the Catholic Reformation. In the late fifteenth and early sixteenth centuries, several religious orders were reformed to adhere more strictly to their rules for life and founding principles. The sixteenth century also saw the foundation of several new orders, including the Jesuits (see below, §XXVII), the Capuchins, Theatines, Ursulines, and the Oratory of Divine Love. Mysticism, too, saw a resurgence during this period. Christian mystics seek union with the divine through prayer and contemplation, and many experience visions or other extraordinary phenomena. Although by no means exclusive to monks and nuns, we often encounter mysticism in the monastic context. Reinvigorated monasticism and famous mystics helped to revitalize the faith of ordinary Catholics and increased trust in the church as an institution.

From early in the history of Christianity, the only way women could distinguish themselves in the church was as nuns or mystics. Thus, the study of monasticism and mysticism during the late fifteenth and sixteenth centuries is particularly important for understanding women's spirituality and their role in the Catholic Reformation. One of the reformed women's orders that arose during the Catholic Reformation was the Discalced Carmelites, established by Teresa of Ávila (1515–82). St. Teresa's monastic reforms sought to overturn what she saw as lax discipline in the Carmelite order and instead emphasized strict enclosure,[4] poverty, and equality among the nuns. Her mystical visions affected her deeply, and she wrote several books about them, including *The Interior Castle* and *The Way of Perfection*, which is excerpted below (doc. 50). Teresa came to be one of the best loved saints of the Catholic Reformation, and in 1970, Pope Paul VI named her a Doctor of the Church, the first woman ever to receive that distinction.

Mysticism, however, posed a potential danger to its practitioners. By definition, it seeks a profound personal religious experience outside the normal structures and practices of the church. As such, church officials viewed it warily, particularly during the Reformation, when Protestants were shrugging off the need for the Catholic Church. Mystics whose spirituality appeared to reject or circumvent church authority, therefore, risked being caught up in the Holy Office of the Inquisition, the body charged with rooting out heresy in the church. The second document below (doc. 51) is from the Inquisition trial of one of Teresa's contemporaries, Francisca de los Apóstoles (also Francisca de Ávila, 1539–after 1578), accused of being an *alumbrado*, a term used by the Inquisition, usually against women, to describe "false illumination" by visions achieved through contemplation. Needless to say, at least from a modern perspective, the line between revered mysticism and heretical *alumbradismo* in early modern Spain could be a fine one. While Teresa of Ávila was canonized and made a Doctor of the Church, Francisca of Ávila was whipped and then disappeared from the historical record.

Focus Questions

1. Although mystics' visions are often deeply personal experiences, they generally write about them to convey a lesson to others. What lessons

---

[4] Enclosure, which was also enjoined by the Council of Trent, meant that nuns were not allowed to leave the monastery, and no outsider was allowed to enter the monastery except under extraordinary circumstances and with the permission of the bishop.

do Teresa and Francisca seem to be trying to convey in the description of their visions?

2. From the excerpts below, what differences do you see that might make Teresa's visions seem legitimate but Francisca's false to inquisitors and church officials?

3. What decision was made in Francisca's case, and how did she respond to it?

50. Teresa of Ávila, *The Way of Perfection*, 1583[5]

1. Nature and Definition of the Prayer of Recollection

It is called the Prayer of Recollection because in it the soul collects or gathers together all her powers and enters into her own interior with God.

I wish I knew how to describe to you this holy intercourse which, without disturbing in the least her perfect solitude, is carried on between the soul and her divine spouse and companion, the Holy of Holies, and which takes place as often as ever she pleases to enter into this interior paradise in company with her God, and to shut the gate to all the world besides. I say, "as often as she pleases," for you must understand that this is not altogether a supernatural thing but is quite within our own power, and we can do it whenever we choose; I mean, of course, with God's help, for without this we can do nothing at all, not so much as have a single good thought. For you must observe that this recollection is not a suspension of the powers of the soul, but only a shutting them up, as it were, within ourselves.

2. The Truth or Foundation on which the Prayer of Recollection Rests

You know that God is everywhere (therefore, he is in our interior). Now it is clear that wherever the king is, there the court is too; therefore, wherever God is, there is heaven; and you can readily believe that wherever this Divine Majesty is, all glory is with him. Then consider what St. Augustine says: that he "sought God in many places, and found him at last within himself."

It is, then, of the utmost importance to bear this truth in mind, that our Lord is within us, and that we ought to strive to be there with him.

On a certain occasion, when I was assisting at the divine office with the rest of the sisters,

---

[5] Source: James, Bishop of Hexham and Newcastle, ed., *St. Teresa's Own Words: Or, Instructions on The Prayer of Recollection, Arranged from Chapters 28 and 29 of Her* Way of Perfection (London: Burns & Oates, 1910), 5–10, text modernized.

I became, on a sudden, thus recollected within myself; and here my own soul was presented before me, and it seemed to me to resemble a bright mirror in which there was no darkness nor shadow, either behind or on either side or above or below, but all clear and resplendent; and in the midst of it there appeared Christ our Lord in the form under which I am accustomed to see him. It seemed to me that his image was shining forth from every part of my soul, as though reflected in the mirror; and then, by a wonderful communication of love, which I know not how to describe, this same mirror of my soul seemed to be reproduced and again represented in a wondrous manner within the form of my divine Redeemer.

Again, on a certain occasion, it was shown to me that my soul was like a sponge in the midst of the ocean of the divinity and that it drank in this heavenly substance, so as, in a manner, to embrace within it the three divine persons. But at the same time, I was admonished that though I had the divinity within my soul, yet I myself was much more contained in him than he in me. Thus, while I beheld, as it were, hidden within me the three divine persons, I saw that they, at the same time, communicated themselves to all created things, without ceasing for an instant to abide in me.

On another occasion I was made to understand this truth with great clarity—that all things are seen in God and that he contains everything within himself. I do not know how to describe this, but it has remained deeply impressed upon my mind and is one of the greatest favors our Lord has ever granted me, and one that has filled me, more than any other, with confusion at the remembrance of my sins. If it had pleased our Lord to let me see this before I had sinned, or if others who offend him could only have seen it, I believe that neither they nor I would have ever had the boldness to commit sin. No words that I can use convey any idea of this sublime truth. The only notion I can give of it is this: I beheld the divinity like a most brilliant diamond, far greater than the whole world, and containing everything within itself; and in this diamond was reflected, as it were, everything that is done here below. Wonderful it was, indeed, to behold in so short a time, within this glorious mirror, such a multitude of things assembled together! But to see represented in this pure and unsullied brightness such foul abominations as my sins was a spectacle that fills me with the deepest sorrow whenever I call it to mind. In truth, when I reflect upon it, I know not how I can bear the thought; and at the time when I beheld it, I was so covered with confusion that I did not know which way to turn.

Now it seems to me that this vision may be of much profit to those who are practicing this Prayer of Recollection, to teach them to consider our Lord in the interior of their own souls; for, to repeat what I have so often said before, this consideration fixes the attention far better, and is far more profitable, than to represent him in any other way. If, instead of this, we direct our thoughts to God in heaven, or if, in the end, we turn to any spot beyond ourselves we do but weary our minds and distract our souls, and after all, lose much of the fruit of our labor.

51. The Inquisition Trial of Francisca de los Apóstoles, 1575–1577[6]

[Trial testimony on October 8, 1575] The defendant [Francisca testified that she] fell asleep and then woke up very disoriented, crying out loud, and she felt transported out of herself without knowing how and was as if put on a cross with her arms extended. In this transported state she saw a great Majesty very irate like a terrible judge, and the defendant cried out loudly saying, "Heaven and earth fear to see God made into our judge." Then she saw Our Lord on the cross asking for justice for His wounds to that Majesty. Then she saw Him at the pillar asking for justice for His lashes and for the ingratitude people had for His passion. At this, the defendant began to cry out to Our Lady telling her to favor sinners, and then she saw her with her Son in her arms having just been taken down off the cross, pleading to that Majesty for the same justice, saying how ungrateful we had been at her Transfixion. At this, the defendant cried out to the saints to defend sinners, since in all parts of the world they were helpless. Then she saw Saint Peter come forward, saying to that Majesty, "Eternal Father, may there be a harsh punishment for the priests who have followed You so poorly, because, naked, I followed the naked one, but they go about weighed down by their incomes and vices." At this she saw many hosts, with Christ crucified on each one, flying over her bed, each one asking for justice from that Majesty. The defendant cried out to Our Lord because she saw that God would hand down a great sentence against all the world because of his legitimate complaint against all the estates of humankind. Many other things happened to the defendant in this regard that she does not remember right now, except that she was occupied in this vision from eight o'clock at night until eleven o'clock....

After this they showed her a procession in which she saw priests dressed in coarse, woolen cloth and black bonnets and another procession of nuns all dressed in coarse white wool with white capes of the same width that the canons of the Cathedral of Toledo wear. And then Our Lord said to the defendant, "These are the religious whom I want to make satisfaction to me in the same way that you have vowed. I want them to celebrate each Thursday the feast of the Most Holy Sacrament and I want it to remain in the monstrance until the next Friday. I want the priests and nuns to remain there throughout the entire night, meditating on the torments I suffered that night and forgetting all else in the world. And all day Friday they should occupy themselves in this and on Saturday on the Transfixion of Our Lady." After all these things and other similar ones

---

[6] Source: Gillian T.W. Ahlgren, ed. and trans., *The Inquisition of Francisca: A Sixteenth-Century Visionary on Trial*, The Other Voice in Early Modern Europe (Chicago: University of Chicago Press, 2005), 68–71, 156–58.

had passed, she returned to herself and this entire vision summed itself up in the fact that Our Lord wanted, for the reformation of the entire world and satisfaction of those offenses, that these religious houses be made in all of the dioceses and that there be seminaries for the prelates from which priests could leave to serve the churches; that they have a common income in the apostolic life, without possessing anything of their own; that their occupation consist entirely in uprooting evil and encouraging virtues and attending to the needs of others; and that they have a school for young men to train them in serving the church, because Our Lord wanted to be honored and revered by his priests, as His Majesty deserves....

Ratification of Her Case and Final Questions, August 9, 1577. And afterward she was read word for word all that she has said, and she responded to the publication, letters, and papers about which she has been examined from the audience on the morning of the last day of July until this audience. And having said that she has understood it, she said that it is the truth and that she affirms and ratifies it, and, if necessary that she would say it again and that she has said it just as it happened to her. And that it is true that she told all those people who testified all the things that she has confessed happened to her, as she has known these witnesses, as a woman ignorant of matters pertaining to Our Lord and a person of little insight, because she thought that all those things she saw, since they pertained to the justice against the world, seemed to her to be urgent, and for this reason she told them all. And she wanted to tell everyone, according to her lack of judgment in this matter, with the desire that all might do penance as she had seen that Our Lord was offended. And because she was ignorant about matters pertaining to Our Lord, she did not understand that they could be deceits of the devil to lead her into the state to which he has led her. And thus not recognizing it for what it was but understanding it all to be from our Lord, she spoke of it with everyone so freely. But now that in this Holy Office she has been made to understand the opposite, she renounces all that she has confessed and spoken of in her confessions and only believes and will believe what they have taught her in this Holy Office. And thus she places herself in the hands of Our Lord and the Lord Inquisitor, as the person who is appointed to give light in the church of God and take her from errors and ignorance. And because she does not understand herself to have fallen into error and if she has fallen she did not recognize it, she asks for the mercy of Our Lord that she be received into the bosom of the church and that what she has suffered during these past two years in prison be taken as penance for her ignorance, lunacy, and vanity. And with this she has nothing more to say....

Sentence against Francisca de los Apóstoles. We have followed with attention the acts and merits of this case and the guilt of Francisca de Avila, alias de los Apóstoles, and if we were to act within the rigor with which we can rightfully proceed we could punish her most gravely, but we recognize her good confession and the signs of repentance she has given. And for other reasons that move us, using kindness and mercy with her, we order that she be punished for these vanities and errors to give others an example and that she walk in this present auto-da-fé[7] in person with a wax candle in her hands, a rope around her neck, where her sentence will be read, and that she abjure her fault *de levi*.[8] And after that we order that she be given one hundred lashes on the customary streets of this city and her crime be read publicly and she be exiled from this said city of Toledo and five leagues around it for the time of three years, and if that exile is broken, this time will be doubled. And we warn her that from now on she must refrain from committing the crimes or any other similar ones and that if she does the opposite she will be punished with all due rigor. And this our sentence is to be spread as we pronounce it and order it.

XXVII. THE SOCIETY OF JESUS AND *CAMPION'S BRAG*

Ignatius of Loyola (1491–1556) was the founder of arguably the most influential modern Catholic order, the Society of Jesus, also known as the Jesuits. Ignatius had been a soldier in Spain when he suffered a terrible wound from a cannonball. While recovering, he read the lives of the saints and Ludolph of Saxony's *Life of Christ*. These texts, together with a vision of the Virgin Mary, formed the background of a conversion experience that led Ignatius to abandon his military career and pursue a life of piety.

He compiled his devotions in a highly influential book entitled the *Spiritual Exercises*, which would become a manual of pious devotion for the Jesuits as well as many other Catholics. During his studies at the University of Paris, he attracted a group of followers who shared his religious zeal and his desire to convert non-Christians in the Holy Land. In 1534, they took vows of poverty and chastity, and in 1540 they received official approval of their order from Pope Paul III, adding to the traditional monastic vows of poverty, chastity, and obedience a fourth vow to go wherever and do whatever the pope commanded.

---

[7] An auto-da-fé, which means "act of faith," was a ritual of public penance imposed upon those found guilty by the Inquisition.

[8] An abjuration *de levi* is one of only slight suspicion of heresy. Strong suspicion of heresy would be abjured *de vehementi*, and a notorious heretic would have to abjure *de formali*.

During the Reformation, the Jesuits became best known for two things: education, both their own training and the free schooling they offered to poor children, and missionary work overseas and in Protestant Europe. The texts in this section reflect both of these emphases. Edmund Campion (1540–81) was an Englishman who had studied at Oxford and initially took the Oath of Supremacy to Queen Elizabeth I. But he later converted to Catholicism and left the country. He studied at the English College in Douai, Netherlands (today in France), a school established specifically to support and educate expatriate English Catholics. Campion then joined the Jesuit Order in Rome. In 1580, he entered England secretly and began to preach underground to Catholics. Officials soon became aware of his presence, however, and in response, Campion wrote a *Challenge to the Privy Council*[9] (doc. 52), declaring his intentions in England. The text is better known as *Campion's Brag*, for he claimed to be able to defeat anyone at any time in a religious debate.

On publication of *Campion's Brag*, William Charke took it upon himself to compose a response, *An Answer to a Seditious Pamphlet*, which is the second text (doc. 53). Charke was a cleric whose Puritan leanings led to his dismissal from the University of Cambridge in 1572. Not a great deal is known of him, and his fame rests largely on his debate with Campion. Eventually, Campion was arrested and offered the debate he sought—in a manner of speaking. It was held at the Tower of London where he was imprisoned, and although his Protestant opponents—one of whom was Charke—were allowed to bring notes and books, Campion was allowed neither. He was also tortured shortly before the debate and given no time to prepare. Nevertheless, Campion performed well, and the authorities cut the debate short when it became clear that they could not definitively humiliate Campion. They executed Campion two months later.

---

[9] The Privy Council was the English monarch's cabinet of close advisors.

Focus Questions

1. Why does Campion write his *Challenge*?
2. What does he say his purpose was in coming to England?
3. What meetings and discussions does he seek and why?
4. Is the name *Campion's Brag* fair or reflective of Protestant bias?
5. How does Charke address Campion's individual points?
6. What does he make of the Jesuits in general and their emphasis on education?
7. What does his use of the word "seditious" in his title indicate?

52. Edmund Campion, *Challenge to the Privy Council* (*Campion's Brag*), 1580[10]

Whereas I have come out of Germany and Bohemia, being sent by my superiors, and ventured to this noble realm, my dear country, for the glory of God and benefit of souls, I thought it likely enough that in this busy, watchful, and suspicious world, I should either sooner or later be interrupted and stopped of my course. Therefore, providing for all doubts and uncertainties about what may become of me when God shall perhaps deliver my body into captivity, I supposed it necessary to prepare this writing, desiring your good lordships to give it a reading and to know my cause. By doing this, I think I shall ease you of some labor, for that which otherwise you must have sought for by practice of wit, I now lay into your hands by plain confession. And so that this whole matter may be conceived in order and thus be both better understood and remembered, I make hereof these nine points or articles, directly, truly, and resolutely opening my full enterprise and purpose.

1. I confess that I am, albeit unworthy, a priest of the Catholic Church and, through the great mercy of God, vowed now these eight years into the religion of the Society of Jesus; and thereby have taken upon myself a special kind of warfare under the banner of obedience, and also resigned all my interest and possibility of wealth, honor, pleasure, and other worldly felicity....

3. My charge is to preach, free of cost, the Gospel, to administer the sacraments, to instruct the simple, to reform sinners, to confute errors,

---

[10] Source: Henry Foley, *Records of the English Province of the Society of Jesus* (London: Burns & Oates, 1878), 3: 629–31, text modernized.

and, in brief, to cry all spiritual arms against foul vice and proud ignorance, by which many of my dear countrymen are now abused....

5. I ask, to the glory of God, with all humility and under your correction three sorts of indifferent and quiet audiences: the first before your honors, wherein I will discourse of religion so far as it touches the commonweal and your nobilities; the second whereof I make more account before the doctors, the masters, and chosen men of both universities [i.e., Oxford and Cambridge], wherein I undertake to defend the faith of our Catholic Church by invincible proofs, Scriptures, Councils, Fathers, histories, natural and moral reasons; the third before the lawyers spiritual and temporal, wherein I will justify the said faith by the common wisdom of the laws standing yet in force and practice.

6. I would be loath to speak anything that might sound of any insolent brag, or challenge, especially being now as a dead man to this world and willing to cast my head under every man's foot, and to kiss the ground they tread upon. Yet I have such a courage in advancing the majesty of Jesus my King, and such trust in his gracious favor, and such assurance in my quarrel, and my evidence so impregnable, that because I know perfectly that none of the Protestants, not all the Protestants living, nor any sect of our adversaries (howsoever they face men down in pulpits and overrule as in their kingdom of grammarians and of unlearned ears) can maintain their doctrine in disputation, I am to seek most humbly and instantly for the combat with all and every one of them, and the most principal that may be found, protesting that in this trial, the better furnished they come, the better they shall be to me.

7. And because it has pleased God to enrich the Queen [Elizabeth I], my Sovereign Lady, with noble gifts of nature, learning, and princely education, I do truly trust that if her Highness would vouchsafe her royal person and good attention to such conference, as in the second part of my fifth article I have mentioned and requested, or to a few sermons which in her or your hearing I am to utter, such manifest and fair lights by good method and plain dealing may be cast upon those controversies that possibly her zeal of truth and love of her people shall incline her noble grace to disfavor some proceedings hurtful to the realm, and procure towards us oppressed more equity.

8. Moreover, I doubt not but you, her honorable Council, being of such wisdom and drift in cases most important, when you shall have heard these questions of religion opened faithfully, which many times by our adversaries are huddled up and confounded, will see upon what substantial grounds our Catholic faith is built, and how feeble that side is which by sway of the time prevails against us; and so at last for your own souls and for many thousands of souls that depend upon your government, you will discountenance error where it is revealed and listen to those who would spend the best blood in their bodies for your salvation. Many innocent hands are lifted up to heaven for you daily and hourly by those English students whose posterity shall never die, which, beyond the seas, gathering virtue and sufficient knowledge for the purpose, are determined never to give you over but either to win you to heaven or to die upon your pikes. And touching our Society, be it known unto you that we have made a

league—all the Jesuits in the world whose succession and multitude must overreach all the practices of England—cheerfully to carry the cross that God shall lay upon us, and never to despair of your recovery while we have a man left to enjoy your Tyburn,[11] or to be racked with your torments, or to be consumed with your prisons. The expense is reckoned, the enterprise is begun; it is of God, it cannot be withstood. So it was first planted; so it must be restored.

9. If these my offers be refused, and my endeavors can take no place, and I, having run thousands of miles to do you good, shall be rewarded with rigor, I have no more to say but to recommend your case and mine to Almighty God, the searcher out of hearts, who sends us of his grace, and sets us at accord before the day of payment, to the end that we may at the last be friends in heaven, where all injuries shall be forgotten.

53. William Charke, *An Answer to a Seditious Pamphlet*, 1581[12]

It happens that one Edmund Campion, a principal champion of the popish religion, flying far from the field some years past for lack of armor, is now returned... [and] requires disputation before all and with all,... yet his purpose is to disturb all by the very proclaiming of this spiritual fight and by giving aim to those who in the same league attempt otherwise more dangerous matters against the state....

But before I come to the particular points of his letter, I will briefly touch on the chief and only matter therein pretended, which is a desire to have a disputation granted, or solemn audience for some sermons to be made in support of the most worthily abandoned popish religion.

This petition seems necessary to all papists, and I cannot blame them.... But I would wonder if any who profess the Gospel should now look for a disputation to answer every vain challenge, after so many blessed years in which error has been confused in every way and the truth established. For our part, we are so assured of the manifest truth that we make no doubt thereof. For their part, if they sought conference in a good conscience and with a desire to learn, it would be necessary to regard their desires and to relieve their conscience. But returning to the land with ungodly vows and obstinate minds to persist in their errors, and hoping to deceive many with their masks, it is proper to keep them as far from doing harm by their lies as they withhold themselves far from receiving good by our truth.... What then shall we gain by disputing with them, when they will not be gained to the truth?... When did they grant a free disputation, or allow sermons to be made to them about religion,

---

[11] Tyburn, in greater London, near today's Marble Arch, was where many public executions took place.
[12] Source: William Charke, *An Answere to a Seditious Pamphlet lately cast abroade by a Jesuite...* (London: Christopher Barker, 1581), text modernized.

unless they were forced on them? Yea, at this very time, howsoever this "Champion" and some others challenge and call for disputation, yet their forerunners and fathers in popery refused the same....

In the first article, he confesses his calling, "That, albeit unworthy, he is a priest of the Romish church," which he falsely honors with the name of the *Catholic Church*. Such as this church is, such is his priesthood also: the Antichristian church, and its priests ministers of Antichrist, taking upon themselves, against the manifest word of God, to offer up a sacrifice [in the Mass] for the living and the dead, an intolerable blasphemy against the all-sufficient sacrifice of the Lord Jesus, offering himself once for all and forever....

In this place, because these scorpions, the Jesuits, are unknown among us in England, I have occasion to speak of them, that the godly may take heed of their leaven, and that their lovers may justly be ashamed of such love. The Jesuits are a kind of regular clergy, professing obedience to the pope and their general, at whose sending they must truly of free cost preach, wherever they be sent. They had an obscure conception about forty-five years ago, not long after the restoring of the Gospel, one Loyola, a Spaniard, being their father.... These new Jesuits must be called the Society of Jesus, as if they alone were in the society of Jesus and all others utterly excluded, whereas rather these Jesuits are excluded for their heresies, and only those are included in the fellowship and body of Jesus Christ who follow his doctrine and have the anointing of his Spirit, contenting themselves with the name of Christians, made to them expressly lawful and honorable by the word of God. Therefore, these who corruptly have called themselves Jesuits may be called Jebusites [cf. 2 Sam. 5:6–10], without offense to the Lord Jesus and most aptly in respect of their dealings....

Their practices are yet more detestable. For they gather learning, as the spider gathers poison, only so that they may infect the heart and stomach of their disciples.... These monkish friars, or friarly monks (O heavy judgment of God), these Jebusites, I say, from whose contagion we have been free to this point, they have recently ventured into England, as scouts to the Irish rebels, and prepare to establish again popish superstitions....

His assigned charge is laid down in the third article, which is, "of free cost to preach the Gospel and administer the sacraments": cunning words to cloak an evil matter. For he speaks in words fit for the Gospel, to avoid the usual and proper speeches of his popish priesthood and order that are full of derogation against the truth. For they preach not the Gospel but against the Gospel in the traditions and ordinances of the pope. Their ministry of the sacraments is the saying or singing of the Mass and corrupt baptism, with other actions which they call sacraments but are not by any warrant out of the word of God....

That he thinks "his poor countrymen abused with proud ignorance," I marvel that he means to blame ignorance in any. For we who profess the Gospel lament and cry out against ignorance; our adversaries, they always have made much of it, as the mother of devotion; yea, even the most famous order of the Franciscans... have a rule that "the unlettered among them should not care to learn letters." But the Jesuits, they profess and teach knowledge. Let us see what knowledge and for what cause. It is the very same knowledge which the serpent performed who promised the knowledge of evil, to take away the knowledge of good, who promised life and brought in death. Therein also the cause appears; for this master promises "to root out proud ignorance," minding indeed to root out the sincere knowledge of the Gospel, which is the power of God to salvation.... Popery is that proud ignorance that must not re-enter, and this disease remaining in many is that which must be more and more rooted out....

In the sixth article, he first shows how little power he has over his tongue, or over his pen. For "being loath to speak anything that might sound of any insolent brag, or challenge," yet he most insolently brags more than any, and challenges more than all.... As one said of another matter, "It is easier to commit murder than to defend it," so it is easier to fall into the error of popery than to support it. Nevertheless, this challenger undertakes the support as if nothing could be replied against him.... [He says,] "I know perfectly that no one Protestant, nor all the Protestants living can maintain their doctrine." They have maintained it by the word of might and truth against all the adversaries in writing and solemn disputation, as has been noted. And can they not now maintain it against one man, of but eight or nine years standing in his profession, as little in deed as he is great in his own conceit? Yes, the meanest of many by the grace of God can maintain it and shall prevail. And if our adversaries will look into our defenses already published, they shall see the defense of our religion so great, and the cause so manifest, that I may truly use these words against the challenger on the other side: No one Jesuit nor all the Jesuits living shall be able to answer

that which is written, or to root out that which is planted....

Again, the Jesuit flaunts in words and vaunts of "his innocent hands lifted up to heaven every day and every hour," as for the good of their honors [on the Privy Council]. To make your hands no fouler than they are, yet those "innocent hands" have written no innocent books; they have cast abroad no innocent libels; they held out no innocent banner of popish obedience in their actual rebellions heretofore in England and presently in Ireland. But if those hands may be "innocent" that have done these things, and moreover crucify the Son of God again every day in their most blasphemous sacrifice of the Mass, yet when you hold up those hands in prayer, I do not doubt but that it is with desire to have popish religion restored, to have the lords of the Council removed, to have way made for you to return from your beggarly estate to the dignities and regency of the land.... He adds the praise "of English students beyond the sea," saying, "Their posterity shall not die." No more shall the posterity of Antichrist, until they and their abominations be brought into judgment. As for the "virtue and sufficient knowledge which they gather," I would know whether it be virtue or knowledge that causes them in some places to carry letters and to enter into seditious matters secretly, in other places to carry arms against her Majesty openly....

Therefore, briefly to see into all this matter and to conclude, these letters of Edmund Campion the Jesuit, which were cast abroad without a direction to comfort the papists and sweetly to feed them with hope of a great conquest against the religion, are found upon examination to sound a false alarm, having nothing for the papists to feed upon but vain hope, or venom to satisfy a heart nourished with reproaches, nothing to trust unto but a broken reed, and that not yet in hand. Touching the Protestants, the same libel has nothing that can either strike the least fear into them or cast the least discredit upon them or their religion. Notwithstanding, against the papists and for the Protestants, ... the pamphlet has (besides the vanity) many points also revealing great mischief intended against her Majesty's peaceable and godly government, as against the heavenly and most fruitful preaching of the Gospel.

FURTHER READING

Ahlgren, Gillian. *Teresa of Avila and the Politics of Sanctity*. Ithaca, NY: Cornell University Press, 1996.

Bilinkoff, Jodi. *The Avila of Saint Teresa: Religious Reform in a Sixteenth-Century City*, 2nd ed. Ithaca, NY: Cornell University Press, 2014.

Bireley, Robert. *The Refashioning of Catholicism, 1450–1700: A Reassessment of the Counter-Reformation*. Washington, DC: Catholic University of America Press, 1999. http://dx.doi.org/10.1007/978-1-349-27548-9.

Jedin, Hubert. *History of the Council of Trent*. 2 vols. Translated by Ernest Graf. London: T. Nelson, 1957–1961. Note: two additional volumes are available in German.

Holleran, James V. *A Jesuit Challenge: Edmund Campion's Debates at the Tower of London in 1581*. New York: Fordham University Press, 1999.

Mullett, Michael. *The Catholic Reformation*. London: Routledge, 1999.

Olin, John C. *The Catholic Reformation: Savonarola to Ignatius Loyola, Reform in the Church, 1495–1540*. New York: Fordham University Press, 1969.

O'Malley, John W. *The First Jesuits*. Cambridge, MA: Harvard University Press, 1993.

O'Malley, John W. *Trent: What Happened at the Council*. Cambridge, MA: Harvard University Press, 2013.

Weber, Alison. *Teresa of Avila and the Rhetoric of Femininity*. Princeton, NJ: Princeton University Press, 1990.

VIII

Wars of Religion

Throughout this book, we have been looking at the intellectual and theological battles among the various figures in the Reformation. Ultimately, these differences resulted in actual warfare as well, revealing just how important religion was in civic as well as personal life at this time. For well over a century, from the First Battle of Kappel in 1529 through the Thirty Years' War, which ended in 1648, nearly all of Europe was affected at one time or another by religious warfare. Of course, factors other than religion often played a role these conflicts. In many cases, however, the opposing sides were divided not so much by political allegiance, economic grievances, or diplomatic disputes as they were by religious differences. This seems to have been especially the case in the conflicts between Protestants and Catholics within a single country: the Kappel Wars in Switzerland (§XXVIII), the Schmalkaldic War in Germany (§XXIX), and the French Wars of Religion (§XXX). The role of religion in international conflicts—for example, the War of the Spanish Armada, the Dutch Revolt, and the Thirty Years' War—is more difficult to evaluate. At the very least, most scholars today would agree that religious differences stemming from the Reformation constituted an aggravating factor in these conflicts. As terrible and as bloody as they were, however, these wars were an important step in the modernization of the West. Indeed, the horror of the Wars of Religion following the Reformation was probably an unfortunate but necessary prerequisite to the development of modern Western notions of religious toleration, religious pluralism, the separation of church and state, the right of armed resistance to tyrannical government, and perhaps even popular sovereignty.

XXVIII. THE WARS OF KAPPEL, 1529–1531

While there were certainly religious elements to the German Peasants' War of 1525 (see above, §XII), the first conflict that can truly be called a religious war—one that pitted Catholics against Protestants within the same state—were the Wars of Kappel, in which the Protestant and Catholic cantons of the Swiss Confederation faced each other. Ever since Zurich had broken from the Catholic Church, its Catholic neighbors grew increasingly nervous. With Bern's adoption of Protestantism in 1528, the situation grew tenser. The Catholic cantons formed an alliance with Archduke Ferdinand of Austria, a member of the Habsburg family and brother of Emperor Charles V. This partnership was shocking, for the Swiss Confederation had originally been established as an alliance against imperial influence in the region. The First Kappel War stemmed from conflicts in the so-called common lordships, which were subject territories governed jointly by two or more Swiss cantons. These dual jurisdictions became a problem when the ruling cantons were divided religiously. When a Catholic priest was killed in Thurgau and then a Protestant pastor was burned at the stake in Schwyz, the two sides declared war. In the First Kappel "War" in 1529, the parties actually avoided armed conflict, hammering out an agreement that was decidedly favorable to the Protestant cantons. But two years later, the two sides came to physical blows in the Second Kappel War, in which the Catholic forces overwhelmed the Protestants from Zurich. One of the soldiers who lost his life on the battlefield that day was none other than Ulrich Zwingli. We are fortunate to have two accounts of Zwingli's death at Kappel, one written by his successor in Zurich, Heinrich Bullinger, and the other by a Catholic witness to the battle.

Focus Questions

1. What justifications do Zurich and the Catholic cantons use in declaring war in the two Wars of Kappel? Are they chiefly religious, or do they indicate other considerations?
2. What does the participation of Zwingli, a pastor in Zurich, seem to indicate about his ideas regarding the relationship of church and state?
3. What specific events do the two accounts of Zwingli's death agree on? In what ways do the two accounts conflict? How can historians reconcile these conflicting accounts?

54. Kappel Declarations of War[1]

A. Zurich's Declaration of War, June 8, 1529

[The] men of Unterwalden ... in time of peace, made a pact with Ferdinand's party and the other four states [Lucerne, Uri, Schwyz, Zug] to attack our faith, and added their names to an agreement that anything that they, in conjunction with the aforesaid Ferdinand, might win in our territory on this side of the Rhine, should go to the Five States. In that easy fashion they thought, with the help of a foreign force, to separate us from our possessions, a thing that is contrary to all natural law; not only was this against the federal bond, in that they joined with our hereditary enemies against whom, from the beginnings of the Confederation, we have so often stood by one another with complete confidence, but it also threatened us with vast damage and utter devastation. We have not taken anyone into co-citizenship in order to oppress or threaten for the sake of our religion, whereas they have already divided up our land and sold the bear's skin before killing the bear.[2]

It is also widely known how for many years now the Five States have outraged, slandered, damaged, and oppressed us and in so many ways have defamed and attacked us. None the less, we have considered in all this disgraceful business what our Lord Jesus Christ suffered for us, and,

---

[1] Source: G.R. Potter, ed., *Huldrych Zwingli* (London: Edward Arnold, 1978), 116–17, 141.
[2] A reference to the Protestant city of Bern, whose symbol is the bear.

so long as we hoped to see any improvement on their part, we took no action but submitted, for God's sake, to suffer such unbearable insults. But when we were further pressed by more harsh intolerable behaviour, ... seeing that it so manifestly involved repression of the gospel and denial of common justice, we determined rather to suffer death than to let this wicked behaviour before God and the world continue. In spite of all our efforts at improvement, we find ourselves and our friends harmed: they [our opponents] care neither for right nor for justice, neither for peace nor for treaties, but they are absolutely determined to make war on us, to damage and destroy us. Hence with difficulty, for we are not unaware of what war means, we have found ourselves obliged to consider how, while upholding the cause of freedom and righteousness ourselves, we can invade and make war on them, so that they, who neither rule well nor can be made any better by our patience, may be disciplined by punishment.

B. The Catholic Cantons' Declaration of War, 1531

For a long time, both individually and together we have put forward our proper, honourable, traditional and just requests and demands all in accordance with the sworn Confederation and accepted peace agreements.

Now against God, honour, law, conformity to the Confederation and what is just, you have separated us and our people from you and your dependants against Christian decency and unity, federal truth, love and friendship, against all natural law and equity and have made us both dependent on you and separate from you.... You have deposed us from the influence and rights which we enjoy in the government of St Gall and as deputy governors in the Rheintal. Moreover, by many cunning devices you have tried to make us discontented and disunited among ourselves and have dangerously endeavoured to separate us from our true, Christian, ancient traditional faith, proclaiming that we will not hear God's word, nor let the Old and New Testaments be read, and have called us godless, wicked flesh-sellers, traitors and evil doers. Further, because we do not adhere to your newly thought-up faith you strike us by denial of food and commerce and so try to intimidate by hunger not only us but also the innocent unborn children.... All this is manifestly and mischievously opposed to the Confederation and the accepted peace of the land which you have clearly infringed as against us....

All our willingness and moderation and appeal to law have been of no avail and so, as neither the honour nor the righteousness of God is esteemed, neither we nor ours will suffer or bear any further scandal, ignominy, scorn, blasphemy and insolence but justify ourselves before God and the world.... We are willing to settle the score with you by combat and force of arms and to tolerate wanton violence no longer.

55. Zwingli's Death at the Battle of Kappel: Two Accounts, 1531[3]

A. A Catholic Version

Zwingli was found in the front line where the Zurich force had been drawn up. He was lying on his face which had not been scratched or wounded. A catholic soldier, not knowing who he was, turned him over and shook him so that he might have air and be able to breathe. He opened his eyes and looked round. Then he was asked if he wished to confess his sins. He shook his head and indicated that he did not wish to do so. Thereupon another warrior standing by struck Zwingli a fatal blow on the neck under the chin with his broadsword. Then a number of men arrived who had known Zwingli when he was alive, looked at him and sought for identification marks on his body. They found that it really was Zwingli. Then they had much to say, rejoicing in his death and calling him a good many entirely suitable names. They added their repeated thanks to almighty God whose vengeance lay there in the blood of the miscreant who had been the true founder, originator, creator and initiator of all their evils, calamities and alarms. Even so God had graciously allowed him to die in the presence of, and surrounded by, good, honourable men, perhaps because he had once been a priest. It would not have been remarkable if there had been more devils by him at his end than there were soldiers in the field. For the whole evening, more and more catholics came up to look at the dead body of one who had been responsible for bringing more discontent, disorder, trouble, need and anxiety than had all the princes, lords, peoples and cities. He now lay there given by God's instrumentality into their hands and he had paid the price for his wickedness. There, at last, was the representative of all the Confederates and (by the grace of God) all his schemes perished with him.

B. Heinrich Bullinger's Account

On the battlefield, not far from the line of attack, Mr. Ulrich Zwingli lay under the dead and wounded. While men were looting... he was still alive, lying on his back, with his hands together as if he was praying, and his eyes looking upwards to heaven. So some approached who did not know him and asked him, since he was so weak and close to death (for he had fallen in combat and was stricken with a mortal wound), whether a priest should be fetched to hear his confession. Thereat Zwingli shook his head, said nothing and looked up to heaven. Later they told him that if he was no longer able to speak or confess he should yet have the mother of God in his heart and call on the beloved saints to plead to God for grace on his behalf. Again Zwingli shook his head and continued gazing straight up to heaven.

---

[3] Source: Potter, *Huldrych Zwingli*, 143–46.

At this the catholics grew impatient, cursed him and said that he was one of the obstinate cantankerous heretics and should get what he deserved. Then Captain Fuckinger of Unterwalden appeared and in exasperation drew his sword and gave Zwingli a thrust from which he at once died....

Above all there was tremendous joy when Zwingli's body was found among the dead. All the morning crowds came up, every one wanting to see Zwingli. The vituperation and insults hurled against him by many jealous people are beyond description....

The crowd then spread it abroad throughout the camp that anyone who wanted to denounce Zwingli as a heretic and betrayer of a pious confederation should come on to the battlefield. There, with great contempt, they set up a court of injustice on Zwingli which decided that his body should be quartered and the portions burnt. All this was carried into effect by the executioner from Lucerne with abundance of abuse; among other things he said that although some had asserted that Zwingli was a sick man he had in fact never seen a more healthy-looking body.

They threw into the fire the entrails of some pigs that had been slaughtered the previous night and then they turned over the embers so that the pigs' offal was mixed with Zwingli's ashes.

XXIX. THE SCHMALKALDIC WAR AND THE PEACE OF AUGSBURG, 1546–1555

In the 1521 Edict of Worms, Emperor Charles V declared Luther and his followers outlaws in the Holy Roman Empire. Through most of the 1520s, however, the emperor needed the support of the Lutheran noblemen of Germany to help fight the Ottoman Turks, so the imperial diet meeting in Speyer in 1526 temporarily suspended the Edict of Worms. Three years later, however, the imperial diet met again in Speyer and voted to reinstate the Edict. In 1531, the Lutheran princes and city officials, meeting in the city of Schmalkalden, formed a defensive alliance called the Schmalkaldic League. For years, Charles V remained preoccupied with his wars elsewhere against the Turks and the French. Finally, in 1546, with his other conflicts settled, Charles was ready to wage war on the German Lutherans. The emperor signed an agreement with the pope (doc. 56) to work together to defeat the Lutherans and force them to accept the decisions of the Council of Trent, which had just opened.

The Schmalkaldic War of 1546–47 ended in a rousing success for the emperor and his Catholic forces. At the Battle of Mühlberg, Charles's forces routed the Lutherans. Charles was less successful in the aftermath, however. First, a long diet held at Augsburg passed a temporary religious settlement known as the Augsburg Interim. This was intended to be a temporary religious arrangement until a more permanent settlement could be reached by the Council of Trent. The Interim was roundly, almost universally, rejected by Protestant pastors all over Germany. The Interim allowed pastors to remain married and permitted communion in both kinds, but otherwise it prescribed solidly Catholic belief and practice.

At least partly in opposition to the Interim, the Lutherans launched a revolt against the emperor in 1552, with the support of King Henry II of France. This time they were successful, and Charles V fled south across the Alps, never again to return to Germany. It took a long time to hammer out a peace treaty—until 1555—but when it came, the Peace of Augsburg (doc. 57) established the important principle of *cuius regio, eius religio* ("whose region, his religion").

Focus Questions

1. What are the terms, rationale, and goal of the alliance between the pope and emperor?
2. Based on the text of the Peace of Augsburg itself, explain more fully what *cuius regio, eius religio* means.
3. Whom does the Peace of Augsburg exclude? Why? What are the implications of this exclusion?
4. What is to be done with ecclesiastical lands? Why were decisions about such land so important to Reformation-era peace treaties?
5. What does the document say about proselytization? What about moving to a different territory for the sake of religion?

56. Alliance between Emperor Charles V and Pope Paul III, 1546[4]

Whereas Germany has been disturbed for many years by gross error and false belief, and some now continue to act in such a way that great harm, corruption, and destruction may occur in Germany; and whereas now for some time there have been those who have wanted to take some action with respect to such false belief in order to avoid divisions and errors and to maintain the unity of Germany; so an open and general council has been convoked and assembled at Trent. The Protestants, however, together with the Schmalkald League said that they did not want to submit to or attend the council that began to meet on the third Sunday in Advent just past and has since then, by the grace of God, been able to make some progress.

2. Therefore, His Holiness, the Pope, and his Majesty, the Emperor, have considered it advisable and productive that they should put together and accept the articles described below, agreeing to comply with them faithfully, to the honor and praise of Almighty God and for the sake of the unity of all people, especially in Germany.

3. First, that his Imperial Majesty in the name of God and with the help and assistance of his Holiness, the Pope, should, in the upcoming month of June, supply himself with soldiers and military equipment to prepare for war against those who have protested against the council, against the Schmalkald League, and also against all those in Germany who persist in false belief and error. With all his power and might, he should bring them back again into the ancient, true, and undoubted faith and into obedience to the Holy See. At the same time, his Imperial Majesty should endeavor with all his zeal and perseverance to see whether he can bring the rebels back to the old Faith and to obedience to the Holy See in an amicable manner, without war. In any case, he should prepare himself so that if they cannot be persuaded peaceably within the announced time, his Imperial Majesty will still be armed and ready for war....

4. Furthermore, that his Imperial Majesty should not propose or accept any agreement with the above-mentioned parties, which might be detrimental to this war effort or the faith of the Holy Christian Church, unless he has obtained the permission and consent of his Holiness, the Pope, or the Legate of the Holy See....

---

[4] Source: Eric Lund, ed., *Documents from the History of Lutheranism, 1517–1750* (Minneapolis: Fortress Press, 2002), 161–62.

57. The Peace of Augsburg, 1555[5]

15. In order to bring peace to the Holy Roman Empire of the Germanic nation between the Roman Imperial Majesty and the electors, princes, and estates, let neither his Imperial Majesty nor the electors, princes, etc., do any violence or harm to any estate of the empire on account of the Augsburg Confession, but let them enjoy their religious belief, liturgy, and ceremonies, as well as their estates and other rights and privileges in peace; and complete religious peace shall be obtained only by Christian means of amity, or under threat of punishment of the imperial ban.

16. Likewise the estates espousing the Augsburg Confession shall let all the estates and princes who cling to the old religion live in absolute peace and in the enjoyment of all their estates, rights, and privileges.

17. However, all who do not belong to the two above-named religions [Catholicism and Lutheranism] shall not be included in the present peace but be totally excluded from it.

18. And since it has proved to be a matter of great dispute what was to happen with the bishoprics, priories, and other ecclesiastical benefices of such Catholic priests who would in course of time abandon the old religion, we have in virtue of the powers of Roman Emperors ordained as follows: Where an archbishop, bishop, or prelate, or any other priest of our old religion shall abandon the same, his archbishopric, bishopric, prelacy, and other benefices, together with all their income and revenues which he has so far possessed, shall be abandoned by him without any further objection or delay. The chapter and such as are entitled to it by common law, or the custom of the place shall elect a person espousing the old religion who may enter on the possession and enjoyment of all the rights and incomes of the place without any further hindrance and without prejudging any ultimate amicable transaction of religion.

19. Some of the abbeys, monasteries, and other ecclesiastical estates having been confiscated and turned into churches, schools, and charitable institutions, it is herewith ordained that such estates which their original owners had not possessed at the time of the Treaty of Passau [1552] shall be comprised in the present treaty of peace.

20. The [Catholic] ecclesiastical jurisdiction over the Augsburg Confession, dogma, appointment of ministers, church ordinances, and ministries hitherto practiced (but apart from all the rights of electors, princes and estates, colleges and monasteries to taxes in money or tithes) shall from now cease, and the Augsburg Confession shall be left to the free and untrammeled enjoyment of their religion, ceremonies, and appointment of ministers, as is stated in a subsequent

---

[5] Source: Emil Reich, ed., *Select Documents Illustrating Mediæval and Modern History* (London: P. S. King, 1905), 230–32, text modernized.

separate article, until the final transaction of religion will take place.

23. No estate shall try to persuade the subjects of other estates to abandon their religion nor protect them against their own magistrates. Those who had from olden times the rights of patronage are not included in the present article.

24. In case our subjects, whether belonging to the old religion or the Augsburg Confession, should intend leaving their homes with their wives and children in order to settle in another, they shall be hindered neither in the sale of their estates after due payment of the local taxes nor injured in their honor.

XXX. THE FRENCH WARS OF RELIGION, 1562–1598

Apart from the Thirty Years' War (1618–48), no armed religious conflict was bloodier or more protracted than the French Wars of Religion. Protestants, known as Huguenots in France, never constituted more than about ten per cent of the French population, but they were able to achieve majorities in certain areas, especially in the south, and many nobles were drawn to the new faith. Thus, the Huguenots were able to fight more effectively than their numbers might indicate.

From the 1530s through the 1550s, the French crown tried to deal with Protestants through individual trials for heresy. Indeed, hundreds of evangelicals were put to death as a result of these trials. But by the 1560s, Protestants in the realm had grown too numerous to prosecute on an individual basis. Militant Catholics, represented particularly by the noble family of Guise, began to agitate for more aggressive tactics, while Huguenots began to organize and raise money for their own defense.

The first War of Religion broke out in 1562 when the duke of Guise and his soldiers broke into an illegal Huguenot worship service and slaughtered those inside in what is known as the Massacre at Vassy. Several phases of the French Wars of Religion followed, each one ending in a temporary peace treaty that allowed Protestant worship in certain locations. Each treaty, however, was invariably followed by renewed fighting within a few years.

The bloodiest episode of the wars was the St. Bartholomew's Day Massacre in 1572. The massacre started when King Charles IX, likely prompted by his mother Catherine de Medici, ordered the assassination of Admiral Gaspard de Coligny, a powerful Huguenot leader who was in Paris, along with many other prominent Huguenot noblemen, for the wedding of the king's sister Margaret to the Protestant Prince Henry of Navarre (the future King Henry IV). The killing soon moved beyond the assassination of Coligny, and over the next several weeks, French Catholics killed thousands of their Protestant neighbors.

This section contains three documents related to the event. The first is an outsider's account of the event itself, provided by Giovanni Michiel, the Republic of Venice's ambassador to France at the time (doc. 58). The second is an address given soon after the event to Pope Gregory XIII by the French humanist Marc-Antoine Muret (doc. 59). Muret (1526–85) is best known for his editions of classical literature and for his own Latin verse and orations. In 1555, he fled France after being accused of both heresy and sodomy. After four years in Venice, he finally settled in Rome, where he delivered the oration below before Pope Gregory XIII soon after the St. Bartholomew's Day Massacre took place in his homeland. The final text in this section is the anonymous *Reveille-Matin*, or *Wake-up Call*. Little is known for sure about either the author or the publication details of this text. The author is most commonly believed to have been Nicholas Barnaud, a Huguenot physician, and the text was not published in Edinburgh, as indicated on the title page, but probably in Basel, Switzerland. The text is an early example of a shift in Protestant political theory following the massacre. From the beginning of the Reformation, most reformers—with the exception of some radical reformers—tried to portray themselves as loyal subjects of the king, not as revolutionaries out to undermine the social and political order. After all, Romans 13 states that resistance to the authorities is wrong, since they were placed there by God. But the killing of thousands of Protestants led several Huguenot writers to adjust their political theory about the nature of monarchy and the rights of the people who live under a monarch, particularly the right to armed resistance.

Focus Questions

1. What events led to the St. Bartholomew's Day massacre? How was it then carried out?
2. According to Michiel's report, how did the Huguenots react to the massacre?
3. What does Michiel conclude about the nature of religion in France?
4. What accusations does Marc-Antoine Muret make against the Huguenots? Why does he defend the massacre?
5. According to the *Reveille-Matin*, what are the limits of a monarch's power, and what is the basis for those limitations?
6. Do Muret and the author of the *Reveille-Matin* have similar or opposing views on the nature of government? Explain.

58. Giovanni Michiel, Venetian Ambassador's Report on the St. Bartholomew's Day Massacre, 1572[6]

Then, at the dinner hour on Friday,[7] while the admiral[8] was returning on foot from the court to his lodgings and reading a letter, someone fired an arquebus[9] at him.... So the arquebus shot tore off a finger on his left hand and then hit his right arm near the wrist and passed through it to the other side of the elbow. If he had simply walked straight ahead it would have hit him in the chest and killed him....

Great numbers of Huguenots and the admiral's friends and followers were in Paris at this time for the marriages of Condé and the king

---

[6] Source: James C. Davis, ed. and trans., *Pursuit of Power: Venetian Ambassadors' Reports on Spain, Turkey, and France in the Age of Philip II, 1560–1600* (New York: Harper & Row, 1970), 232–38.

[7] This was Friday, August 22, 1572.

[8] Gaspard de Coligny.

[9] An arquebus is an early hand-held, muzzle-loaded gun invented in the fifteenth century.

of Navarre....[10] Some of their leaders went to where the king was dining and complained violently and bitterly. They demanded swift and stern justice and said that otherwise there was no lack of men who would provide it. Among them was a certain Captain Briquemault, who was later dragged out of the English ambassador's house, where he had hidden, and was jailed and ultimately hanged. According to what Briquemault revealed, the Huguenots assembled that same day bearing arms and came very close to carrying out a plan to march on the Louvre (where the king lives and also the duke of Guise), overpower the royal guards and any others who blocked their way, and kill the duke in his apartment. If it had come to this there would have been great danger of an all-out battle in which most of the nobility would have been killed, because there were a great many of them in both factions....

Late Saturday night, just before the dawn of Saint Bartholomew's Day, the massacre or slaughter was carried out. The French say the king ordered it. How wild and terrifying it was in Paris (which has a larger population than any other city in Europe), no one can imagine. Nor can one imagine the rage and frenzy of those who slaughtered and sacked, as the king ordered the people to do. Nor what a marvel, not to say a miracle, it was that the common people did not take advantage of this freedom to loot and plunder from Catholics as well as Huguenots, and ravenously take whatever they could get their hands on, especially since the city is incredibly wealthy. No one would ever imagine that a people could be armed and egged on by their ruler, yet not get out of control once they were worked up. But it was not God's will that things should reach such a pass.

The slaughter went on past Sunday for two or three more days, despite the fact that edicts were issued against it and the duke of Nevers was sent riding through the city along with the king's natural brother to order them to stop the killing. The massacre showed how powerfully religion can affect men's minds. On every street one could see the barbarous sight of men cold-bloodedly outraging others of their own people, and not just men who had never done them any harm but in most cases people they knew to be their neighbors and even their relatives. They had no feeling, no mercy on anyone, even those who kneeled before them and humbly begged for their lives. If one man hated another because of some argument or lawsuit, all he had to say was, "This man is a Huguenot," and he was immediately killed. (That happened to many Catholics.)... Some estimate the number who were killed as high as four thousand, while others put it as low as two thousand.

The killing spread to all the provinces and most of the major cities and was just as frenzied there, if not more so. They attacked anyone, even the gentry, and as a result all the leaders who did not escape have been killed or thrown in prison....

---

[10] Henri de Bourbon Prince of Condé and Henri de Bourbon King of Navarre were first cousins. Condé married Marie of Cleves (another first cousin) in July 1572.

At present, sermons, meetings, and all other activities of the new sect are forbidden. Both nobles and commoners are returning to the Church, especially since the leading families are showing them the way.... The king of Navarre has recanted and ordered that Catholicism be reestablished in his lands, monasteries set up again, and the churches allowed to have their revenues. And that's not all. The Huguenot ministers themselves, including the most important ones, want to become Catholics again! But with these men they will handle the abjurations more carefully than they did with the others.

There were two kinds of Huguenots in France. One group was made up of rebels and atheists who used religion only as a pretext and encouraged the growth of the sect because it led to wars in which they profited from the plundering and the looting and the good pay they got as soldiers and officers. These men would fight against anyone, even the king. The other kind had flocked to the new sect only because they wanted to enjoy more freedom and license, but they kept out of the riots and rebellions and obeyed the king. There is nothing to fear now from the first group because the leaders and others who could disturb the peace are all dead or being killed. The second group may not change their real beliefs but they have no choice but to continue to obey the king if they want to enjoy the presents and favors and titles he distributes. The king is an absolute ruler and just as he can shower rewards on those he likes, so he can ruin and make life miserable for those he despises and chooses to forget. The French are so constituted that they cannot and will not live anyplace but in France; they would never dream of it. They have no God but the king, and the common people fall on their knees and worship him when he passes by, just as if he were God. So we can state this as a general proposition: everywhere, but especially in France, whatever religious beliefs the king holds, his subjects must do the same.

59. Marc-Antoine de Muret, *Oration before Pope Gregory XIII*, 1572[11]

On The Happy and Admirable Success of the Most Christian King of France, Charles IX, in Punishing the Chiefs of the Rebel Heretics

The venom that was already conceived during the reign of Henry II [r. 1547–59] hid itself in the veins and intestines of France and could not be remedied (although he greatly desired to do so) due to the unexpected and perpetually regretted death of this good-natured prince. This same venom continued to stir under

---

[11] Source: Marc-Antoine de Muret, *Oraison prononcée devant le Pape Gregoire XIII, par M. Antoine de Muret, I.C. touchant l'heureux et admirable succes de Charles IX. tres-Chrestien Roy de France, en la punition des chefs des Heretiques rebelles* (Lyon: Benoist Rigaud, 1573), A3r–B1v, translated by the editor.

Francis II [r. 1559–60], who slowed but could not drain or purge it because of his untimely death. At last, it spewed forth at the accession of Charles IX. And as water that has long been retained and slowed by a levee or rampart made of rocks and wood becomes more violent if such an obstacle is finally removed or broken, so these assemblies of unruly men, which the fear and dread of the law and of the authority of kings had held bound and reined in until this time, having finally broken the barriers, began to run wild with all dissolution throughout this noble realm. They justified their exorbitant license by their self-righteous piety and confounded all things human and divine by their murders and burnings.

And as the ancients left us their fables in which two serpents of great size came from on high to Hercules reborn in order to devour him in his crib, so to this new Hercules... on the throne came an infinite multitude of serpents who arrived not from on high but were sent forth from hell. With their breath, they corrupted all things and spread their dangerous and wicked venom far and wide, trying not only to take away the life of the young king, but also to strip from this realm the true religion and divine worship which preserve the only hope for eternal life. They have for a long time rejected the fear of God, and taking advantage of the young age of the king, they have trampled on the authority of the law and justice. What slaughter, what misery, what spoils and destruction, and what examples of new and execrable deeds have they caused in France! My hair stands on end when I recall what has happened after these plagues and hellish furies have been unleashed by the enemy of the human race: churches polluted, ruined, and burned, altars defiled with the blood of priests, holy virgins taken from their churches, towns pillaged and sacked, blood soaking the fields, rivers choked with human bodies, the astonishing cruelty in the defeat and dismemberment of men, the stubbornness and inhumanity that spared not even the ashes and bones of the dead.

Who—unless an enemy of the French, or rather Christian, name—could witness such things without tears? O France, France, mother of such valiant men, of such excellent princes, of such sovereign pontiffs who have presided in the Church of God with great praise, are you not the one who received the faith of Jesus Christ from the disciples of the apostles themselves without ever abandoning it? Who so many times has chased and exiled heretics and adversaries of the Christian name far away, not only from your borders but also from those of other provinces? Who has won renown in Europe, Africa, and Asia for the wars fought for the faith of Jesus Christ? Who so many times has restored the faith that has been altered by others and placed it back under the dignity of the Apostolic See, which it has also so well supplied and decorated? Who so many times has delivered the city of Rome from the threat of its total ruin?

And truly we can boast, Holy Father, without injury to anyone else, that since the coming of Jesus Christ, our nation has always flourished and excelled above all others principally in two points: First, that our people have been diligent and intent not only on the preservation of the Christian religion, but also on its enlargement and expansion; second, that they have always been quick to obey all the commands of their kings. And all the efforts of these diabolical men aim only toward spoiling France of these two ornaments and praises, removing it from obedience to God and king; or, not being able to achieve these two goals, turning it at least from the observance of the sovereign pontiffs and seducing it away from the union of the Roman Catholic Church. This principal goal they have conceived in their spirits; this they await; this has been their objective and intention from the beginning....

Rejecting the advice and propaganda of the wicked, the king lost hope for the soft and moderate remedies and was constrained, to his great regret and displeasure, to go to extremes and use violence against his own innards, as those do who burn or cut off the corrupt and rotten parts of their body after having tried all other remedies in vain, for fear that their contagion might harm the rest of the body. He was forced to wage war on his own people, which is always accompanied and followed by all the evils and miseries that one can contemplate, and to extinguish the fire by ruin, for fear that it might enflame all of France.

In this war there had been several battles and several thousands of people killed; the enemies had often been chased and almost ruined. Nevertheless, the gentle king desired rather to bring his people back to health than to lose and exterminate them, and tried to appease them by all possible means, agreeing to such conditions that even the most sinful and perverse would judge most equitable. Everything seemed peaceful, and there was hope that several of these miserable people would recognize their error and return to the bosom of the Church.

These plagues and parricides of the fatherland had almost covered all of France with dead bodies lying motionless across the land and deprived of burial; their swords, which were accustomed to massacring the innocent, demanded only murders and blood. They then thought that they would hardly be in conformity with their past life if they didn't augment and complete their infamous deeds, the memory of which was still recent, with a new crime. The conscience of such iniquities wickedly committed against God and man tortured them. Pushed by such wickedness and deprived of counsel and understanding, they did not fear to conspire against the life and estate of this king, from whom, after such heinous crimes, they had not only obtained pardon but had been kindly received and embraced by him. This conspiracy was divinely discovered, around the time it was supposed to be executed, and what they had plotted against the king and his family was turned around onto the heads of these abominable traitors. O memorable night, which by the ruin of a few seditious men delivered the king from the peril of imminent death and the kingdom from a perpetual fear of civil wars! I believe that the stars shone more brightly that night and the Seine swelled more than usual in order to sweep the bodies more swiftly into the sea.

60. Nicholas Barnaud(?), *Reveille-Matin: Wake-Up Call for the French and Their Neighbors, 1574*[12]

I say with the ancient Roman people that among all generous acts, the most illustrious and magnanimous is to kill a tyrant....

First, one must establish the maxim that there is only one infinite empire, namely, that of God Almighty; consequently, the power of all magistrates and princes is enclosed within certain limits and barriers, beyond which the prince may not go. Nor should the subject obey him if he does; otherwise, this would equate the empire of the magistrate with that of the sovereign God, a blasphemy too horrible even to consider....

With this foundation established, namely, that we owe total obedience without exception to God alone, it follows that we must not obey the profane or sinful edicts of any magistrate or prince. Consequently, subjects cannot obey the king in good conscience when he commands profane or sinful things....

It remains to be seen now whether one can also resist them and for what reasons.... First, there is a mutual and reciprocal necessity and obligation between the magistrate and his subjects, as is easy to see when one considers the origin, cause, and end of the institution of magistrates. It is certain that magistrates were created for the people, and not the people for the magistrates.... Therefore, there must have been some assemblies and groups of people before the creation of the magistrates. Today one can still find people without a magistrate, but never a magistrate without people. It is thus the people who created the magistrate and not the magistrate the people; the people created the first magistrates out of common consent for the necessity that they felt for the preservation of a place and way of life....

Those who gave the government to a single person elected and elevated him over themselves to govern and act like a monarch and sovereign. But there has never been found a people so stupid and ill-advised who elevated a magistrate over their shoulders to whom they gave absolute power and authority to command whatever they wanted to the people who elected him. On the contrary, in submitting to the magistrate, the people always also bound him to certain laws and conditions, which he is not permitted to break or surpass.

Having seen the origin and form of the creation of magistrates, let us now see what is the cause and occasion for which they were created. We find that there is none other than the welfare of the people....

---

[12] Source: *Le Reveil-Matin des François, et de leurs voisins* ([Basel?], 1574), II, 75–77, 80–83, 86–87, 89, 92–93, 186, 190, translated by the editor.

The authority of the ancient Roman kings was sovereign, but it was restrained by the senate.... Such is the case today with the prince-electors in the Holy Roman Empire, who have the right not only to establish the emperors, but also to depose them.... The same was observed with the kings of France from the time when the authority of the Estates was in force (which the Valois[13] have abolished). Their authority extended to the point where the king was not permitted to declare or wage war, nor to impose tribute or new taxes without the consent of the three Estates, which did not include any churchmen but only the judiciary, the nobility, and the people.

At their coronation, the kings of France promise and vow to preserve each person in his order, rank, and degree. When they do the contrary and violate the good laws and good edicts, they are no longer kings but tyrants....

The magistrate is established as a terror for the wicked [cf. Rom. 13:3]. Those who violate the divine law are more wicked than those who simply contravene human law. Now, if it is permitted to remove oneself from obedience to the magistrate who violates human law, there is all the more reason to do so from one who has violated all things holy, even humanity itself, who has stripped all natural affections and shaken off as much as possible the yoke and knowledge of the deity, and has corrupted and dispelled religion, which is the principal bond of human society....

It is, therefore, the people who enslave themselves, who cut their own throat, who, having the choice to remain serfs or to be free, abandon their liberty and take the yoke. Able to live under the protection of the Estates, they want to live under iniquity, oppression, and injustice, at the simple desire of this tyrant. It is the people who consent to his evil, or rather embrace it....

From such indignities that even beasts do not allow themselves to suffer, you can deliver yourselves if you try, not in actually delivering yourselves but simply in desiring to do so. Be resolved to serve no longer, and you will be free. I do not mean that you should push or shake off tyranny, but only that you should no longer support it; do that, and you will see it like a great Colossus, which has lost its base, fall to the ground and break apart under its own weight.

FURTHER READING

Brady, Thomas A., Jr. *Protestant Politics: Jacob Sturm (1489–1553) and the German Reformation*. Atlantic Highlands, NJ: Humanities Press, 1995.

Franklin, Julian H., ed. and trans. *Constitutionalism and Resistance in the Sixteenth Century: Three Treatises*. New York: Pegasus, 1969.

---

[13] The Valois family was the royal dynasty at the time, which ruled France from King Philip VI's accession in 1328 to King Henry III's death in 1589.

Gordon, Bruce. *The Swiss Reformation*. Manchester: Manchester University Press, 2002.

Holt, Mack. *The French Wars of Religion, 1562–1629*. 2nd ed. Cambridge: Cambridge University Press, 2005. http://dx.doi.org/10.1017/CBO9780511817922.

Jouanna, Arlette. *The Saint Bartholomew's Day Massacre: The Mysteries of a Crime of State (24 August 1572)*, translated by Joseph Bergi. Manchester: Manchester University Press, 2013.

Kingdon, Robert M. *Myths about the St. Bartholomew's Day Massacres, 1572–1576*. Cambridge, MA: Harvard University Press, 1988. http://dx.doi.org/10.4159/harvard.9780674182202.

Knecht, R. J. *The French Wars of Religion*. 3rd ed. Boston: Longman, 2010.

Tracy, James. *Emperor Charles V, Impresario of War: Campaign Strategy, International Finance, and Domestic Politics*. Cambridge: Cambridge University Press, 2002.

IX

Cultural Impact of the Reformation, Part 1: Christian Life and Practice

One of the most important advances in scholarship on the Reformation in the late twentieth and early twenty-first centuries has been a much greater attention to the cultural impact of the Reformation. While scholars of earlier generations tended to focus on either the finer points of Reformation theology or the political and diplomatic context of the period, recent historians have tried to show how the Reformation affected the whole spectrum of human life, from birth and baptismal practices to ideas about sex and marriage; to attitudes toward women, Jews, and other minorities; to funeral practices and ideas about the afterlife; and so much more. The lesson we have learned was that the Reformation did far more than simply create a variety of new churches with their own religious doctrines and practices; it created divisions and drove change that affected many aspects of everyday life, with effects that persist even today. This chapter and the next explore debates that arose during the Reformation on several of these issues.

XXXI. BAPTISM

Baptism was one of the two sacraments retained by Protestants (along with the Eucharist), and apart from the Anabaptists, most continued to practice infant baptism. Catholic doctrine held that the sacrament of baptism was absolutely necessary for salvation, so almost every child was baptized soon after birth. An unbaptized infant, Catholics believed, would go to limbo, an area of hell believed not to involve painful torment but out of which there could be no escape. Because of this, parents tried desperately to keep sick infants alive and often resorted to emergency baptisms performed by midwives or other laypersons. Ideally, however, the child would be baptized in the church in an elaborate ceremony, one of which is partially described below. You will see that the Catholic rite involved much more than the sprinkling of water on the child's head, and the additional ritual elements became the focus of much Protestant criticism. In general, Protestants vastly simplified the ritual, removing what they saw as the "superstitious" elements of the Catholic rite. The Reformed churches also tried to do away with emergency baptisms, emphasizing that salvation depended on God's election, not on a human ritual. Thus, they taught that infants who died without baptism might still go to heaven, as long as they had been predestined for it.

Both Protestants and Catholics continued to baptize in the name of the Father, Son, and Holy Spirit, and because of that commonality, they all generally accepted the legitimacy of baptisms performed by "heretics." For both groups, rebaptism, such as the Anabaptists performed, was deemed far worse than infant baptism by "the enemy" (whether Protestant or Catholic, depending on one's perspective), while the Anabaptists saw the continued practice of infant baptism by Lutherans and the Reformed church as proof that they still clung to "papist" traditions.

Focus Questions

1. What are the chief similarities and differences between the Protestant and Catholic rituals?
2. What differences in theology that you have already explored help to explain the differences between the two rituals?

3. What role do the godparents play? What about the parents? The priest/pastor?

4. What meaning might the traditional Catholic ritual have had for the lay participants? How did the Protestant ritual alter that meaning? How do you think people accustomed to the Catholic ritual might have reacted when seeing the Protestant ritual for the first time?

61. Catholic Rite of Baptism from the *Sarum Missal*, 1543[1]

We beseech thee, Lord, mercifully to hear our prayers: and this thine elect (*Here let the godfathers and godmothers name the child*), *N.*, do thou guard with the power of the Lord's cross, with the imprint of which ... we sign him (*or* her): so that preserving the first beginnings of the worship of thy majesty, through the keeping of thy commandments he (or she) may be found meet to enter the glory of the new birth. Through Christ our Lord. Amen....

The exorcism of salt without Let us pray.

I exorcize thee, creature of salt, in the name of God the Father almighty, and in the love of our Lord Jesus Christ, and in the power of the Holy Spirit.... Therefore, we ask thee, O Lord our God, that this creature of salt (*Here let the priest look at the salt*) thou wouldest sanctify ✠[2] and bless ✠, so that for all who receive it, it may become a perfect medicine remaining in their bowels, in the power of the same our Lord Jesus Christ, who is to come to judge the quick and the dead and the world by fire.

R.[3] Amen.

Afterwards, let the priest ask the name of the child, and let some of the salt be placed in his (*or* her) mouth as he says:

N., receive the salt of wisdom for a propitiation of God unto eternal life. Amen....

Adjuration over a male[4] *without* The Lord be with you, *and without* Let us pray, *the priest saying thus:*

Therefore, accursed devil, hearken to thy sentence, and give honor to the living and true God: give honor to Jesus Christ his Son and to the Holy Spirit, and depart from this servant of God, *N.*, because our God and Lord Jesus Christ

---

[1] Source: J.D.C. Fisher, *Baptism in the Medieval West: A Study in the Disintegration of the Primitive Rite of Initiation* (Litvrgy Training Publications 2004), 178–201.

[2] Wherever this symbol of the cross (✠) appears in the text, the priest was to make the sign of the cross with his hands.

[3] "R." indicates a response made by the congregation.

[4] The adjuration over a female is the same except with "handmaid" used instead of "servant."

has vouchsafed to call him to himself by the gift of the Holy Spirit to his holy grace and blessing and to the fount of baptism. And this sign of the holy cross, (*Here let the priest make the sign of the cross on the forehead of the infant with his thumb, saying thus:*) which we place upon his forehead, do thou, accursed devil, never dare to violate. Through him who is to come to judge the quick and the dead and the world by fire....

Exorcism over a male[5] only, without Let us pray.

I exorcize thee, unclean spirit, in the name of God the Father, and of the Son, and of the Holy Spirit, that thou come out and depart from this servant of God (*look upon him*), N., for he himself commands thee, accursed one, damned and to be damned, even he who walked on his feet on the sea, and stretched out his right hand to Peter as he was sinking....

Goodfaders and goodmoders[6] and all that be here about, say in the worshyppe of god and our ladye and of the xii apostellys an *Our Father*, and *Hail Mary*, and *I believe in God*, that we may so mynyster thys blessed sacrament, that yt may be to the pleasure of almyghty god, and confusyon of our gostly enmy, and salvacyon of te sowle of thys chylde.

Godfaders and godmodyrs of thys chylde whe charge you that ye charge the foder and te moder to kepe it from fyer and water and other perels to the age of vii yere, and that he lerne or se yt be lerned the *Our Father, Hail Mary,* and *I believe,* after the lawe of all holy churche and in all goodly haste to be confermed of my lorde of the dyocise[7] or of hys depute....

The Litanies follow.

Lord, have mercy.
Christ, have mercy.
Christ, hear us....
Holy Mary, pray for us....
Holy Michael, pray....
All ye holy angels and archangels of God, pray for us.
All the holy orders of blessed spirits, pray for us.
Holy John Baptist, pray for us.
All the holy patriarchs and prophets, pray.
Holy Peter, pray.
Holy Paul, pray....
All the holy apostles and evangelists, pray.
All the holy disciples and innocents, pray.
Holy Stephen, pray.
Holy Linus, pray....
All the holy martyrs, pray for us.
Holy Silvester, pray.
Holy Leo, pray....
All the holy confessors, pray.
All the holy monks and hermits, pray.
Holy Mary Magdalene, pray.
Holy Mary of Egypt, pray....

---

5 The exorcism over a female is similar but uses "handmaid" and refers to Christ raising Lazarus from the dead rather than walking on water.

6 The original text shifts from Latin to the English vernacular of the sixteenth century here. "Goodfaders" and "goodmoders" should be read as godfathers and godmothers.

7 Here meaning the bishop.

All the holy virgins, pray.
All the saints, pray....

[*Blessing of the font*]

May the same Holy Spirit make fruitful this water prepared for the regeneration of men by the secret admixture of his light, so that, sanctification having been conceived in it from the immaculate womb of the divine font, a heavenly offspring may come forth reborn unto a new creature.... At thy command, therefore, O Lord, let every unclean spirit depart far from hence: let all the wickedness of the devil's deceit be removed away.... Be this fount living, this water regenerating, this wave purifying, so that all who are to be washed in this saving laver by the operation of the Holy Spirit in them, may obtain the favor of a perfect cleansing. Therefore, I bless thee ✠, creature of water, through the living ✠ God, through the true ✠ God, through the holy ✠ God....

O God almighty, mercifully be present, do thou favorably inspire us. (*Here, let the priest breathe three times into the font in the form of a cross; then let him say as if reading thus:*) Do thou with thy mouth bless these simple waters, so that besides the natural cleansing which they can impart for the washing of men's bodies they may be also able to purify their minds. (*Here let the priest drop wax from a candle in the font in the form of a cross: next let him say as if reading a preface:*) May there descend into the fullness of this font the virtue of the Holy Spirit, and may it make the whole substance of this water fruitful with the power to regenerate. (*Here, let the priest divide the water with the candle in the form of a cross, saying:*) Here be the stains of all sins blotted out. Here may the nature created in thine image and restored to the honor of its beginning be cleansed from every filth of age... so that every man who enters into this sacrament of regeneration may be reborn in a new infancy of true innocence....

[*The Baptism*]

Then let the infant be carried to the fonts by those who are to receive him at baptism, they themselves holding the child in their hands over the fonts: and let the priest place his right hand over him: and his name being asked, let those who hold him reply, *N*. So let the priest say:

N., dost thou renounce Satan?
Let the godfathers and godmothers reply:
I renounce.
Again the priest asks:
And all his works?
R. I renounce.
Again the priest:
And all his pomps?
R. I renounce.
Next let the priest touch the breast of the infant and between his shoulders with holy oil, making the cross with his thumb, saying:
N., I also anoint thee *upon the breast* with the oil of salvation, *between the shoulders*, in Christ Jesus our Lord that thou mayest have eternal life and live for ever and ever. Amen....

N., dost thou believe in God the Father almighty maker of heaven and earth?
Let them reply: I believe.
Again the priest:
Dost thou believe also in Jesus Christ his only Son, our Lord, who was born and suffered?
Let them reply:
I believe.
Again the priest:

Dost thou believe also in the Holy Ghost, the holy catholic Church, the communion of saints, the remission of sins, the resurrection of the flesh and eternal life after death?

Let them reply:

I believe.

Then let the priest ask the name of the infant saying:

What seekest thou?

Let them reply:

Baptism.

Again the priest:

Dost thou wish to be baptized?

Let them reply:

I wish.

Then let the priest receive the infant sideways in his hands: and having asked his name let him baptize him with a threefold dipping invoking the Holy Trinity once, saying thus:

N., I also baptize thee in the name of the Father *(and let him dip him once with his face turned towards the north and his head towards the east) and of the Son (and again let him dip him once with his face turned towards the south)* and of the Holy Ghost. Amen *(and let him dip him the third time with his face towards the water.)*...

Next, let the infant be clad in his chrismal robe, the priest asking his name and saying thus:

N., receive a white robe, holy and unstained, which thou must bring before the tribunal of our Lord Jesus Christ, that thou mayest have eternal life for ever and ever. Amen....

Then having asked the name let him place a burning candle in the hand of the infant, saying:

N., receive a lamp burning without fault: guard thy baptism: keep the commandments, so that when the Lord comes to the wedding thou mayest meet him together with the saints in the heavenly hall, that thou mayest have eternal life, and live for ever and ever. Amen.

62. Protestant Baptism: A Rite of Baptism Used at Strasbourg, 1525–1530[8]

You shall no longer use oil, chrism and enchanted water at baptism: for they have caused a false trust in such things on the part of the people when they ought to trust in Christ alone. Instead, you shall explain and present the whole of baptism as an initial sign of faith and an entry into the Christian life, whereby the parents testify before the church that they will bring up their child to the glory of God and will teach and explain to him what happened at his baptism, so that he may remember to order his life in a Christian manner and not to live like the heathen....

---

[8] Source: J.D.C. Fisher, *Christian Initiation, the Reformation Period: Some Early Reformed Rites of Baptism and Confirmation and other Contemporary Documents*, Alcuin Club Collections 51 (London: SPCK, 1970), 35–37.

You shall explain to the curious and warn them not to rush with their ailing infants to baptism in disorder and anxiety, as if the whole of salvation depended on an outward washing alone, for God has not confined his grace to any external element, but gives it freely to those whom he has chosen as and when it pleases him. On the other hand you shall say that baptism is not to be neglected, since instead of circumcision and like circumcision in Judaism it is given to the little child as a sign of his initiation into Christianity, whereby we testify for our part that the infant must be of God's people (until he shows himself otherwise by a wicked life afterwards) because he is born of Christian parents....

And this is the order of baptism:

The minister asks:

Are you willing that this child be baptized?

Answer: Yes.

Name this child.

Answer: N.

The minister says:

Remember then that our Saviour Jesus Christ has said that all that we ask in our prayer, if only we believe that we shall receive it, so will it be done to us: so let us pray with comfortable assurance that this infant may be given faith, which is a gift of grace, and does not increase by nature, reason or long experience over the years and cannot otherwise be obtained but comes only by the operation of the invisible power of God, which is bound neither by time nor place, youth nor age. Let us pray, therefore, that the Lord will baptize him with water and the Holy Spirit, so that the outward washing which he will perform through me may inwardly be fulfilled in deed and in truth by the Holy Spirit; for that second birth which is signified by baptism takes place in water and in the Holy Spirit, as the Lord says in John 3.

And so let us say in true faith and confidence an *Our Father....*

And let us affirm our faith: *I believe in God....*

Almighty, eternal God, merciful Father, since the righteous lives only by faith alone and without faith it is impossible for anything to please thee, we beseech thee that thou wilt grant to this child, who is thy creature, the gift of faith, and that thou wilt seal and confirm his heart in the same with the Holy Spirit according to thy Son's promise, so that thy inward renewal and the regeneration of the Spirit may truly be signified by this our baptism, and so that, as he is baptized into the death of Christ Jesus, he may be buried with him and raised by him from the dead to walk in newness of life to the praise of God's majesty and to the edification of his neighbors. Amen....

Seeing that we have now prayed to God, our Father, as we are taught by his Spirit to pray for all men, that he would make this infant a fellow heir, fellow member and fellow partaker of the promises in Christ, therefore let us now impart to him the sign of faith and through baptism recognize him as a member of the body and of the congregation of Christ for a confirmation of his faith, as Abraham received circumcision for a seal of the righteousness which was already his by faith; and let us on his behalf call upon the name of the Lord, in which he is to be baptized, as the apostle Paul after the vision and wonderful enlightenment and reception of grace arose and was baptized by the prophet Ananias, and suffered him to wash away all his sins.

Then they proceed to the baptism and the minister says:

You godparents and you brothers and sisters shall each of you teach this child Christian order, discipline and fear of God, each of you, as God gives him grace?

Answer: We will.

The minister takes the child and says:
Name the child.
Answer: N.
The minister says while pouring the water: I baptize thee in the name of the Father and of the Son and of the Holy Spirit. Amen.

And he gives the child to the godparents and says to the people:

God give you all his grace and lead you on in the knowledge of him. Amen.

XXXII. FOOD AND FASTING

You may have noticed that during Lent (the period between Ash Wednesday and Easter) many Catholic churches hold Friday night fish fries and that Lent is usually the only time of year when fast food chains advertise their fish sandwiches. This is because the Catholic Church still prohibits the eating of meat, but not fish, on Fridays during Lent. In the sixteenth century, the fast was much more rigorous, with meat prohibited during the entire season of Lent. Lent was to be a season of abstinence and self-denial, a 40-day fast that recalled Jesus's 40 days of fasting in the desert (Matt. 4).

Protestants believed, however, that the Catholic Church's food prohibitions and fasting requirements trampled on the "freedom of a Christian" and encouraged a sense of "works righteousness," that is, the belief that one is justified by works rather than by faith alone. The Reformation in Zurich, in fact, began with a challenge to the Lenten prohibition on eating meat. In the first document below (doc. 63), Ulrich Zwingli (see above, chapter 4) offers support to that challenge.

The second text (doc. 64) presents a sermon on fasting given by St. Francis de Sales (1567–1622) on Ash Wednesday. De Sales was from Savoy (in present-day France), a region conquered in 1536 by the Swiss canton of Bern. The new Swiss rulers had imposed Protestantism there, but in 1564, Bern restored the territory to the Catholic duke of Savoy. De Sales spent a significant part of his career attempting to convert more fully the people in the region back to Catholicism. He was later named bishop of Geneva, a position he held in exile, since Geneva remained thoroughly Protestant during his life.

Focus Questions

1. What is Zwingli's position with regard to required fasting, and how does he support it?
2. Does he reject fasting altogether? Why or why not?
3. According to de Sales, what effect can proper fasting have?
4. What are the three things he says need to be done to fast properly?
5. What does he say about people who decide for themselves whether or how to fast?

63. Zwingli, *Concerning Choice and Liberty Respecting Food*, 1522[9]

Dearly beloved in God, after you have heard so eagerly the Gospel and the teachings of the holy apostles now for the fourth year, teachings which Almighty God has been merciful enough to publish to you through my weak efforts, the majority of you, thank God, have been greatly fired with the love of God and of your neighbor. You have also begun faithfully to embrace and to take unto yourselves the teachings of the Gospel and the liberty which they give, so that after you have tried and tasted the sweetness of the heavenly bread by which man lives, no other food has since been able to please you.... Some now at last during this fast—and it was their opinion that no one else could be offended by it—at home, and when they were together, have eaten meat, eggs, cheese, and other food hitherto unused in fasts. But this opinion of theirs was wrong, for some *were* offended.... Indeed, all these have so troubled the matter and made it worse, that the honorable council of our city was obliged to attend to the matter. And when the previously mentioned evangelically instructed people found that they were likely to be punished, it was their purpose to protect themselves by means of the Scriptures, which, however, not one of the council had been wise enough to understand well enough to accept or reject them. What should I do, as one to whom the

---

[9] Source: Samuel Macauley Jackson, ed., *The Latin Works and Correspondence of Huldreich Zwingli*, 2 vols. (New York: G.P. Putnam's Sons, 1912), 1:71–74; 80, 86–89, 112, text modernized.

care of souls and the Gospel have been entrusted, except search the Scriptures again and bring them as a light into this darkness of error, so that no one from ignorance or lack of recognition, injuring or attacking another, come into great regret, especially since those who eat are not triflers or clowns, but honest folk and of good conscience?... I have therefore made a sermon about the choice or difference of food, in which sermon nothing but the Holy Gospels and the teachings of the apostles have been used, which greatly delighted the majority and emancipated them. But those whose mind and conscience is defiled, as Paul says [Titus 1:15], it only made mad....

First, Christ says, in Matthew 15:17, "What goes in the mouth does not defile a man," etc. From these words, anyone can see that no food can defile a man, provided that it is taken in moderation and thankfulness....

Secondly, as it is written in Acts 10:10, when Peter was in Joppa, he went one day to the rooftop around noon and desired to pray: "He became hungry and wanted something to eat; and while it was being prepared, he fell into a trance. He saw the heavens opened and something like a large sheet coming down, being lowered to the ground by its four corners. In it were all kinds of four-footed creatures and reptiles and birds of the air. Then he heard a voice saying, 'Get up, Peter; kill and eat.' But Peter said, 'By no means, Lord; for I have never eaten anything that is profane or unclean.' The voice said to him again, a second time, 'What God has made clean, you must not call profane.'" Now, God has made all things clean, and has not forbidden us to eat, as his very next words prove. Why do we burden ourselves willfully with fasts?

[*Zwingli continues by citing 1 Cor. 6:12, 1 Cor. 8:8, 1 Cor. 10:25, Col. 2:16, 1 Tim. 4:1, Titus 1:15, Heb. 13:9.*] No Christian can deny these arguments, unless he defends himself by denying the Scriptures. Then he is, however, no Christian, because he does not believe Christian doctrine. There are, nevertheless, some who take exception to this, either to the times, or the fasting, or human prohibitions, or giving offense....

They will now raise as objections the fasts, or all fast days, saying that people will never fast if they are allowed to eat meat. Answer: Have you until now fasted because you were not allowed to eat meat, as naughty children who will not eat their broth, because they are not given meat? If anyone desires to fast, does he not have as much the power to do so when laborers eat meat, as when they are forced to fast with the idle, and are thus less able to do and to endure their labors? In a word, if you will fast, do so; if you do not wish to eat meat, do not eat meat. But leave Christians free choice in the matter. You who are an idler should fast often, should often abstain from foods that make you lustful. But the laborers' lusts pass away at the hoe and plough in the field....

Here the first difficulty will occur, when one speaks to those who, complaining, ask: "Is one to let go the ordinances of our pious fathers?" Where have the Fathers or the councils forbidden the use of meat during fasts?... Finally, they must help themselves out with custom, and they consider abstinence from food to be a custom. How old the custom is supposed to be, we cannot really know, especially with regard to meat, but of abstinence from eggs the custom cannot be so very old, for some nations even today eat eggs without permission from Rome, as in Austria and elsewhere.

Milk food became a sin in the Swiss Confederation in the last century and was again forgiven....

These points have forced me to think that the church officers have not only no power to command such things, but if they command them, they sin greatly; for whoever is in office and does more than he is commanded is liable to punishment. How much more, then, when they transgress that which is forbidden them; and Christ forbade the bishops to beat their fellow servants. Is it not beating when a command is placed upon a whole people, to which command the general assembly has not consented? Therefore, in these articles I leave to each free judgment, and I still hope that I have made this clear to those thirsting for Christian freedom, in spite of the enmity to me that will grow out of it.... Given at Zurich, 16 April 1522.

64. Francis de Sales on Fasting, Sermon for Ash Wednesday, c. 1620[10]

Fasting done well has these effects: to fortify the spirit and elevate it to God, to mortify the flesh and sensuality and to subject them to reason, to give strength to conquer and diminish the passions, and to defeat temptations. And by fasting, the heart is better disposed to serve God more purely and to be occupied with spiritual matters....

Now, among all the conditions required to fast properly, I will be content to say something to you about three of the principal ones. The first condition is that one must fast with one's whole heart, generally and entirely. St. Bernard... says that fasting was instituted by our Lord as a remedy for our mouths and for our gluttony. Since sin entered the world through the mouth, it is the mouth that must do penance, by taking away the foods prohibited and forbidden by the Church and abstaining from them for forty days during Lent. "But," this glorious saint says, "since it is not our mouth alone that offends God but also all the other senses and parts of the body, our fast must be general and entire, and we must make them all fast by mortification. For," as this great saint says, "if we have offended God by the eyes, by the ears, by the tongue, and by all the other senses of the body, why will we not make them fast?"...

And to show us that during these holy forty days, one must accompany the exterior fast with the interior, the Church says to us today these words of Genesis: "Remember, you are dust, and to dust you shall return" [Gen. 3:19],

[10] Source: François de Sales, *Œuvres complètes de Saint François de Sales, Évêque et Prince de Genève*, nouvelle édition (Paris: Berche et Tralin, 1898), 1:143–53, translated by the editor.

as if it wants to say to us, "Remember that you are mortal; remember your final end and that this remembrance causes you to leave behind all pleasant, joyous, and agreeable considerations, in order to fill your understanding and your memory with bitter, harsh, and unpleasant thoughts, making not only your body to fast by abstinence from prohibited meats, but also your spirit by such thoughts and considerations."

In order to observe the holy Lenten season better, the Christians of the primitive Church abstained during the whole time from ordinary conversations with their friends and retired into solitude and places shut off from the business of the world. And the Christians from around 400 A.D. were so careful to observe Lent well that they were not content simply to abstain from prohibited meats, but they also did not eat fish, milk, or butter but nourished themselves only on roots and herbs....

The second principal point is not to fast by vanity but by charity and with humility, for if our fast is not done in charity, it will be neither meritorious nor agreeable to God.... For if you discipline yourself every day and make great prayers but do not have charity, this does you no good; and if you perform great miracles but do not have charity, it is nothing; even if you suffer martyrdom, without charity your martyrdom is worth nothing, nor would it be meritorious in the eyes of God.

Moreover, I say that if you perform your fast without humility accompanied by charity, it is worth nothing, nor can it be agreeable to God. Some pagan philosophers fasted, but since their fast was without humility, it was not regarded by God. Several great sinners fast, but since they are without charity and without humility, they gain no profit. All that you do without charity, says the great Apostle, profits you nothing [cf. 1 Cor. 13:1–3]; one can say the same about humility....

But what is fasting with humility? It is not to fast with vanity, which is done in several ways, but I will limit myself to talk to you about one, so as not to tax your memory with many things. Thus, to fast with vanity is to fast by one's own will. And what is fasting by one's own will? It is fasting as we like, not as others like. It is fasting in a fashion that pleases us and not as we are ordered and counseled.

You will find people who want to fast more than they must and others who do not want to fast as much as they should; what is this, except vanity and willfulness? For all that comes from ourselves always seems to us better and easier to do that which is ordered for us and imposed on us by others, even though the latter is more useful and more appropriate for our perfection....

Those who fast during Lent should not hide themselves, since the Church ordains it, for it is good for each one to know that we are keeping its commandments and observing the fast, and because we are obliged to provide good edification and to take away every object of scandal from our brothers. But when our Lord says to fast in secret, he means: Do not do it in order to be seen or esteemed by creatures; do not do what you do for the eyes of humans; be careful to edify them, but do not perform your works so that you will be thought holy and virtuous; do not act like the hypocrites, do not attempt to appear holier

216

than others in performing greater fasts and penance than they....

The third condition that must be met when fasting... is to have regard for God alone and to do all in order to please him, retiring into oneself and contenting ourselves that his divine Majesty and his angels see and know our good works.... One must fast, therefore, in humility and in truth, that is, for God and to please him alone and not in falsehood and hypocrisy. And one must not amuse oneself with vain questions, like whether or not all are obliged to fast, or why it is commanded; it suffices to know that it is ordained for the sake of penitence, because of the sin that our first father Adam committed in breaking the fast that was commanded to him by God's order not to eat of the fruit of the forbidden tree; and therefore, the mouth must do penance and abstain from meats prohibited by the holy Church. This is what many have trouble with, but I am not here to respond to them; I say simply that those who contravene the ordinances and commandments of God and of the holy Church, and who make interpretations on what has been commanded to them and want to quibble over the things commanded put themselves in peril of death and eternal damnation. For all the reasons conjured by one's own will and human discretion, contrary to the will of God, are worthy of nothing but the eternal fire.

XXXIII. CARNIVAL AND LENT

By abolishing the Lenten fast, Protestants also removed the rationale for holding carnival. Better known as Mardi Gras[11] in North America, carnival was widely celebrated in medieval Europe as one last chance to feast and blow off steam before the penitence and asceticism of the season of Lent. Carnival nearly always featured feasting, drinking, dancing, singing, and some form of role reversal. Masks were common, giving revelers the license that comes with playing the role of another. Lay commoners assumed the roles of priests and lords, often using caricature or burlesque, while priests and lords sometimes agreed to play the part of commoners.

---

[11] Technically, *mardi gras*, or "fat Tuesday," refers only to the day before Ash Wednesday, which marks the start of Lent, but celebrations in New Orleans and elsewhere use the term for the period lasting several weeks before Lent.

The first text below (doc. 65) is a description of carnival in the French city of Rouen, which was organized and led by the Abbey of the Conards. This was a social organization, not a group of actual monks. Typical of the "world turned upside down" nature of carnival, however, the abbey had its own "abbot" who presided over carnival, as well as "cardinals," "patriarchs," and "chancellors" (none of whom were real churchmen).

After reading Zwingli's defense of eating meat during Lent (see above, doc. 63), one might think that by eliminating the Lenten fast, Protestants hoped to make carnival a year round event. In fact, the opposite is true. The very first of Luther's Ninety-Five Theses states, "When our Lord and Master Jesus Christ said 'Repent,' he meant that our whole lives should be ones of repentance." Remember also Calvin's emphasis on moral discipline (above, §XX). Protestants pushed for the victory of Lent over carnival, only without the required fasting. Among no group, perhaps, was this clearer than among England's Puritans. Upset over Queen Elizabeth's failure to get rid of all the trappings of "papist superstition" and hierarchy, they also railed against the immorality of society. Puritans also wanted to shut down the English theater and launched the original "war on Christmas," believing the holiday to be another "papist" feast day. During the Interregnum of the 1650s,[12] for example, they made it illegal for merchants to close shop or for people to attend special church services on Christmas Day. Philip Stubbs's *Anatomy of Abuses* (doc. 66) reflects well this Puritan disgust with English immorality. The selection below is a tiny excerpt of a very long list of complaints about English morals.

The Puritans remained a minority in England, however, and Elizabeth's "middle way" seems to have taken hold in attitudes toward holidays and recreation as well. Her successor, King James I, was worried about Puritan moves to shut down leisure activities like archery practice on Sundays,

---

[12] The Interregnum was the period in English history between the execution of King Charles I in 1549 and the restoration of the monarchy in 1660 by Charles II. During this period, England was governed not by a king but by Parliament and the Lord Protector Oliver Cromwell.

and he issued the *Book of Sports* (doc. 67), ordering that many traditional Sunday recreations remain in place, while forbidding certain others.

Focus Questions

1. In the Description of Carnival in Rouen, what are the chief carnival events? Which seem the most controversial? The most innocuous?
2. What are Philip Stubbs's chief complaints about morality in England?
3. How does he think the Sabbath should be observed, and how does he find it actually being observed?
4. What is King James's attitude toward the Puritans, and why does he feel this way?
5. What activities does he specifically order to be kept? Which does he want abolished? In making distinctions between licit and illicit activities, what criteria does he appear to apply?

65. Description of Carnival in Rouen, 1541[13]

The day of the parade thus over, the bands and companies retired into different places, holding open houses and having flaming lanterns in the windows. And after supper, they decided to go out masked in order to see each other and the other companies in the homes of the elites, in which there were a great number of women and girls, who rejoiced to see such joyful companies, some playing with masks, others with rods, bracelets, and other rings and new fantasies. Others danced, which all the women and girls liked a lot.

And the next days, Monday and Tuesday, several of the bands and others changed clothing in order to wear masks. I do not remember having seen masks or mummers more daring or in greater number, some joyful, others distressed, as happens in a battle....

The next day, fat Monday, after supper, the abbot held an open house, and the council assembled, and it was decided to hold a dinner the next day, not in the usual manner, but an exceptional one, in much greater triumph....

---

[13] Source: Marc de Montifaud, ed., *Les triomphes de l'Abbaye des Conards* (Paris: Librairie des Bibliophiles, 1874), 76–80, translated by the editor.

The next day, fat Tuesday, the dinner was prepared in the abbot's palace at 10:00 a.m., and a masked company carried the crozier through town, holding lanterns and drums in order to summon the dinner, as is the custom. Immediately, the tables were found full of an inestimable number of people, and others not able to find a place had to go away.

This was the order of the dinner: There were six tables of the same length with all the seats along one side, as in the convent, each facing the other. In the middle, there was a stage for playing the farces, comedies, and Morris dances, made so that one could walk below it for the dinner service. And above it, there was a person clothed like a hermit, seated in a chair, who read continually, not the Bible but the Chronicle of Pantagruel.[14]

At the end of the room, there was an elevated theater, richly tapestried, on which the lord abbot was in the middle, and on his two sides, the chancellor, patriarch, and cardinals, dressed in their pontifical habits, his bailiff holding his rod at the tip, and the sergeant on the other side holding his mace, in good order and seriousness. At both ends, there were trumpets and oboes, and at the bottom were fifes and drums. At one end, a spinet played with singers. To write to you about the variety of meats, dishes, and desserts would be wasted time, for it is an ordinary thing. Therefore, let us come to the end of the dinner, when several farces and comedies were played, as well as a great number of dances and Morris dances, with good morals and audacity.

66. Philip Stubbs, *Anatomy of Abuses*, 1583[15]

Preface, dedicated to Philip, Earl of Arundel. As your Lordship knows, the reformation of manners and amendment of life was never more needful, for was pride (the chief argument of this book) ever so ripe? Do not both men and women (for the most part), everyone in general, go attired in silks, velvets, damasks, satins, and whatnot, which are attire only for the nobility and gentry, and not for others? Are not unlawful games, plays, interludes, and the like used everywhere? Are not whoredom, covetousness, usury, and the like daily practiced without all punishment or law?...

The people in England are marvelously given to dainty fare, gluttony, good-cheer, and many also to drunkenness.... Today, if the table is not

---

[14] Written by the irreverent French poet Rabelais, *The Deeds of Pantagruel* was a satirical book that poked fun at nearly all of French society, especially the church.

[15] Source: Philip Stubbs, *Anatomy of the Abuses in England in Shakespeare's Youth*, ed. Frederick Furnivall (London: N. Trübner & Co., 1877), viii, 102–7, 136–37, text modernized.

covered from one end to the other, as thick as one dish can stand by another, with delicate meats of various sorts, each one different from the other, and for every dish a special sauce that goes with it, it is thought to be unworthy of the name of *dinner.*... And you shall have this many for the first course, and this many at the second, and perhaps more at the third, apart from other sweet condiments and delicate confections.... And to these dainties, all kinds of wines are not lacking, you may be sure. Oh, what nicety is this! What vanity, excess, riot, and superfluity are here! Oh, farewell former world! For I have heard my father say that in his days, one dish or two of good wholesome meat was thought sufficient for an honorable man, and if they had three or four kinds, it was reputed a sumptuous feast.... And to be plain, there are three cankers, which in course of time will eat up the whole commonwealth, if a speedy reformation is not undertaken, namely dainty fare, gorgeous buildings, and sumptuous apparel.... God remove them from here, for his Christ's sake....

Drunkenness is a horrible vice, and far too much used in England. Every county, city, town, and village has an abundance of alehouses, taverns, and inns, which are so filled with drunks night and day that you would wonder to see them. You shall see them there sitting at the wine and good ale all day long, indeed, all night too, perhaps a whole week altogether, as long as any money is left, swilling, guzzling, and carousing from one to another, until no one can speak a ready word. Then, when with the spirit of wine they are thus possessed, a world it is to consider their gestures and demeanor, how they stutter and stammer, stagger and reel to and fro like madmen, some vomiting, spewing, and disgorging their filthy stomachs, others pissing under the table as they sit, and what is most horrible, some start swearing and cursing, interlacing their speech with terms of blasphemy, to the great dishonor of God and offense to the godly ears present....

The Manner of Sanctifying the Sabbath in England. The Sabbath day is well observed by some, namely in hearing the word of God read, preached, and interpreted in private and public prayers, in singing of godly psalms, in celebrating the sacraments, and in collecting for the poor and indigent; these are the true uses and ends for which the Sabbath was ordained. But others spend the Sabbath day (for the most part) in attending bawdy stage plays and interludes, in maintaining lords of misrule (for so they call a certain kind of play which they use), May games, church ales, and feasts, in piping, dancing, playing dice and cards, bowling, and playing tennis, in bear-baiting, cock fighting, hawking, hunting, and the like, in keeping of fairs and markets on the Sabbath, in keeping courts, in playing football, and such other devilish pastimes, reading of lascivious and wanton books, and an infinite number of similar practices and profane exercises used on that day, by which the Lord God is dishonored, his Sabbath violated, his word neglected, his sacraments disregarded, and his people marvelously corrupted and carried away from the true virtue and godliness. Lord, remove these exercises from your Sabbath!

67. King James I, *Book of Sports*, 1618[16]

Whereas we did justly in our progress through Lancashire rebuke some Puritans and precise people, and took order that the like unlawful carriage should not be used by any of them hereafter, in the prohibiting and unlawful punishing of our good people for using their lawful recreations and honest exercises upon Sundays and other holy days, after the afternoon sermon or service, we now find that two sorts of people wherewith that country is much infected (we mean papists and Puritans) have maliciously traduced and calumniated those our just and honorable proceedings.... We have, therefore, thought good hereby to clear and make our pleasure to be manifested to all our good people in those parts....

With our own ears we heard the general complaint of our people that they were barred from all lawful recreation and exercise upon Sunday afternoons after the ending of all divine service, which cannot but produce two evils: the one, the hindering of the conversion of many, whom their priests will take occasion hereby to vex, persuading them that no honest mirth or recreation is lawful or tolerable in our religion, which cannot but breed a great discontentment in our people's hearts, especially of such as are peradventure upon the point of turning. The other inconvenience is that this prohibition bars the common and meaner sort of people from using such exercises as may make their bodies more able for war,

when we or our successors shall have occasion to use them. And in place thereof sets up filthy tipplings and drunkenness, and breeds a number of idle and discontented speeches in their alehouses. For when shall the common people have leave to exercise if not upon Sundays and holy days, seeing they must apply their labor and win their living in all working days?

Our express pleasure, therefore, is that ... no lawful recreation shall be barred to our good people, which shall not tend to the breach of our laws and canons of our Church.... Our pleasure likewise is that the bishop of that diocese take the like straight order with all the Puritans and precisians within the same, either constraining them to conform themselves, or to leave the county according to the laws of our kingdom and canons of our Church, and so to strike equally on both hands against those who disregard our authority and the adversaries of our Church.

And as for our good people's lawful recreation, our pleasure likewise is that after the end of divine service, our good people be not disturbed, letted, or discouraged from any lawful recreation, such as dancing, either men or women, archery for men, leaping, vaulting, or any other such harmless recreation, nor from having of May games, Whitsun ales, and Morris dances, and the setting up of Maypoles and other sports therewith used, so as the same be had in due and convenient time,

---

[16] Source: King Charles I, *Declaration to His Subjects Concerning Lawful Sports to Be Used on Sundays, 1633* (London: Chiswick Press, 1862), 4–12, text modernized.

without impediment or neglect of divine service; and that women shall have leave to carry rushes to the church for the decorating of it, according to their old custom. But withal we do here account still as prohibited all unlawful games to be used on Sundays only, as bear- and bull-baitings, interludes, and at all times in the meaner sort of people by law prohibited, bowling.

XXXIV. MUSIC

Music in the medieval church was long dominated by Gregorian chant, a style of singing usually performed in unison, without harmony or much musical accompaniment. By the time of the Renaissance, however, pipe organs were in widespread use, and composers such as Josquin des Prez, Palestrina, and Thomas Tallis were composing increasingly complex polyphonic music, mostly for use in church.

Luther recognized the potential power of music in worship. Early in his career, he began to encourage his friends to write hymns (doc. 68) and wrote several himself, the best known of which is "A Mighty Fortress." Luther departed from both Renaissance-style polyphony and from Gregorian chant to embrace the style of the simple German folk song. Indeed, scholars believe Luther adapted some of the music for his hymns from existing popular songs. Moreover, just as Luther wanted the people to be able to read the Bible in the German language, so also he wanted them to sing his hymns in the German tongue. Both the simple musical style and the vernacular lyrics reflected Luther's desire for the entire congregation to sing, whereas much singing in the medieval church was done only by the choir. Luther's hymn writing campaign was so successful that a later Jesuit complained, "Luther's hymns destroyed more souls than his writings and sermons."

Luther's radical archrival in Germany, Thomas Müntzer (see above, §XI), also introduced German singing in his church services and composed a German liturgical setting several years before Luther. Not all Protestants agreed with this push for music in the church, however. In the second document below (doc. 69), Conrad Grebel, an Anabaptist from Zurich, criticizes Müntzer's musical program. And although

Grebel and Zwingli bitterly parted ways over infant baptism, the two largely agreed about the use of music in the church, despite the fact that Zwingli himself was one of the best musicians among the Protestant reformers. For Zwingli, music was to be enjoyed outside of church but had no place in it.

Calvin took a middle way between Luther and Zwingli (as he often did). He was not as enthusiastic as Luther about popular styles of music in the church, but he believed that Psalm-singing was perfectly acceptable in Christian worship. While the Lutherans published many different editions of new hymnals, adding new hymns all the time, Calvinists continued to revise and republish the *Huguenot Psalter* as their primary musical guide. Calvin's preface to the *Psalter* is the third document below (doc. 70).

Focus Questions

1. What reasons does Luther give for wanting to compose and collect German hymns?
2. What guidelines does he follow (or want others to follow) in writing hymns?
3. Why does Grebel believe that music has no place in the church?
4. How can Luther and Grebel both cite the Bible and come up with completely different conclusions about music's place in the church?
5. What encouragements and warnings does Calvin give about music? Is he closer to Luther or to Grebel?

68. Luther on Music

A. Luther to George Spalatin on Hymns, 1523[17]

There is a plan afoot to follow the example of the prophets and the fathers of the early church and compose for the common people German psalms, that is spiritual songs, so that the word of God may remain among the people in the form of song also. We are seeking everywhere

---

[17] Source: Smith and Jacobs, *Luther's Correspondence and Other Contemporary Letters*, 2:211–12, text modernized.

for poets, and since you are gifted with such knowledge of the German language and command so elegant a style, cultivated by much use, I beg that you will work with us in this matter and try to translate some one of the psalms into a hymn, like the sample of my own which you have here.[18] But I wish that you would leave out all new words and words that are only used at court. In order to be understood by the people, only the simplest and commonest words should be sung, but they should also be pure and apt and should give a clear sense, as near as possible to that of the psalter. The translation, therefore, must be free, keeping the sense, but letting the words go and rendering them by other appropriate words.

B. Luther, Preface to the Hymnal of 1524[19]

That it is good and pleasing to God for us to sing spiritual songs is, I think, a truth no Christian can be ignorant of, since not only the example of the prophets and kings of the Old Testament (who praised God with singing and music, poetry and all kinds of stringed instruments) but also the similar practice of all Christendom from the beginning, especially in respect to psalms, is well known to everyone. Indeed, St. Paul also calls for the same

(1 Cor. 14) and commands the Colossians, in the third chapter, to sing spiritual songs and psalms from the heart unto the Lord, so that the word of God and Christian doctrine might be in every way furthered and practiced.

Accordingly, to make a good beginning and to encourage others who can do it better, I have myself with some others put together a few hymns in order to bring into full play the blessed Gospel, which by God's grace has risen again, that we may boast, as Moses does in his song (Exod. 15), that Christ has become our praise and our song, and that, whether we sing or speak, we may not know anything except Christ our Savior, as St. Paul says (1 Cor. 2).

These songs have been set in four parts, for no other reason than because I wished to provide our young people (who both will and ought to be instructed in music and other sciences) with something by which they might rid themselves of amorous and carnal songs, and in their place learn something wholesome, and so apply themselves with pleasure to what is good, as is appropriate to the young.

Beside this, I am not of the opinion that all sciences should be beaten down and made to cease by the Gospel, as some fanatics pretend; instead, I desire to see all the arts, and music in particular, used in the service of him who has given and created them.

---

[18] We do not know which hymn Luther attached.

[19] Source: Leonard Woolsey Bacon, ed., *The Hymns of Martin Luther Set to Their Original Melodies* (London: Hodder and Stoughton, 1884), xxi, text modernized.

69. Conrad Grebel, Letter to Thomas Müntzer, 1524[20]

We understand and have noted that you have translated the mass into German, and have begun to use German hymnody. That cannot be right, when we find no teaching in the New Testament about singing, and no example of singing. Paul scolds the learned at Corinth more than he praises them because they chanted in the church service, just as if singing, as the Jews and Italians pronounce their words in a singsong manner. Second, since singing in the Latin tongue arose without divine teaching and apostolic precedent and practice, and neither resulted in good nor brought edification, it will much less edify in German, but will result in an outward make-believe faith. Third, Paul quite explicitly forbids singing in Ephesians 5 and Colossians 3, when he teaches that they shall teach and admonish one another with psalms and spiritual songs, and if anyone wishes to sing, he shall sing and give thanks in his heart. Fourth, that which is not taught by clear instruction and example we shall regard as forbidden to us—just as if it stood written, Do not do this; do not sing. Fifth, the only command Christ gave His ambassadors in the Old (Testament) was to preach the Word; the same in the New. Paul likewise commands that the Word of Christ shall dwell in us, not singing. He who sings poorly is vexed; he who is able to sing well becomes conceited. Sixth, a person is not to do what seems right to him; it is the Word which we are to follow, with no additions. Seventh, if you wish to abolish the mass, do not introduce German singing. That is perhaps your idea, or it originated with Luther.

70. Calvin, Preface to the *Huguenot Psalter*, 1543[21]

There are two types of public prayers: The first are made by simple words, the others with song. And this is not something invented recently. For this has been done since the very origin of the church, as it appears in the histories. And even St. Paul speaks not only about praying with speech, but also about singing. Truly, we know by experience that song has great strength and power to move and inflame the people's hearts to invoke and praise God out of a stronger and

---

[20] Source: William R. Estep, Jr., ed., *Anabaptist Beginnings (1523–1533): A Source Book*, Bibliotheca Humanistica & Reformatorica 16 (Nieukoop: B. de Graaf, 1976), 32–33.

[21] Source: Clement Marot and Théodore de Bèze, *Les Pseaumes mis en rime Françoise* ([Geneva]: François Jaquy, 1562), *iiii^v–*v^v, translated by the editor.

more ardent zeal. One must always be careful that the song be neither frivolous nor capricious, but serious and majestic (as St. Augustine says), and so there is a significant difference between the music that one makes to entertain people at dinner and in their homes, and the Psalms that are sung in church in the presence of God and his angels.

Now when one would like to judge rightly about the form which is presented here, we hope that one will find it holy and pure, seeing as it is simply shaped for the edification we have discussed, although the use of song might extend further. Even in houses and in the fields it might incite us as a means to praise God and raise our hearts to him, to console us in meditating on his virtue, goodness, wisdom, and justice, which is more necessary than one can say....

Now, among the things which are appropriate for refreshing and delighting man, music is either the first or one of the first, and we must believe that it is a gift of God intended for that purpose. Therefore, it is all the more important that we be careful not to abuse it, for fear of polluting and contaminating it, transforming it into our condemnation, when it was given for our profit and salvation. When there is no other consideration than this one: that we must be moved to moderate the use of music, to make it serve all honesty, and that it not provide an occasion for us to relax the reins into dissolution or to soften us in disordered delights, and that it not be an instrument of lechery or shamelessness.... Therefore, we must be all the more diligent to regulate music in such a way that it be useful and not at all pernicious. For this reason, the ancient doctors of the church often complained about the people of their times being addicted to dishonest and shameful songs, which they deservedly called mortal and Satanic poison for corrupting the world....

We will not find better songs, nor more appropriate ones, than the Psalms of David, which the Holy Spirit spoke to him and composed. And therefore, when we sing them, we are certain that God put the words in our mouths, as if he himself were singing through us to exalt his glory. Therefore, [John] Chrysostom exhorts men, women, and children to become accustomed to singing them, to the end that this might be like a meditation for joining the company of angels. Moreover, we must remember what St. Paul said, that the spiritual songs cannot be better sung than from the heart.

XXXV. DEATH AND DYING

Protestantism altered the entire conception of the supernatural world. From its origins, and arguably at its core, Protestantism entailed a rejection of the Catholic doctrine of purgatory. Much of late medieval religious practice—indulgences, masses for the dead, pilgrimages, jubilee years, saintly intercession, doing penance for one's sins—was meant to expiate sin and thus to reduce or eliminate one's time in purgatory. The Protestant doctrine of justification *sola fide* eliminated the need for purgatory altogether. Thus, the three areas of the Catholic afterlife, famously described in Dante's *Inferno, Purgatorio*, and *Paradiso*, were reduced to two, heaven and hell. For Protestants, one's eternal destination was determined at the moment of death, and nothing could change it between that time and the Last Judgment.

This theological shift carried with it significant changes in practice. Catholicism had a porous border between the living and the dead. The living could pray for the dead to help reduce their time in purgatory. Similarly, the saints could intercede on behalf of both the living and the souls in purgatory. Protestants, by contrast, slammed shut the door between the living and the dead. Prayers for the dead, they insisted, had no effect; the saints did not intercede for the living; only Christ could intercede for humans with God. Burial practices shifted as well. Catholics liked to keep the dead with them, in cemeteries attached to churches or, for prominent or saintly people, inside the churches themselves. Protestants, by contrast, increasingly built cemeteries outside the city walls. Protestant belief even affected the way people wrote wills. Catholic wills frequently mentioned "Holy Mother Church," the Virgin Mary, and the saints, and the wealthy often directed that a portion of their estate fund masses for their souls. Protestant wills eliminated language about Mary and the saints, and while they might still leave some money to the church, it was not for the purpose of saying masses for their souls.

The first documents below discuss purgatory. St. Catherine of Genoa (1447–1510) was an Italian mystic, although not a nun, who had visions of the afterlife. These visions were the basis of her *Treatise on Purgatory*, excerpted below (doc. 71). The text is partly a mystical vision and partly a theological explanation of purgatory, and it explains orthodox Catholic thought on purgatory. The second document (doc. 72) is anonymous but comes from the circle of Guillaume Farel, the early reformer of French-speaking Switzerland. It was published in Neuchâtel in 1534, before Calvin's arrival in nearby Geneva. The treatise is a scathing critique of the doctrine of purgatory and the practices associated with it.

The remaining two documents are descriptions of Catholic and Protestant funerals. The first is from Erasmus's *Colloquies* (see above, doc. 9). This colloquy, "The Funeral," describes the deathbed scene of George Balearicus, a fictional nobleman and soldier. Much of the dialogue mocks the haggling of the doctors and friars while the man is on his deathbed, but the excerpt below is a description of the funeral that is planned for him. The second document is from an anonymous Catholic (known by his irreverent pen name, the *Passevent Parisien*, or "Parisian Passwind") who had spent time in Geneva. It is a polemical work critical of the Protestant church and its leaders. One must note that funeral practices varied widely across Europe, not just between Protestants and Catholics, but also both geographically and across socioeconomic lines. Still, even though both texts mock the practices they are describing, other sources tell us that they are fairly faithful descriptions of certain types of funerals in Reformation Europe.

Focus Questions

1. How does Catherine of Genoa portray the souls in purgatory? What imagery does she use? With what effect?
2. What lessons does she think her readers should draw from her discussion of purgatory?
3. What are the chief criticisms—theological and otherwise—of purgatory in the second document?
4. Compare the funeral descriptions in the last two documents. How does each reflect the doctrinal perspectives of its author? What seem to be the main contrasts? Are there any similarities?

71. Catherine of Genoa, *Treatise on Purgatory*, c. 1510[22]

The souls in purgatory, as far as I can understand the matter, cannot but choose to be there, and this by the ordinance of God, who has justly decreed it so.... They are so completely satisfied with what God has ordained for them and that he should be doing all that pleases him and in the way it pleases him, that they are incapable of thinking of themselves even in the midst of their greatest sufferings. They behold only the goodness of God, whose mercy is so great in bringing men to himself that they cannot see anything that may affect them, whether good or bad; if they could, they would not be in pure charity.... They are in that fire of purgatory by the appointment of God, which is all one with pure love; and they cannot in anything turn aside from it, because as they can no more merit, so they can no more sin....

The souls are covered by a rust—that is, sin—which is gradually consumed away by the fire of purgatory; the more it is consumed, the more they respond to God their true sun. Their happiness increases as the rust falls off and lays them open to the divine ray, and so their happiness grows greater as the impediment grows less, till the time is accomplished. The pain, however, does not diminish, but only the time remaining in that pain.... They suffer a torment so extreme that no tongue could describe it, no intellect could form the least idea of it, if God had not made it known by special grace; which idea, however, God's grace has shown my soul, but I cannot find words to express it with my tongue, yet the sight of it has never left my mind. I will describe it as I can: They will understand it whose intellect the Lord shall vouchsafe to open.

All the pains of purgatory take their rise from sin, original or actual. God created the soul perfectly pure and free from every spot of sin, with a certain instinctive tendency to find its blessedness in him. From this tendency it is drawn away by original sin, and still more by the addition of actual sin, and the farther off it gets, the more wicked it becomes because it is less in conformity with God....

God is all mercy and stands with open arms to admit us to his glory. But still I see that the being of God is so pure (far more than one can imagine), that should a soul see in itself even the least mote of imperfection, it would rather cast itself into a thousand hells than go with that spot into the presence of the divine majesty. Therefore, seeing purgatory ordained to take away such blemishes, it plunges therein and deems it a great mercy that it can thus remove them.... It appears to me that the greatest pain the souls in purgatory endure proceeds from

---

[22] Source: Catherine of Genoa, *Treatise on Purgatory*, 4th ed., trans. Cardinal Manning (London: Burns & Oates, c. 1858), 2–5, 7–9, 22–24, 29–30, 40–41, text modernized.

their being sensible of something in themselves displeasing to God and that it has been done voluntarily against so much goodness, for being in a state of grace, they know the truth and how grievous is any obstacle which does not let them approach God....

Look at gold: The more it is melted the better it becomes, and it could be melted so as to destroy every single defect. Such is the action of fire on material things.... In like manner the divine fire acts on souls: God holds them in the furnace until every defect has been burnt away, and he has brought them, each in his own degree, to a certain standard of perfection. Thus purified, they rest in God without any alloy of self; their very being is God....

"Would that I could cry out" (said this blessed soul when under divine illumination she saw these things), "loud enough to strike with fear every person upon the earth, and say, 'Miserable beings, why do you allow yourselves to be so blinded by this world as to make no provision for the dire strait you will find yourselves in at the hour of death? You all shelter yourselves under the hope of God's mercy, which you say is so great, and you do not consider that this very goodness of God will rise up in judgment against you for having opposed the will of so good a master; his mercy ought to constrain you to do all his will and not encourage you to do evil. Be assured that his justice cannot yield, but must in one way or other be fully satisfied. Let no one buoy himself up saying, "I shall confess, and then I shall receive a plenary indulgence, by which I shall be cleansed from all my sins and get through safely." Know that a plenary indulgence requires confession and contrition; and the latter is so difficult to obtain, that if you knew how difficult, you would tremble with fear, and rather make sure of not gaining than of gaining the indulgence.'"

72. Anonymous (Guillaume Farel's Circle), *Treatise on Purgatory*, 1534[23]

One does not find mention of any purgatory in the word of God other than the blood of Jesus Christ, by which the sins and iniquities of the world are purged.... In order to show that the papistical purgatory is nothing but a phantom, illusion, and horror giving terror, fear, and wonder to people without faith, it is necessary to call to mind some passages of the Holy Scripture against it.

---

[23] Source: "Traicté de Purgatoire" in *Le Sommaire de Guillaume Farel*, ed. J.-G. Baum (Geneva, 1867), 128–39, translated by the editor.

First, it is written in St. Matthew and in St. Mark, "He who believes and is baptized shall be saved; but he who does not believe will be condemned" (Matt. 28, Mark 16). By these words, the path of damnation is shown to us: namely, by unbelief. And the way of salvation is given to us, namely, by faith. Now, it is certain that we will die either faithful or unfaithful. If we die in the faith, we will be saved, for it is said, "He who believes will be saved." If we die unfaithful, we will be damned, according to what is said, "He who does not believe will be condemned."...

Also, the thief who was crucified near Christ was never in purgatory to do penance for his sins. For Christ said to him, "Today you will be with me in paradise" [Luke 23:43]. Where, therefore, is his purgation? Is it not by the blood of Christ, by the washing of regeneration which he poured out on us abundantly, and by the faith which purifies hearts?...

If, therefore, our Lord forgives us all our sins when we request it of him, there is no more need to be bothered for them, seeing as they are erased for us by the faith that we have in the death and passion of Jesus Christ, whose death is either perfect or imperfect. If it is perfect, nothing more can perfect it, for that would be to blaspheme Christ's passion, as those smelters of souls do when they want to make satisfaction for their sins by their works in the furnace of purgatory....

It is not, therefore, pain that purges sin, but the faith that we have in God through Jesus Christ, which, as St. Paul says, is the purgation of our sins (Rom. 3). And so, to want to find a purgatory other than the blood of Christ is noth-ing else than to empty his passion and to say that his works are imperfect....

And so, it is clear that the frivolous invention of purgatory that is cried and emblazoned throughout the world is vain and contrived by Satan, putting ambition in the hearts of the ministers of the church, who have searched more for their individual profit than for the salvation of souls; indeed, it appears that this fire has been more profitable to them than the furnaces of the practitioners of alchemy. For by it, they have converted a great portion of the goods of the world into gold and silver which returns to the profit of their table. O Lord God, how full of patience you are to suffer that your word be profaned by the inventions, dreams, and lies of men! For how long, O Lord, will you let these poor blind men create monthly and annual masses for the dead and other doubtful services, when they should be providing for you in your poor members, by building schools to instruct the ignorant, marrying off poor girls, teaching poor orphans a craft, nourishing the old, the weak, the poor, and the sick? These are the works of faith operating through charity that are commanded by you.

Extend, O Lord, the arm of your power, and by the rigor of your justice rend, break, and annihilate these false prophets, seducers, big-ots, hypocrites, and abusers who daily deceive your people by their frivolous inventions full of greed.... Woe to you Scribes, Pharisees, hypocrites, thieves, and murderers who aban-don the commandment of God (which is to provide for the poor), in favor of your tradi-tions and your great abyss of purgatory, where all the goods of the world are swallowed up.

232

It is the sack with a hole in it, which the prophet speaks of, which will never be full (Hag. 1). Certainly, it is well named *purgatory*, for by

this fire, everything is cleared away, everything is purged: grain stores, cellars, purses, coffers, fields, and towns.

73. Protestant and Catholic Funerals

A. Catholic Ritual: Erasmus, Colloquies, *"The Funeral," 1526*[24]

Marcolphus and Phaedrus

PHAEDRUS: ... After this, the funeral procession came up for discussion—but not without argument. Finally they agreed that from each of the five orders nine members should attend, in honour of the five books of Moses and the nine choirs of angels: each order to carry its own cross before it and sing funeral dirges. With these and the relatives should march thirty torchbearers dressed in black (thirty being the number of coins for which the Lord was sold), and—to lend distinction—twelve mourners (the number sacred to the band of apostles, that is) should accompany them. The bier was to be followed by George's horse, draped in black, with head tied down to his knees to suggest that he was looking along the ground for his master. The pall was to display on each side George's coat of arms. Likewise each torch and mourning garb should have his arms. Now the corpse itself was to rest at the right of the high altar in a marble tomb four feet high. On top of the tomb was to be George's

effigy carved in Parian marble, in full armor from head to foot. His helmet was to have his crest (a pelican's neck), and his left arm a shield bearing as insignia three boars' heads of gold in a field of silver. Nor was his sword with the golden hilt to be missing from his side, nor his gold baldric adorned with jewelled studs, nor his gold spurs from his feet; for he was a gilded knight. At his feet he was to have a leopard. The borders of the tomb were to have an inscription worthy of such a man. He wanted his heart to be buried separately in the chapel of St. Francis. His entrails he bequeathed to the parish priest for honourable burial in a chapel sacred to the Virgin Mother.

MARCOLPHUS: A splendid funeral, no doubt, but too costly. At Venice any cobbler would be accorded a more splendid one for a minimum of expense. His guild gives a fine bier; and sometimes six hundred monks, dressed in tunics or cloaks, accompany a single corpse.

PHAEDRUS: I too have seen and laughed at this inappropriate ostentation of the poor. Fullers and tanners march in front, cobblers in the rear, monks in the middle; you'd say they were chimeras. Nor would you have seen any

---

[24] Source: Erasmus, *Colloquies*, Collected Works of Erasmus 39–40, trans. Craig R. Thompson, 2 vols. (Toronto: University of Toronto Press, 1997), 2:772–73.

difference here. George stipulated also that Franciscan and Dominican were to settle by lot which of them should have first place in the procession; then the rest, too, were to draw lots, to prevent any disorder on this account. The parish priest and his clerks were to have the lowest place—that is, at the front—for the monks would consent to no other arrangement.

Marcolphus: He was skilled in drawing up not only battle lines but parades as well.

Phaedrus: It was stipulated, too, that the funeral rites, conducted by the parish priest, should be accompanied by the harmonious singing of the choir, in George's honour.

B. Calvinist Ritual: The Parisian Passwind on Geneva Funerals [25]

As soon as the man or woman has died, those in the house dress them as they like, and then tell their other close relatives and neighbors to join them. Those who ring the bells for the sermon, who also have the duty of carrying and burying the dead, dig the grave in the appointed place, and the funeral proceeds as follows: The two appointed for the task carry on their shoulders the deceased, who is covered with a sheet or cloth, just as among us Catholics the reliquaries are carried in processions. Then the men follow two-by-two, and after them the women in the same order. Some laugh, others cry, and in this way they go to throw the body into the grave without saying anything and without having any ceremony, no more than you would do for a dog or a horse. And then all those who participated return to the lodging of the deceased, and at the door, each one says to those closest, "God preserve you in life," and they respond, "And you also." And they are very careful to avoid any prayer or alms for the soul of the deceased, lest they be summoned to their consistory and held for a papist and idolater.

FURTHER READING

Albala, Ken, and Trudy Eden, eds. *Food and Faith in Christian Culture*. New York: Columbia University Press, 2011. http://dx.doi.org/10.7312/columbia/9780231149976.001.0001.

Ariès, Philippe. *The Hour of Our Death*. Translated by Helen Weaver. New York: Oxford University Press, 1991.

Brown, Christopher Boyd. *Singing the Gospel: Lutheran Hymns and the Success of the Reformation*. Cambridge, MA: Harvard University Press, 2005. http://dx.doi.org/10.4159/9780674028913.

Burke, Peter. *Popular Culture in Early Modern Europe*. 3rd ed. Farnham, UK: Ashgate, 2009.

---

[25] Source: *Passevent Parisien, Respondant à Pasquin Romain* (Paris, 1875), 72–73, translated by the editor.

Durston, Christopher, and Jacqueline Eales, eds. *The Culture of English Puritanism, 1560–1700*. New York: St. Martin's Press, 1996. http://dx.doi.org/10.1007/978-1-349-24437-9.

Karant-Nunn, Susan. *The Reformation of Ritual: An Interpretation of Early Modern Germany*. London: Routledge, 1997.

Koslofsky, Craig. *The Reformation of the Dead: Death and Ritual in Early Modern Germany, 1450–1700*. New York: St. Martin's Press. 2000. http://dx.doi.org/10.1057/9780230286375.

Spinks, Bryan. *Reformation and Modern Rituals and Theologies of Baptism: From Luther to Contemporary Practices*. Aldershot, UK: Ashgate, 2006.

X

Cultural Impact of the Reformation, Part 2: Social Relations and Customs

In the last chapter, we explored the impact of the Reformation on Christian life and customs. In this chapter, we will examine how the Reformation affected views of women, marriage, Jews, religious toleration, and slavery. It should become clear through this chapter why scholars refer to this period as "early modern." You will encounter ideas that seem strikingly modern alongside others that decidedly seem to belong to an older era. The early modern period was a time of transition between the Middle Ages and modernity, and thus a time when the attitudes typical of both eras began to clash. Other developments—such as Renaissance humanism, global exploration, and the beginning of the scientific revolution—contributed to this ideological transformation, but it is clear that the Reformation played an important role.

XXXVI. WOMEN

One of the most important advances over the past few decades in Reformation studies (and in historical studies generally) has been the growing integration of women into the historical narrative and examination of issues such as gender, sexuality, and marriage. Scholars have studied prominent women of the Reformation, such as Marie Dentière, Katharina Schütz Zell, and Anne Askew. They have also exploited new sources and taken new approaches to well-known sources to study the perspective and experience of women more broadly.

The first document in this section, John Knox's *First Blast of the Trumpet against the Monstrous Regiment of Women* (doc. 74), sets the stage by presenting a typically misogynistic but common male view of women during this era. Knox (c. 1513–72) is best known as the founder of the Scottish Presbyterian Church. He fled England during Queen Mary I's reign and composed this text while in exile in Geneva. In the text, Knox had chiefly in mind three powerful Catholic Marys: Queen Mary I of England, Mary Queen of Scots, and her mother Mary of Guise. Unfortunately for Knox, he published the text just before Mary I died and the Protestant Queen Elizabeth took the throne.

The next two texts were written by learned Protestant women.[1] The author of the first, Marie Dentière (1495–1561), had been a nun in Tournai before embracing Protestantism early in the 1520s, leaving the convent, and marrying a former priest. She moved to Strasbourg, where she probably would have met Jacques Lefèvre d'Etaples, Gérard Roussel, Guillaume Farel (see above, chapter 5), and Katharina Schütz Zell (more on her below). Dentière and her husband later joined Farel in his missionary efforts in French-speaking Switzerland. When her husband died, she married again, this time to Antoine Froment, another of the early reformers of Geneva. Soon after Calvin and Farel were exiled from Geneva in 1538, Dentière wrote the *Epistle to Marguerite of Navarre* (doc. 75). The excerpt below contains a defense of women engaged in theological discourse.

---

[1] See doc. 79 in the section below for another text on a related topic by a Catholic woman.

Katharina Schütz Zell (1498–1562) wrote the third document, a letter to the Spiritualist pastor Caspar Schwenckfeld (doc. 76). Schütz Zell was the most popular and prolific female author of the German Reformation. She embraced Protestantism early after listening to the Lutheran sermons of Matthew Zell in her hometown of Strasbourg (at that time a German-speaking city). She married Zell in 1523 in an early act of clerical marriage (Luther himself did not marry Katharina von Bora until 1525), which she defended in her first published writing. Schütz Zell became Matthew Zell's lifelong companion and assisted in his public ministry at Strasbourg until his death in 1548. She wrote the text below in 1553 at a time of increasing religious factionalism in Strasbourg. In particular, Caspar Schwenckfeld, who had grown increasingly radical over the years, alienated Schütz Zell by falsely claiming her as a disciple and then criticizing her for not attending his worship services. Her letter to Schwenckfeld asserts her independence from all factions and defends her life and learning.

Focus Questions

1. What are Knox's chief arguments against women rulers? Do they seem to apply to women generally, or does he seem to have in mind specific individuals or categories of women?
2. How does Marie Dentière defend the participation of women in public discussions of religion?
3. How does Schütz Zell describe her marriage? How does she describe her religious identity? What relationship would she claim between the two?
4. How does she characterize her learning? How does she claim others characterize it?
5. How do you think Dentière and Schütz Zell would respond to Knox? Would you label them proto-feminists? Why or why not?

74. John Knox, *First Blast of the Trumpet against the Monstrous Regiment of Women*, 1558[2]

To promote a woman to bear rule, superiority, dominion, or empire above any realm, nation, or city, is repugnant to nature, contumely to God, a thing most contrary to his revealed will and approved ordinance, and finally it is the subversion of good order, of all equity and justice....

And first, where I affirm that the empire of a woman is repugnant to nature, I mean not only that God by the order of his creation has deprived woman of authority and dominion, but also that man has seen, proved, and pronounced just causes why it should be so. Man, I say, in many other cases blind, in this matter sees very clearly. For the causes are so manifest that they cannot be hidden. For who can deny that it is repugnant to nature that the blind shall be appointed to lead and conduct those who see? That the weak, the sick, and the impotent shall nourish and keep those who are whole and strong, and finally, that the foolish, mad, and frenetic shall govern the discrete and give counsel to those of sober mind? And all women are like this compared to man in the bearing of authority. For their sight in civil rule is but blindness; their strength, weakness; their counsel, foolishness; and their judgment, madness, if it be rightly considered.

I make an exception of those whom God, by singular privilege and for certain causes known only to himself, has exempted from the common rank of women. I am speaking of women as nature and experience do this day declare them. Nature, I say, paints them to be weak, frail, impatient, feeble, and foolish; and experience has declared them to be inconstant, variable, cruel, and lacking the spirit of counsel and rule. And men in all ages have seen these notable faults in them, for which they have not only removed women from rule and authority, but some have also thought that men subject to the counsel or empire of their wives were unworthy of all public office....

But now to the second part of nature, in which I include the revealed will and perfect ordinance of God, and I say that it is clearly repugnant to this part of nature that any woman shall reign or hold dominion over man. For God, first by the order of his creation and then by the curse and malediction pronounced against the woman because of her rebellion, has pronounced the contrary. First, I say that woman in her greatest perfection was made to serve and obey man, not to rule and command him, as St. Paul explains in these words: "Indeed, man was not made from woman, but woman from man. Neither was

---

[2] Source: John Knox, *First Blast of the Trumpet against the Monstrous Regiment of Women*, ed. Edward Arber (London, 1878), 11–16, text modernized.

man created for the sake of woman, but woman for the sake of man. For this reason a woman ought to have a symbol of authority on her head (that is, a covering in sign of subjection) (1 Cor. 11[:8–10])." From these words, it is plain that the Apostle means that woman in her greatest perfection should have known that man was lord above her and, therefore, that she should never have claimed any kind of superiority above him, no more than do the angels above God the creator, or above Christ Jesus their head. So I say that in her greatest perfection woman was created to be subject to man.

But after her fall and rebellion committed against God, a new necessity was put upon her, and she was made subject to man by the irrevocable sentence of God, pronounced in these words: "I will greatly increase your pangs in childbearing; in pain you shall bring forth children, yet your desire shall be for your hus-

band, and he shall rule over you (Gen. 3:16)." By this, anyone who is not altogether blind may plainly see that God by his sentence has dejected all women from empire and dominion above man....

But, alas, ignorance of God, ambition, and tyranny have strived to abolish and destroy the second part of God's punishment. For women are lifted up to be heads over realms, and to rule above men at their pleasure and appetites. But horrible is the vengeance which is prepared for the one and for the other, for the promoters and for the persons promoted, unless they quickly repent. For they shall be dejected from the glory of the sons of God to the slavery of the devil, and to the torment that is prepared for all those who exalt themselves against God. Against God can nothing be more manifest than that a woman shall be exalted to reign above man.

---

75. Marie Dentière, *Epistle to Marguerite of Navarre*, 1538[3]

Not only will certain slanderers and adversaries of truth try to accuse us of excessive audacity and temerity, but so will certain of the faithful, saying that it is too bold for women to write to one another about matters of scripture. We may answer them by saying that all those women who have written and have been named

in holy scripture should not be considered too bold. Several women are named and praised in holy scripture, as much for their good conduct, actions, demeanor, and example as for their faith and teaching: Sarah and Rebecca, for example, and first among all the others in the Old Testament; the mother of Moses, who, in spite of the

---

3   Source: Marie Dentière, "Epistle to Marguerite de Navarre and Preface to a Sermon by John Calvin", *The Other Voice in Early Modern Europe*, ed. and trans. Mary McKinley (Chicago: University of Chicago Press, 2004), 54–56.

king's edict, dared to keep her son from death and saw that he was cared for in the Pharaoh's house, as is amply declared in Exodus 2; and Deborah, who judged the people of Israel in the time of the Judges, is not to be scorned.... If we are speaking of the graces that have been given to women, what greater grace has come to any creature on earth than to the virgin Mary, mother of Jesus, to have carried the Son of God? It was no small grace that allowed Elizabeth, mother of John the Baptist, to have borne a son miraculously after having been sterile. What woman was a greater preacher than the Samaritan woman, who was not ashamed to preach Jesus and his word, confessing him openly before everyone, as soon as she heard Jesus say that we must adore God in spirit and truth? Who can boast of having had the first manifestation of the great mystery of the resurrection of Jesus, if not Mary Magdalene, from whom he had thrown out seven devils, and the other women, to whom, rather than to men, he had earlier declared himself through his angel and commanded them to tell, preach, and declare it to others?

Even though in all women there has been imperfection, men have not been exempt from it. Why is it necessary to criticize women so much, seeing that no woman ever sold or betrayed Jesus, but a man named Judas? Who are they, I pray you, who have invented and contrived so many ceremonies, heresies, and false doctrines on earth if not men? And the poor women have been seduced by them. Never was a woman found to be a false prophet, but women have been misled by them.... Therefore, if God has given grace to some good women, revealing to them by his holy scriptures something holy and good, should they hesitate to write, speak, and declare it to one another because of the defamers of truth? Ah, it would be too bold to try to stop them, and it would be too foolish for us to hide the talent that God has given us, God who will give us the grace to persevere to the end. Amen.

76. Katharina Schütz Zell, Letter to Caspar Schwenckfeld, 1553[4]

On account of my sins... God has taken away my simple, good, upright husband. As you also well know, my husband denied me nothing. He did not rule over or compel my faith; he also never put any obstacles in the way of my faith but rather much more he actively furthered and helped me. He granted and allowed me space and will to read, hear, pray, study, and be active in all good things, early and late, day and night: indeed, he took great joy in that—even

---

[4] Source: Katharina Schütz Zell, "Church Mother: The Writings of a Protestant Reformer in Sixteenth-Century Germany", *The Other Voice in Early Modern Europe*, ed. and trans. Elsie McKee (Chicago: University of Chicago Press, 2006), 188, 191–92, 195–97.

when it meant less attention to or neglect in looking after his physical needs and running his household. . . .

However, I must say, as my good upright husband Matthew Zell often said to me, "God will take the capacity for speech away from me." Why? Because he knew that the world no longer deserved it. Oh this great word, that I did not then understand, but now understand very well! Yes, I could say that and more: but why should I do so much, or bestir myself? I am now a poor solitary woman, fit only (as some say!) to spin or wait on the sick. But no matter which side I were on, if I were pleased with everything about them, those who say these things would speak differently about me, indeed they would idolize me. I well believe that if I agreed that everything said on the preachers' side was right and pleased me, they would count me the most devout and learned woman in Germany. But since I do not do that, they regard me instead as a presumptuous spirit and (as some mockingly say) "doctor Kathrina." . . .

But what else should I say about all this except that I thank my God that, from my youth on, He has given me good judgment, without love or hate, and at the age of discretion He made me completely free from all others in Christ my spouse. Yes, He, the same Lord Christ Himself as the true Son, has freed me and taught me through His apostles that I should no longer be a servant of any person, nor allow a halter to be laid on my neck. With His help that is what I will do: I will demonstrate my love and service everywhere to whoever seeks it, but I will not give myself as a prisoner to anyone. I will also not liken any element or creature to my spouse Christ, nor give to them the throne in my heart that He Himself once took through His grace. I will never cast Him from that same throne, and so He will also not abandon me or allow me to be torn out of His hand [cf. John 8:36; 1 Cor. 7:23; Acts 15:10; Eph. 3:17]. . . .

You do me wrong to think that I would then leave church, preaching, and sacraments out of disregard for them: wherever I am or whatever I do, I would never leave the church of Christ, in whose communion I always seek to remain. . . . However, that I leave the outward church gathering and preaching, and cannot always visit it (as you think I should do), for that I will not lay a halter on my neck or allow myself to be bound to place and time [cf. Acts 15:10; Gal. 4:10]. . . . And—God willing—I would like often to pray with the parish and to hear preaching. . . . Still I would gladly do this if you preached Christ rightly and did not hatefully abuse those who love Him.

For I also am no longer a young schoolchild who is still drinking milk and learning the ABCs; but I am an old student who has studied a long time, when you were still children and played in the sand. I ought now to be a Master, while you would be a student who lights the fires. (Please accept this little joke well.) I have exercised myself in the Holy Scriptures and godly matters for more than forty-eight years now and never abandoned the grace of God; I have heard the old teachers and let them be my counselors and made the wine new (to put in new skins) since I was ten years old [Matt. 9:16–17; Mark 2:22]. I never got bogged down hearing, learning, and following until the day (sad to me but happy to him) of the death of my dear and good husband.

I could now teach others and with the elderly Anna prophesy about Christ to those who are waiting for redemption and praise the Lord [cf. Luke 2:36–38]. But considering that I must appropriately be submissive under the man's office, according to the teaching of Saint Paul [cf. 1 Cor. 14:34; 1 Tim. 2:12], I myself seek to hear others and to be exhorted as far as they speak the truth! But where that is not so, then I would tell you and not keep silent, but speak, point out, and answer your wrong preaching and insulting words about the innocent.

XXXVII. SEX, CHASTITY, AND MARRIAGE

Protestants' rejection of monasticism required rethinking the appropriate roles for women and men in society. No longer were individuals to pursue solitary lives of prayer and contemplation. Instead, Protestants, starting with Luther himself, encouraged everyone, of both sexes, to get married. This admonition included the clergy, and thus represented yet another stark contrast with Catholicism, which for several hundred years had insisted on a celibate priesthood. This shift had enormous social ramifications as thousands of men and women left the monasteries during the Reformation. While former monks had little difficulty finding positions as Protestant clergymen, women had no such option. They either had to return to their families or find husbands. Luther himself would marry one of these former nuns, Katherina von Bora.

Two other important shifts with regard to marriage took place in the Reformation. First, under certain, very limited circumstances, Protestants permitted divorce. This permission is easy to blow out of proportion; for a long time, divorce remained exceedingly rare in Protestant lands, but the Reformation did crack open the door to the possibility for the first time in centuries. Catholicism did not permit divorce, but under specific circumstances, the church granted annulments—declarations that no true marriage had actually occurred. Second, while marriage had long been subject to canon law and thus controlled by the church rather than by the state, the

Reformation placed control over marriage squarely in the hands of the secular magistrate.

The first document below is from one of Luther's early treatises on the subject of sexuality and marriage (doc. 77). His arguments in this text would be important for Protestants throughout the Reformation. Protestants had one major vulnerability in their arguments against the celibate life: The letters of St. Paul seem to indicate a strong preference for a life of celibacy. Luther's nemesis, Johannes Eck (see above, §VI), makes this point clearly in the second document (doc. 78).

Finally, the *Autobiography* of Ana de San Bartolomé (doc. 79) depicts the struggle some Catholic women faced when their family's desire that they get married clashed with their own desire to "marry" Christ and live the chaste life of a nun. Ana de San Bartolomé (1549–1626) was the daughter of well-to-do peasants in Spain. After the struggles recounted in the text below, she entered the convent of the Discalced Carmelites in Ávila, where she met Teresa of Ávila, the founder of the order (see above, §XXVI), eventually becoming her personal assistant. She wrote her autobiography toward the end of her life.

Focus Questions

1. What is Luther's main argument for encouraging marriage for everyone, or at least nearly everyone?
2. Under what circumstances does he find divorce acceptable?
3. What is his advice for someone with a spouse who is an invalid? Is his argument on this point consistent with his earlier arguments? Why or why not?
4. How does Eck counter the Protestant position on marriage?
5. Why is Ana de San Bartolomé so reluctant to marry? What steps does she take to avoid marrying?
6. What role do her visions play in her story? How does she characterize her relationship with Jesus?
7. How do you think Ana would have responded to Luther?

77. Luther, *The Estate of Marriage*, 1522[5]

[A]fter God had made man and woman he blessed them and said to them, "Be fruitful and multiply" [Gen. 1:28]. From this passage we may be assured that man and woman should and must come together in order to multiply. Now this [ordinance] is … inflexible … and [not] to be despised and made fun of … since God gives it his blessing and does something over and above the act of creation. Hence, as it is not within my power not to be a man, so it is not my prerogative to be without a woman. Again, as it is not in your power not to be a woman, so it is not your prerogative to be without a man. For it is not a matter of free choice or decision but a natural and necessary thing, that whatever is a man must have a woman and whatever is a woman must have a man.

For this word which God speaks, "Be fruitful and multiply," is not a command. It is more than a command, namely, a divine ordinance which it is not our prerogative to hinder or ignore. Rather, it is just as necessary as the fact that I am a man, and more necessary than sleeping and waking, eating and drinking, and emptying the bowels and bladder. It is a nature and disposition just as innate as the organs involved in it. Therefore, just as God does not command anyone to be a man or a woman but creates them the way they have to be, so he does not command them to multiply but creates them so that they have to multiply. And wherever men try to resist this, it remains irresistible nonetheless and goes its way through fornication, adultery, and secret sins, for this is a matter of nature and not of choice….

From this you can now see the extent of the validity of all cloister vows. No vow of any youth or maiden is valid before God, except that of a person in one of the three categories which God alone has himself excepted. Therefore, priests, monks, and nuns are duty-bound to forsake their vows whenever they find that God's ordinance to produce seed and to multiply is powerful and strong within them. They have no power by any authority, law, command, or vow to hinder this which God has created within them. If they do hinder it, however, you may be sure that they will not remain pure but inevitably besmirch themselves with secret sins or fornication. For they are simply incapable of resisting the word and ordinance of God within them. Matters will take their course as God has ordained….

In the second part, we shall consider which persons may be divorced. I know of three grounds for divorce. The first, which has just been mentioned and was discussed above, is the situation in which the husband or wife is not equipped for marriage because of bodily or

---

5 Source: Martin Luther, "The Estate of Marriage, 1522," in *Luther's Works*, American Edition, ed. Jaroslav Pelikan and Helmut T. Lehmann, 55 vols. (Philadelphia: Muehlenberg and Fortress, and St. Louis, MO: Concordia, 1955–86), 45:18–19, 30–31, 33–35, 46.

natural deficiencies of any sort. Of this enough has already been said.

The second ground is adultery. The popes have kept silent about this; therefore we must hear Christ, Matthew 19[:3–9].... Here you see that in the case of adultery Christ permits the divorce of husband and wife, so that the innocent person may remarry. For in saying that he commits adultery who marries another after divorcing his wife, "except for unchastity," Christ is making it quite clear that he who divorces his wife on account of unchastity and then marries another does not commit adultery....

The third case for divorce is that in which one of the parties deprives and avoids the other, refusing to fulfil the conjugal duty or to live with the other person. For example, one finds many a stubborn wife like that who will not give in, and who cares not a whit whether her husband falls into the sin of unchastity ten times over. Here it is time for the husband to say, "If you will not, another will; the maid will come if the wife will not."[6] Only first the husband should admonish and warn his wife two or three times, and let the situation be known to others so that her stubbornness becomes a matter of common knowledge and is rebuked before the congregation. If she still refuses, get rid of her; take an Esther and let Vashti go, as King Ahasuerus did [Esther 1:12–2:17]....

Notice that St. Paul forbids either party to deprive the other, for by the marriage vow each submits his body to the other in conjugal duty. When one resists the other and refuses the conjugal duty she is robbing the other of the body she had bestowed upon him. This is really contrary to marriage and dissolves the marriage. For this reason the civil government must compel the wife, or put her to death. If the government fails to act, the husband must reason that his wife has been stolen away and slain by robbers; he must seek another....

What about the situation where one's wife is an invalid and has therefore become incapable of fulfilling the conjugal duty? May he not take another to wife? By no means. Let him serve the Lord in the person of the invalid and await His good pleasure. Consider that in this invalid God has provided your household with a healing balm by which you are to gain heaven. Blessed and twice blessed are you when you recognize such a gift of grace and therefore serve your invalid wife for God's sake.

But you may say: I am unable to remain continent. That is a lie. If you will earnestly serve your invalid wife, recognize that God has placed this burden upon you, and give thanks to him, then you may leave matters in his care. He will surely grant you grace, that you will not have to bear more than you are able. He is far too faithful to deprive you of your wife through illness without at the same time subduing your carnal desire, if you will but faithfully serve your invalid wife....

But the greatest good in married life, that which makes all suffering and labor worth while, is that God grants offspring and commands that they be brought up to worship and serve him.

---

[6] This was a well-known proverb and not penned by Luther.

In all the world this is the noblest and most precious work, because to God there can be nothing dearer than the salvation of souls. Now since we are all duty bound to suffer death, if need be, that we might bring a single soul to God, you can see how rich the estate of marriage is in good works.

78. Eck, *Enchiridion*, "The Celibacy of the Clergy," 1529[7]

God commanded, "Be fruitful and multiply," (Gen. 1[:28]) when the earth had yet to be filled, but now heaven does. At that time, there were few creatures procreating, now countless ones are. Therefore, that law is not permanent. Otherwise, John the Baptist, who remained a virgin, would have sinned. Mary, who held up virginity, would have sinned. Paul, who counseled virginity, would have sinned. And Christ would not have praised eunuchs.

The church does not prohibit marriage, but when certain individuals are bound by a vow, it forbids them to break that vow. Before the vow, they were free to marry; once married, they cannot marry again. In the same way, the church does not want those who have given power over their bodies to Christ to give it to another....

There heretics object, "It is better to marry than to be aflame with passion" (1 Cor. 7[:9]), but Paul also says, "It is well for a man not to touch a woman." [1 Cor. 7:1]. The apostle does not want someone who is tempted by the flesh to burn. In the case of someone who burns and is overcome by the flames of passion, it is better to marry than to roll around forever in filth....

I confess that it is difficult to control oneself, and "the kingdom of heaven has suffered violence, and the violent take it by force" (Matt. 11[:12]). All are tempted by the flesh, but "God is faithful, and he will not let you be tested beyond your strength, but with the testing he will also provide the way out so that you may be able to endure it" (1 Cor. 10[:13]).

You say that this vow is impossible. If you look at nature, many other things are impossible for us. But if you look at God's assisting grace, nothing is impossible. Those to whom it is given can succeed. Therefore, the wise person says, "But I perceived that I would not possess" chastity "unless God gave it to me, and it was a mark of insight to know whose gift it was" (Wis. 8[:21]). The heretic gives us a new way to overcome the temptations of the flesh, namely, to give in to its desires, which is contrary to all of Scripture.

---

[7] Source: Johannes Eck, *Enchiridion locorum communium adversus Lutheranos* (Ingolstadt, 1529), 78v–79v, translated by the editor.

79. Ana de San Bartolomé, *Autobiography*, 1625[8]

My brothers and sisters, seeing that I had grown up, tried to marry me off. I had no such ideas. I called upon the Virgin, whom I had taken as my mother, and all my saints, and I increased my devotion and penitence. I went to church and hid in a chapel of the Conception of Our Lady the Virgin, and with bare feet and my bare knees on the ground, I called upon her to help me. A thousand terrible temptations against my wishes tormented and afflicted me. The trickery of the devil was never lacking on these occasions. But I took scourges and lay down naked on the ground in a cave, even though it was damp, until the fury of the temptation died down. I slept on brambles and other rough things instead of wearing a shift, which I gave to the poor so they wouldn't know at home that I went about without it. At other times I put on a hair shirt of pig's bristles.

One day they told me to sleep with a sister who was afraid. I hadn't prayed the rosary, and so as not to fall asleep I took with me a big, sharp rock; after putting out the light I got into bed with it, since I had used it many times as a pillow. This time I put it beneath my naked body so as not to sleep, but it was not enough because before I finished the rosary I fell asleep. In dreams I saw the Mother of God enter the room in great splendor; she carried the Child Jesus in her arms and sat down on the bed with him. The Child began to pull on the rosary, as though wanting to play. He pulled so hard that he woke me up, and the Mother [of God] told me, "Don't be afraid or worried. I will take you where you'll be a nun and wear my habit." With this she disappeared. I was very comforted, with greater desires to serve God.

Another day, since my family was after me, I was wondering if there were a man nearby who hadn't sinned and was very intelligent and handsome; because I didn't think I had seen such a one as I was imagining—for they were all ugly; if only there were this man who didn't sin and didn't have any other involvement and if they [i.e., her family] would let me alone [I would marry him], but if he were not like that, I wouldn't want him for anything in the world. One day Jesus appeared to me all grown up, about my age, very beautiful and completely lovely, because ever since I was a little girl out in the fields and he had appeared to me, it seemed to me that he was growing up with me. This time, coming to me as I have said, he told me, "I am the one you want and whom you will wed" and then disappeared.

But my soul remained on fire and inflamed with his love; from then on I went about ordinarily with such impulses that they took away my natural strength. Day and night I had no other thoughts than what I would do for the Beloved.

---

[8]   Source: Ana de San Bartolomé, *Autobiography and Other Writings*, The Other Voice in Early Modern Europe, ed. and trans. Darcy Donahue (Chicago: University of Chicago Press, 2008), 39–41.

I wanted to suffer trials and dishonors and be taken for crazy.

Once my sister, who was married, sent for me to come to her house, and I asked the maid who was there with her, and she told me, "A brother of her husband who is unmarried." I knew that they wanted to marry me to him and were making great efforts. I dressed myself in a completely disheveled way with some kitchen rags and went there dressed that way. My sister, when she saw me come in, was extremely angry and said, "What are you doing? Are you crazy? Get out of here." I returned home completely happy.

I avoided talking with men or giving them occasion to speak to me; and if my brothers' friends came into the house I would go outside, or I would make a face at them as though they were a bad vision. I used this type of caution because I saw myself, as I have said, often [as a person] with great willfulness, and on the other hand, [as a person] with great obligations to God, which required perfect purity and faithfulness. The one and the other fought in my spirit with violence.

Sometimes they sent me a quarter league from the village to the wheat fields and pastures, with my sisters and people from the house. I went, keeping quiet the whole way, and when we got there, I withdrew among the trees and told them to leave me alone and began to pray. And the good Jesus came with me and sat on my lap, as I have said. I said to him, "Let's go, Lord, alone," and although he seemed to be pleased, it wasn't convenient. He gave me to understand this without speaking, smiling at me. I wanted to go to some very high ground near there, and this time he gave me to understand that it wasn't advisable; and asking him again to take me there, I slept a little, and he showed me the monastery of Avila, which is the first that our Holy Mother[9] and the nuns with that habit had founded. I asked them to give me something to drink, because I was thirsty. All this was in dreams. And they gave it to me. The glass in which they gave it to me I recognized later when I went to the monastery.

With this, I abandoned the desires I had to be a hermitess in the desert and began to want to be a nun.

XXXVIII. THE JEWS

In medieval Europe, Jews constituted a small, marginalized, and often oppressed minority, but they were the only religious minority with any substantial presence. For many years, Jews played a significant

---

[9] That is, Teresa of Ávila.

socioeconomic role as the moneylenders of Europe. Biblical prohibitions against usury (e.g., Deut. 23:19)—at least before Christian bankers gradually worked their way around them—were understood to prohibit charging any interest when a Christian lent money to a fellow Christian (or a Jew to a fellow Jew). Although the role of moneylender was essential to the economic function of Europe, it did not endear Jews to their borrowers. More difficult for the Jews was the rise in persecution that started around the time of the crusades (c. 1096). Increasingly, Christians labeled Jews "Christ killers" and accused them of "ritual murder," an ungrounded accusation that Jews would kidnap and ritually crucify a Christian boy before the Passover. During the Black Death, some Christians also accused the Jews of causing the disease by poisoning wells. An increasingly hostile Christian population turned on the Jews all over Europe, sometimes murdering groups of them and sometimes expelling them from their kingdoms.

The Renaissance complicated Christian Europeans' relationships with the Jews. On the one hand, the full establishment of banking by this time eliminated the need for Jews to serve as moneylenders, and some of the largest expulsions of Jews took place at this time, particularly the mass expulsion from Spain in 1492. On the other hand, the humanist cry to go *ad fontes* (back to the sources) necessarily entailed for Biblical humanists the need to learn Hebrew, which very few Christians had bothered to learn during the Middle Ages. Thus, a new interest in Hebrew language and books emerged during the Renaissance, and the first new Hebrew grammars and dictionaries were written to satisfy this need.

With the new Jewish books, however, came the fear that they would "pollute" the Christian reader, much like some early Christians feared the continued use of the classics of pagan antiquity. This is the attitude of the first author below, Johannes Pfefferkorn (1469–1523). A converted Jew himself, Pfefferkorn's *The Jews' Mirror* (doc. 80) is in large part an attempt to explain why more Jews had not converted to Christianity. Among the reasons he cites is the anti-Christian content of their books, in particular the Talmud, a collection of rabbinical interpretations of the Hebrew Scriptures. Pfefferkorn's call to burn copies of the Talmud was more than a theoretical exercise. In 1509, Pfefferkorn received permission from Emperor Maximilian I to confiscate all anti-Christian Jewish books. Not long afterwards, however, the emperor halted the confiscation and asked the archbishop of Mainz to look into the matter. He, in turn, sought the advice of Johannes Reuchlin (1455–1522), one of the leading Hebrew scholars of the time. Reuchlin disagreed with Pfefferkorn and produced the text below in response (doc. 81). This was the start of the so-called Reuchlin affair, which dragged on for years and involved inquisitors, faculties of theology, and German humanists, all of whom weighed in on the affair and were deeply divided between traditionalists and humanists. Occurring on the eve of the Reformation, it was perhaps the most divisive religious debate in Germany, and it helped to draw the ideological battle lines for the doctrinal conflicts that followed.

Luther was not involved in the Reuchlin affair, but his views on the Jews were influential. Early in his career, he was sympathetic, believing that their refusal to convert to Christianity should not be surprising, since he believed the Catholic Church had "obscured the Gospel." His treatise below, *That Jesus Was Born a Jew* (doc. 82) was a remarkably tolerant tract on the Jews for its time. By the end of his life, however, Luther had grown frustrated that the Jews still refused to convert even though he had reintroduced the Gospel. In contrast with his earlier work, Luther's *On the Jews and Their Lies* (doc. 83) is a classic anti-Semitic work.

Focus Questions

1. What three reasons does Pfefferkorn give for the Jews' refusal to convert to Christianity? What remedies does he suggest?
2. How does he answer the foreseen objection to taking away their property?
3. What reasons does Reuchlin offer in support of not burning the Talmud?

4. What is Luther's early advice for dealing with Jews? How does it change in his later years?

5. Does Luther end up agreeing more with Pfefferkorn or with Reuchlin?

6. The Reuchlin affair was an early case of book censorship, but the issue has never gone away. Can you think of more recent examples of efforts to ban certain books, films, or artworks? How do the arguments for and against censorship resemble the arguments made by Pfefferkorn and Reuchlin?

80. Johannes Pfefferkorn, *The Jews' Mirror*, 1507[10]

Hereafter follows the second part which advises how one should treat the Jews in order to bring them to faith.... [There are three reasons they remain obstinate in their Judaism:]

Firstly, because they are granted such great freedom and are allowed to hold their high positions and because they are permitted to take usury which, of course, is strictly forbidden by law. By doing that they collect great treasures and goods, and because they think about how to get them constantly, day and night, they have been prevented from thinking about the path to salvation....

The other reason why the Jews persist in their unbelief is the fact that they are deprived of God's word, for they do not hear it and therefore cannot really come to know the Christian faith.... Although the Jews have the Holy Scripture of the Old Testament and know the text,

they cannot learn the Christian faith without guidance. Therefore, be advised to think carefully about these two points which concern the Jews and the Christian churches, and do not accommodate them or give them any houses, unless they are willing to accept these two points, i.e., to support themselves by working and to listen to sermons. As long, however, as they are possessed by the devil, it will be difficult for them to do this and, especially, to listen to God's word, as you can see in the case of possessed people who are terribly afraid of God's word....

Now someone could say: "Why do they not come to listen to sermons since, after all, the doors of the churches stand open to them? What business do we have with the Jews? If we can preach to the Christians to lead a Christian life, we could just let the Jews be what they are."

---

[10] Source: Johannes Pfefferkorn, *The Jews' Mirror (Der Juden Spiegel)*, trans. Ruth I. Cape (Tempe: Arizona Center for Medieval and Renaissance Studies, 2011), 77, 85, 87, 89, 91.

To this I respond that we owe it to them, to ourselves, and to others to give good instruction so that they can come to enjoy eternal salvation.... [T]he Jews adore idols now, and as long as we do not come to teach them, they will not come to accept the Christian faith....

The third reason why the Jews do not change their ... religious belief, is the increasingly bad content of their books, which are full of lies about Christ, Mary, His blessed Mother, and the whole heavenly host and were devised out of carnal desire for temporal goods. This discredits the Christian faith and does so increasingly every day. Therefore, as you have the power to do so, you should take these books away from them and leave them only the text of the Holy Scripture, i.e., the Bible that was given to us from God to comfort us and for the salvation of all men....

[T]he Jews who have been led by the false Talmud to a wrong path, continue to walk on it in good spirits. If, however, learned people were to come to them to make them knowledgeable about the Holy Scripture and were to take the false Talmud away from them, they would learn the right way and would indeed have to follow it. Therefore, confiscate their books and burn them. Then you will steer them onto the path of truth all the easier.

One could object to my arguments by saying that it is not right to deprive someone of his possessions by force. Answer: Where you do not do it they will be wronged and oppressed much worse by taxes, customs fees, interest, and fees for protection, than if one seizes their books. Their salvation must be sought more by this than by money. Moreover, I believe that God, Mary, and the whole heavenly host would be greatly displeased by the books; and because one tolerates such bad books and all kinds of blasphemies in Christianity, although one could get rid of them, I am surprised that God has not punished us yet as he punished Sodom and Gomorrah, etc. So, you rulers, who hold power over people, have heard the three reasons why the Jews remain so obstinate. You could indeed confront them and help them find the way to eternal salvation.

81. Johannes Reuchlin, *Recommendation Whether to Confiscate, Destroy, and Burn All Jewish Books*, 1510[11]

If such a book is found among the holdings of a Jew who knowingly harbors it, a book that expressly and clearly heaps scorn, offense and dishonor upon our sacred Lord Jesus, his venerable mother, the saints or the Christian Order, then one would have the right by Imperial mandate to

---

[11] Source: Johannes Reuchlin, *Recommendation Whether to Confiscate, Destroy and Burn All Jewish Books: A Classic Treatise against Anti-Semitism*, ed. and trans. Peter Wortsman (New York: Paulist Press, 2000), 35, 37, 39–40, 42, 45–46, 61–62, 64.

confiscate and burn it and duly punish said Jew for having himself failed to tear it up, burn it or otherwise dispose of it....

To begin with,... let me treat the other books, notably the Talmud. This is a collection of the teachings regarding God's commandments....

Now, alas, to my great regret, I have never myself perused this Talmud, even though I would have gladly paid double the price for the chance to read it. Thus, all my efforts to no avail, I have no direct knowledge of the Talmud itself, but only an indirect knowledge based on our [Christian] books written against it....

And I know no Christian in all of Germany who has himself actually studied the Talmud. Never, moreover, in my lifetime has there ever been a baptized Jew in the German realm who could either understand or read it.... For although the Talmud is written in Hebrew letters, its language is not pure Hebrew, as we find in the Bible; but rather, we find in its phrasing diverse strains from other Oriental languages, that is, among others, from the Babylonian, Persian, Arabic and Greek....

Thus, I reply to the question at hand that the Talmud must not be burned or otherwise destroyed, for the aforementioned reasons as for the following: ...

Since the Talmud contains the characteristics of so many languages, as noted above, every Jew, even if he is well versed in Hebrew, cannot possibly understand it in its totality. How then can the Christians justify the condemnation of the Talmud, a work which they themselves do not even understand?...

If someone wished to write against the mathematicians and were himself ignorant in simple arithmetic or mathematics, he would be made a laughing stock. So too would be the case of anyone wanting to argue against the philosophers who are unschooled in their methods and teachings. This, according to canonical law.

Hereto someone might, however, object: I do not need to understand the Talmud, since there are so many books in print written against the Jews, books that maintain that the Talmud is evil. And Magister Raimundus writes such foul things about the Talmud in his *Pugio fidei* that honorable people are inclined to turn away in revulsion.[12]... The same is true of Johannes Pfefferkorn, the plaintiff in this inquiry. They all write that the Talmud is full of scurrilous and reprehensible teachings, and replete with foul language.

To which one might reply: There has never been anyone who in a just and orderly fashion expounded the position of the accused. We have a common saying: Listen to both sides of the story. It is a fundamental principle of law that one may not dismiss as guilty or condemn anyone without first conducting a thorough inquiry and an in-depth investigation into all the circumstances surrounding the case....

---

[12] Magister Raimundus was Ramón Martí, a thirteenth-century Spanish Dominican. *Pugio fidei* means "dagger of faith."

Therefore, I do not feel bound by what our aforementioned coreligionists have written against the Talmud, being apprised that some of these self-appointed critics have never so much as perused its pages....

Have not the books of the ancient poets been preserved, though they contain much more scandalous things than are to be found in the Talmud, and stand in much greater contrast to our Christian Faith than does the Talmud!...

Among all these learned and pious men, the defenders of our Christian Faith, there is not a one who ever desired or wished that such books as those referred to above be burned or suppressed.... Thus, the Holy Christian Church, faithful to these dictates, rules in its canonical law that all books must be preserved so that they may be winnowed and studied, according to the words of the Apostle Paul (1 Thes. 5:21): "Prove all things; hold fast that which is good."

But if we burn them, then our descendants will not be able to sift through them for that which is good....

The Jews ... in matters concerning their faith, must answer to none but their own judges. No Christian can or may pass judgment on their spiritual affairs, except in connection with a secular trial initiated by a proper accusation brought before an established court of law. For they do not belong to the Christian Church and, consequently, their faith is of no concern to us....

And so, concerning the Talmud, I say: Let it neither be suppressed nor burned.

---

82. Luther, *That Jesus Christ Was Born a Jew*, 1523[13]

If the Jews should take offense because we confess our Jesus to be a man, and yet true God, we will deal forcefully with that from Scripture in due time. But this is too harsh for a beginning. Let them first be suckled with milk, and begin by recognizing this man Jesus as the true Messiah; after that they may drink wine, and learn also that he is true God. For they have been led astray so long and so far that one must deal gently with them, as people who have been all too strongly indoctrinated to believe that God cannot be man.

Therefore, I would request and advise that one deal gently with them and instruct them from Scripture; then some of them may come along. Instead of this we are trying only to drive them by force, slandering them, accusing them of having Christian blood if they don't stink, and I know not what other foolishness. So long as we thus treat them like dogs, how can we expect to work any good among them? Again, when we forbid them to labor and do business and have any human fellowship with us, thereby forcing them into usury, how is that supposed to do them any good?

---

[13] Source: Luther, "That Jesus Was Born a Jew, 1523," in *Luther's Works*, eds. Pelikan and Lehmann, 45:229.

If we really want to help them, we must be guided in our dealings with them not by papal law but by the law of Christian love. We must receive them cordially, and permit them to trade and work with us, that they may have occasion and opportunity to associate with us, hear our Christian teaching, and witness our Christian life. If some of them should prove stiff-necked, what of it? After all, we ourselves are not all good Christians either.

83. Luther, *On the Jews and Their Lies*, 1543[14]

What shall we Christians do with this rejected and condemned people, the Jews? Since they live among us, we dare not tolerate their conduct, now that we are aware of their lying and reviling and blaspheming. If we do, we become sharers in their lies, cursing, and blasphemy. Thus we cannot extinguish the unquenchable fire of divine wrath, of which the prophets speak, nor can we convert the Jews. With prayer and fear of God we must practice a sharp mercy to see whether we might save at least a few from the glowing flames. We dare not avenge ourselves. Vengeance a thousand times worse than we could wish them already has them by the throat. I shall give you my sincere advice:

First, to set fire to their synagogues or schools and to bury and cover with dirt whatever will not burn, so that no man will ever again see a stone or cinder of them. This is to be done in honor of our Lord and of Christendom, so that God might see that we are Christians, and do not condone or knowingly tolerate such public lying, cursing, and blaspheming of his Son and of his Christians....

In Deuteronomy 13[:12ff], Moses writes that any city that is given to idolatry shall be totally destroyed by fire, and nothing of it shall be preserved. If he were alive today, he would be the first to set fire to the synagogues and houses of the Jews.... Now the Jews' doctrine at present is nothing but the additions of the rabbis and the idolatry of disobedience, so that Moses has become entirely unknown among them,... just as the Bible became unknown under the papacy in our day. So also, for Moses' sake, their schools cannot be tolerated; they defame him just as much as they do us. It is not necessary that they have their own free churches for such idolatry.

Second, I advise that their houses also be razed and destroyed. For they pursue in them the same aims as in their synagogues. Instead they might be lodged under a roof or in a barn, like the gypsies. This will bring home to them the fact that they are not masters in our country, as they boast, but that they are living in exile and in captivity, as they incessantly wail and lament about us before God.

---

[14] Source: Luther, "On the Jews and Their Lies, 1543," in *Luther's Works*, eds. Pelikan and Lehmann, 47: 268–70, 272.

Third, I advise that all their prayer books and Talmudic writings, in which such idolatry, lies, cursing, and blasphemy are taught, be taken from them.

Fourth, I advise that their rabbis be forbidden to teach henceforth on pain of loss of life and limb. For they have justly forfeited the right to such an office by holding the poor Jews captive with the saying of Moses (Deuteronomy 17[:10ff.]) in which he commands them to obey their teachers on penalty of death, although Moses clearly adds: "what they teach you in accord with the law of the Lord." Those villains ignore that. They wantonly employ the poor people's obedience contrary to the law of the Lord and infuse them with this poison, cursing, and blasphemy. In the same way the pope also held us captive with the declaration in Matthew 16[:18], "You are Peter," etc., inducing us to believe all the lies and deceptions that issued from his devilish mind. He did not teach in accord with the word of God, and therefore he forfeited the right to teach.

Fifth, I advise that safe-conduct on the highways be abolished completely for the Jews. For they have no business in the countryside, since they are not lords, officials, tradesmen, or the like. Let them stay at home....

Sixth, I advise that usury be prohibited to them, and that all cash and treasure of silver and gold be taken from them and put aside for safekeeping. The reason for such a measure is that, as said above, they have no other means of earning a livelihood than usury, and by it they have stolen and robbed from us all they possess. Such money should now be used in no other way than the following: Whenever a Jew is sincerely converted, he should be handed one hundred, two hundred, or three hundred florins, as personal circumstances may suggest. With this he could set himself up in some occupation for the support of his poor wife and children, and the maintenance of the old or feeble. For such evil gains are cursed if they are not put to use with God's blessing in a good and worthy cause....

Seventh, I recommend putting a flail, an ax, a hoe, a spade, a distaff, or a spindle into the hands of young, strong Jews and Jewesses and letting them earn their bread by the sweat of their brow, as was imposed on the children of Adam (Gen. 3[:19]). For it is not fitting that they should let us accursed Goyim toil in the sweat of our faces while they, the holy people, idle away their time behind the stove, feasting and farting, and on top of all, boasting blasphemously of their lordship over the Christians by means of our sweat. No, one should toss out these lazy rogues by the seat of their pants.

But if we are afraid that they might harm us or our wives, children, servants, cattle, etc., if they had to serve and work for us,... then let us emulate the common sense of other nations such as France, Spain, Bohemia, etc., compute with them how much their usury has extorted from us, divide this amicably, but then eject them forever from the country. For, as we have heard, God's anger with them is so intense that gentle mercy will only tend to make them worse and worse, while sharp mercy will reform them but little. Therefore, in any case, away with them!

258

XXXIX. THE SERVETUS AFFAIR AND RELIGIOUS TOLERATION

In 1553, with the support of John Calvin, officials in the city of Geneva burned at the stake a Spanish doctor named Michael Servetus. Servetus has a place in the history of science for having been one of the first to write about the circulation of blood in the human body. His clash with Calvin, however, stemmed from his authorship of books denying the Christian doctrine of the Trinity. Servetus had previously been captured and imprisoned in France but escaped. When he arrived in Geneva, he was once again imprisoned and charged with heresy. This time he was executed.

Not all of Calvin's allies agreed with the decision to kill Servetus. Most importantly, several rallied around the principles contained in an anonymous book published soon after the execution entitled *Concerning Heretics, Whether They are to be Persecuted* (doc. 84), which sharply condemned executions for heresy. The listed author/editor was Martin Bellius, but this was a pseudonym. Several chapters, including the ones below, were also pseudonymous. All are now widely believed to have been the work of Sebastian Castellio (1515–63), a native of Savoy who had received a humanist education in Lyon. He had been one of Calvin's friends in Geneva, but the two men fell out over Castellio's suitability for the ministry, as well as over his interpretation of the Song of Songs. Castellio left Geneva for Basel, where he worked for several years for a pittance in a printer's shop. *Concerning Heretics* revived his career as an author and humanist. It also made him a lifelong enemy of Calvin.

Calvin was unable to write an immediate counterattack to *Concerning Heretics*, but he had his friend and later successor in Geneva, Theodore Beza (1519–1605), write a response on his behalf. Beza was a French humanist and theologian who was highly skilled in Greek. He came to Switzerland in 1548 and found a position teaching Greek at the Lausanne Academy. Later, he would play a prominent role in the establishment of the Academy in Geneva, and he would succeed Calvin as head of the Geneva Company of Pastors. *On the Authority of the Magistrate in Punishing Heretics* (doc. 85) is his direct response to Castellio's book.

Focus Questions

1. What reasons does Castellio cite for not persecuting heretics?
2. What reasons does Beza cite for doing so?
3. What "first principles" underlie each of their arguments? In other words, what principles are most important to each of them?
4. What are their arguments regarding Scriptural interpretation? Do you see any parallels with the debate between Luther and Erasmus on free will (see above, §IX)?

84. Sebastian Castellio, *Concerning Heretics, Whether They Are to Be Persecuted and How They Are to Be Treated*, 1554[15]

"George Kleinberg," On How Persecution Hurts the World

No one in his right mind doubts that our sins are the cause of the many calamities, discords, and wars with which the whole world today, especially Germany, is desolated. But few inquire as to the character of the sins which are the cause. I think they are cruelty and severity.... I speak not only of the blood which has been shed in wars, for which also an answer must be given if it was unjustly done, but chiefly of that which has been shed for religion, which is of such a nature that it stems and staunches the flow of blood, for "they shall beat their swords into ploughshares and their spears into pruning hooks" [Isa. 2:4; Micah 4:3]. Wherefore I cannot see by what perverse human reasoning it has come to pass that scarcely any shed so much blood as those who profess to have the true religion....

From the cruelty first exercised against the Anabaptists arose a long succession of atrocities. They retaliated and slew many of their opponents. Thus blood was expiated by blood. Again the Anabaptists were miserably slain, even those who were not in arms, and what is still more cruel the suppression was carried on not only by the sword, but also in books which reach farther and last longer, or rather forever perpetuate this savagery. Let it be understood that I do not defend homicides, adulterers, or other like criminals. I know that against such the magistrate has received the sword from God. But I am talking

---

[15] Source: Sebastian Castellio, *Concerning Heretics*, trans. Roland H. Bainton (New York: Octagon Books, 1965), 216–21, 225–26.

about the understanding of Scriptural passages, the sense of which is not yet clear. If they were not obscure controversy would have ceased, for who is so demented that he would die for the denial of the obvious? I am talking about errors. If there is any offense here it must be due to error and ignorance.... For error and ignorance, men now in our time and regions are put to death by the sword and afterwards their memory is defamed in books far and wide and for all time to come. He who does not deplore this, in my judgment, has not the heart of a man. God Himself seems to have manifested His displeasure against these murders in that the author of this policy [i.e., Zwingli], a learned man and famous throughout the world, shortly after he had put harmless folk to death, fell himself with many others at the edge of the sword.... Having first burned the persons and the books of their critics at a slow fire, they then tilt against the ashes and vanquish in death those whom they could not overcome in life.... A just judgment indeed is this, to kill a man before we know whether he ought to be killed and not to permit even his books to plead his cause, at least, not after his death.... O unheard-of cruelty! Who was ever so eager to save life as they are to destroy it? O Prince of Peace! O Light of the World! Enlighten the eyes of the princes that henceforth they may no longer serve the cruelty of Satan, but rather Thy mercy and meekness.

Princes and all rulers open your eyes, open your ears, fear God, and consider how you will render an account to Him of your administration. Many have been punished for cruelty, none for mercy. Many will be condemned in the last judgment for having killed the innocent, none for

not having killed. Incline to the side of mercy, and do not obey those who incite you to murder....

Believe me, if Christ were here he would not advise you to kill those who confess His name, however much they might err in certain respects, not to say that they merely seem to err....

Be wise and follow the counsel of Christ, not of Antichrist. Otherwise, I assure you, there will never be an end of seditions and wars, until all of you who have lightly shed blood shall miserably perish. Think not that the exercise of cruelty will eliminate seditions.... If cruelty were the cure, these evils would long ago have been removed, for cruelty has been exercised for more than five thousand years. But this is certain that evil will never be overcome with evil. There is no remedy against murders other than to stop committing murder.

"Basil Montfort," Refutation of the Reasons Commonly Alleged in Favor of Persecution

Some wish to see all heretics put to death, that is, all those who disagree with them, of whatever condition or nation they may be, provided this can be done.... In order to persuade princes and rulers, the persecutors collect all the passages of Sacred Scripture which may enflame princes to bloodshed. Although not a few authors have refuted these opinions, nevertheless, the persecutors persevere and listen to no one unless he is also a persecutor.

Such conduct is not actuated by Christ, as it seems to me, for He did not defend Himself by arms, though He might readily have done so, since He had at His disposal ten legions of angels. The oppressors are actuated rather by the desire to defend their power and worldly kingdom by the arms of the world. This appears from the fact that when they were poor and powerless they detested persecutors, but now, having become strong, imitate them. Abandoning the arms of Christ they take the arms of the Pharisees, without which they would not be able to defend or retain their power. When I see how much blood has been shed since the creation of the world under color of religion and how the just have always been slain before they were recognized, I fear lest the same thing happen in our day, that we kill as unjust those whom our descendants will revere as just.... This is the battle of Christ; we must use the arms of Christ. Let Him be judge and defend the persecuted, as He was persecuted. Let Him open the eyes of the oppressors to see that their sacrifices are not pleasing to God. May they turn again and be healed and saved.

85. Theodore Beza, *The Authority of the Magistrate in Punishing Heretics*, 1554[16]

If there were ever a time when the church of God had need of assistance, today one certainly sees it assailed from without and from within by an infinite number of enemies dedicated to doing it harm.... And we have recently seen a notable example of such wickedness and ingratitude.... For this detestable heretic Servetus was... delivered into the hands of the council of Geneva, so that it might punish for his evil this wicked man, more full of impiety and blasphemy than anyone who ever lived....

Let us now... look at what arguments are brought forth to try to prove that even if the magistrate can reprimand heretics, he should not punish them with death. In this regard, I see that I am dealing not only with our impudent adversaries who want nothing held for certain in religion, but also with certain good and very knowledgeable people who... do not think the magistrate can ever put heretics to death....

Thanks be to God, we remember that we are human, and we are well aware that no one can be compelled to faith and that Christians should be gentle and kind; nevertheless, we ask that this kindness have some limits and be measured by the rule of the word of God. For it is written, "One who justifies the wicked and one who condemns the righteous are both alike an abomination to

---

[16] Source: Théodore de Bèze, *Traitté de l'authorité du magistrate en la punition des hérétiques et du moyen d'y proceder* ([Geneva]: Conrad Badius, 1560), 1–2, 217–19, 288–90, 292, 335–36, 338–40, translated by the editor.

the Lord" [Prov. 17:15]. We ask that one have more regard for the sheep than for the wolves. We ask that one wisely punish those who abuse the gentleness of the church and the kindness of princes in order to throw down and destroy. In short, we ask to remember that Christian charity does not agree with injustice, and that we at least be moved by injuries made to the majesty of God by wickedness and malice....

Heretics are simply those who want to be considered Christians but who, after being duly shown and convicted of their error by the word of God, nevertheless prefer to follow their own judgment and obstinately and persistently support false articles of religion against the church.... Now such monstrous spirits are incredibly dangerous plagues in the church and are the true instruments of the devil for overturning the church.... When the doctrine is corrupt—and corrupt in such a way that the devil is hidden there under a shadow and false appearance of God—what else happens but that many people receive the devil instead of God? Many also abandon all hope of being able to come to the knowledge of the truth, leaving behind all religion; in short, what else will occur but horrible confusion in the church of God?...

As God created all things for himself, the chief end of human society is for God to be honored by humans as he ought to be. Now the magistrate is established as the guard and governor of this society. It follows, then, that in its administration and conduct, the magistrate should have regard for this end above all.... Far be it that he could or should abstain from having regard for the state of religion. And he cannot preserve and maintain religion unless he reprimand by the punishment of the sword those who obstinately hold religion in contempt and form sects....

There are certain crimes which are such that... they are held, as by a common right, for capital crimes among all nations,... such as parricide, premeditated homicide, sacrilege, blasphemy, impiety, or crime against the received religion of the land.... As for parricides and other premeditated murders, as well as sacrilege, I think that the matter is self-evident. But as for the crime of blasphemy and impiety, I am amazed how some people call this into doubt. For everyone agrees that the enormity of the crime should be measured according to the quality of the victim.... And if this is true, it also follows, as I believe, that just as the glory of God is a more excellent thing than the honor of men, so also blasphemy and impiety are great and enormous crimes....

It is, therefore, quite reasonable that in such true Christian [i.e., Protestant][17] churches in

---

[17] A few sentences earlier, Beza defines true Christian churches as those that "adhere to the clear voice of God, not being obscured by any human traditions, and the pure and right administration of the sacraments, which seal the doctrine in the hearts of the faithful."

which the lambs hear the voice of the Shepherd, this rule ought to hold place and be observed: Whoever teaches a doctrine other than that which is commonly received, especially after being admonished twice by the church, this person should be held as one who sins against the church and willingly and deliberately offends against the religion....

But if together with blasphemy and impiety there is also heresy, that is to say, when someone is possessed of an obstinate disregard for the word of God and for the ecclesiastical discipline, and throws himself into a rage for infecting others as well, what crime could one find among humans that is greater and more

outrageous? Certainly, if one wants to order a punishment according to the enormity of the crime, it seems to me that one could not even find a torment corresponding to the enormity of such a crime.... Indeed, anyone who attempts in the assembly and company of the church to corrupt the true service of God lights a fire which could spread, causing the eternal damnation of an infinite number of persons.... Therefore, whether the magistrate aims to maintain the glory of God or wants to preserve human society whole, there is no one whom he should punish with greater rigor and severity than heretics, blasphemers, and those who hold religion in contempt.

XL. SLAVERY

Although chattel slavery was not widely practiced in Western Europe during the Middle Ages, serfdom certainly was. The age of exploration ushered in a new era, however, as Spanish and Portuguese colonists began to enslave Native Americans and Africans to work their lands in the New World. Eastern Europe had a longer tradition of slavery, and while it was on the decline in the sixteenth century, serfdom was growing to take its place.

Christian thought had always accepted the possibility of slavery. It was practiced by the Jews of the Old Testament (cf. Exod. 21, Lev. 25, Deut. 23), and the New Testament contains several exhortations for slaves to "obey your masters" (e.g., Eph. 6:5, Titus 2:9, 1 Peter 2:18, Col. 3:22). The European peasant rebellions of the fourteenth through sixteenth centuries contained some of the first Christian arguments against slavery (e.g., see above, doc. 25, art. 3). But arguably the first substantive Christian debate on slavery took place at Iwie, in the Grand Duchy of Lithuania (now Iŭje, Belarus), from January 20 to 26, 1568.

The Iwie Synod was a meeting of the Minor Reformed Church, an anti-Trinitarian offshoot of the Lithuanian Reformed Church; the split with the Trinitarian "Major" Reformed Church had occurred just three years before. Within the Minor Church, however, a division had emerged between the traditionalist gentry and social radicals influenced by the Hutterites, a branch of the Anabaptists. Thus, although the participants at the Iwie Synod spent several days discussing traditional theological issues, the questions of slavery and serfdom lay at the heart of the division within the church and, consequently, received substantive debate. The proceedings, from which the excerpt below is taken, were published by Simon Budny, the principal pro-slavery advocate in the debate. Budny was a humanist-trained pastor and expert in Hebrew who published a Polish translation of the Bible in 1572. His position won the day at the Iwie Synod, and the anti-slavery faction, led by Jacob Kalinowski, soon left Lithuania to join their more radical Polish coreligionists.

Focus Questions

1. What are the chief arguments and biblical passages used here both for and against slavery?
2. What does Simon Budny say needs to be considered before freeing slaves?
3. What specific issues of bias must one consider in reading this account written by Budny himself?
4. Who do you think made the stronger arguments in the debate? What assumptions, beliefs, and attitudes have changed to bring about the universal condemnation of slavery in the West today?

86. The Iwie Debate, 1568[18]

Jacob Kalinowski: You, Brother Simon, claim that there may be male and female slaves. Tell me, therefore, who may these slaves be—of the faithful, or nonbelievers? Christians or non-Christians?

Simon Budny: Believers or nonbelievers may be slaves of Christians.

Jacob: That cannot be so by any standard. First of all, a Christian cannot have or keep a nonbeliever in bondage, for the apostle has written that Christ cannot be in accord with Belial [2 Cor 6:15], nor a believer with a nonbeliever. If, therefore, there cannot be agreement of a believer with a nonbeliever, how then can the believer keep a nonbeliever in bondage? Regarding a member of the faith, it cannot by any means be that a Christian would have one of these in bondage. The apostle plainly states that with Christ there is neither Jew, nor Greek, there is neither slave, and so on [Gal. 3:28].

Simon: . . . who could be such a simpleton as not to understand that the apostle is not speaking here of bondage, but rather that being a Jew will not be of special benefit before God to anyone; neither will it be of help if one is free, not in bondage, nor will it hurt if one be a slave. . . .

As to your claim that a Christian may not have a pagan as a slave because the apostle wrote that there is no accord between Christ and Belial, nor between a believer and a nonbeliever, in this too the apostle does not speak of Christians not being in bondage to a pagan, or a pagan to a Christian. Rather that Christians are not to be of assistance to pagans in doing evil; to the contrary, that they are to live differently from the pagans, that they have no part of evil or uncleanliness. For a Christian can be in bondage to a pagan and a pagan to a Christian.

This I will prove by the Scriptures. The apostle Paul wrote to Timothy: "Let all who are under the yoke of slavery regard their masters as worthy of all honor, so that the name of God and the teaching may not be defamed" [1 Tim. 6:1]. Here the apostle, speaking of slaves who are also Christians and have pagans as masters, tells Timothy to teach them that they should hold their masters in respectful regard, even though they are pagans, so that they would not defame the teachings of Christ. I say that these were slaves who were Christians and had masters who were nonbelievers. . . .

Jacob: I cannot understand what type of Christianity would have slaves—ruling, commanding, and a brother at that. You have not yet proved that the brethren had nonbelievers in bondage.

Simon: Well now, I will show you, for nothing could be more simply proved, especially with the use of the letter of St. Paul to Philemon. For there it is plainly written that Onesimus, on whose behalf Paul writes this letter, was the

---

[18] Source: Donald J. Ziegler, ed., *Great Debates of the Reformation* (New York: Random House, 1969), 248–51, 260, 267–70.

slave of Philemon. He was not a Christian but a pagan, who, when he had done his master wrong, ran away to Rome where he met Paul.... He listened to him, believed, and even allowed himself to be baptized. All this is revealed in this letter in verses 10–17, wherein Paul states that he had him in bondage, that he is returning him, although he could have been useful to him. It is definite, therefore, in this letter that Philemon, a Christian, had a slave who was non-Christian, the unfaithful Onesimus. If, therefore, it was permissible for Philemon, a minister of the word of God, to have such slaves, hence it is all the more permissible for those who are not ministers.

Jacob: You, brother, have used the term slave for the longest time, but all the other interpreters have been using the term servant in their translation. This I like, because it agrees with Holy Scripture, but it is difficult to accept the slave concept, that a Christian should enslave someone; that is not befitting for one of the brethren....

Simon: the Greek term *dulos* and also the Latin term *servus* mean nothing else but "slave." Therefore, in my translation of the Bible, which I am now doing (if the Lord will permit me to complete it), you shall have in the New Testament... the word *dulos* appearing in translation as "slave," and the same for the Old Testament, where the Hebrew term *ewed* is used. For this is their meaning.

Jacob: It matters little how you translate this word, for all others are not doing it that way, but rather as the word *servus* has always been understood and translated—servant, not slave.

Simon: If *servus* means a free servant, tell me, what does *famulus* mean? Also, what does "min-ister" mean? In addition, tell me, how else would you designate a slave in Latin except *servus*?

Jacob: We did not come here for the purpose of discussing vocabulary, but rather to free ourselves of the falsities of Antichrist. We, through the help of God, realize it is still the evil of Antichrist to have serfs or slaves, and you are attempting to defend this mistake by means of grammar and vocabulary.

Simon: I am not using interpretations of vocabulary here nor Antichrist's terms to refute your conception, but proving by the true word of God that Christians as well as pagans in the time of the apostles had both believing Christians and nonbelieving pagans as slaves....

Jacob: You have talked a long time, brother, but if you had talked ten times as long, you could not have convinced me that it is proper for a Christian to have servants, less so slaves. The Lord Christ does not wish to have his followers gain property by working people like animals, but rather that they should sell properties already in their possession, denying themselves everything to take up the cross and follow him....

Simon: Denial and renunciation do not mean discarding or selling everything. Rather they mean being ready and willing to give up all possessions, wealth, honors, position, friends, even life itself for Christ and his teachings, permitting them to be taken, but not allowing him to be torn away from you, nor you frightened away from him....

Since it is plain from the Scriptures that former Christians had possessions, homes, farms, land, slaves, and so on, therefore they may also have them today. However, they are to use these differently from pagans and nonconverted people. They may have subjects, but not abuse them, so that these would not weep because of them but rather praise God for such masters. They may have male slaves and female slaves, but be merciful to them and not only forgive them some threatened punishment, but, as the apostle writes, to some who served well, honestly, and faithfully, grant them their freedom....

In this situation, however, it is necessary to move cautiously, knowing whom to make free and whom not. There are those among the slaves who can become good people when freed. There are also those, however, who are good in bondage and under threat of punishment, but bad when freed. Our elders tell the story that a certain Rekuć, a sheriff of Żmódź, was persuaded by the Bishop Molus to order freedom for all the slaves. The peasants, who were bad as slaves, became ten times worse in freedom. Some of them who were thieves in former times then became raiders of the manors of their masters and murdered

them. The sheriff and bishop had to recall their law, permitting each of the gentry thereafter to recapture their retinue of slaves and keep them in bondage as before. This should not surprise us, for it is evident that they came to this not so much by birth (they are human beings), as they did by improper rearing. We see that in ancient times, in Lithuania and Ruthenia, although it was against the law, the custom prevailed that slaves were permitted to steal, and even if caught with the evidence, they would be punished only slightly or not at all.

We need to pray to the Lord God, asking that he might stir the hearts of the lords and the gentry, causing them not merely to use the slaves and all their subjects, but rather to rule these people in such a way that they might be worthy of respect.

Synod: Amen.

FURTHER READING

Bell, Dean Philip, and Stephen G. Burnett, eds. *Jews, Judaism, and the Reformation in Sixteenth-Century Germany*. Leiden: Brill, 2006.

Brock, Peter. "Slave and Master in the Congregation of God: A Debate over Serfdom among Antitrinitarians in the Grand Duchy of Lithuania, 1568." *Polish Review* 43 (1998): 79–100.

Guggisberg, Hans. *Sebastian Castellio, 1515–1563: Humanist and Defender of Religious Toleration in a Confessional Age*. Translated by Bruce Gordon. Aldershot, UK: Ashgate, 2003.

Harrington, Joel. *Reordering Marriage and Society in Reformation Germany*. Cambridge: Cambridge University Press, 1995.

Karant-Nunn, Susan C., and Merry E. Wiesner-Hanks, eds. and trans. *Luther on Women: A Sourcebook*. Cambridge: Cambridge University Press, 2003. http://dx.doi.org/10.1017/CBO9780511810367.

Lecler, Joseph. *Toleration and the Reformation.* Vol. 2. Translated by L. Westow. New York: Association Press, 1960.

Leonard, Amy. *Nails in the Wall: Catholic Nuns in Reformation Germany.* Chicago: University of Chicago Press, 2005. On nuns, see also "Further Reading" at the end of chapter 7 of this sourcebook.

McKee, Elsie Anne. *Katharina Schütz Zell.* 2 vols. Leiden: Brill, 1999.

Oberman, Heiko. *The Roots of Anti-Semitism in the Age of Renaissance and Reformation.* Translated by James Porter. Philadelphia: Fortress Press, 1984.

Plummer, Marjorie Elizabeth. *From Priest's Whore to Pastor's Wife: Clerical Marriage and the Process of Reform in the Early German Reformation.* Burlington, VT: Ashgate, 2012.

Price, David. *Johannes Reuchlin and the Campaign to Destroy Jewish Books.* Oxford: Oxford University Press, 2011.

Wiesner-Hanks, Merry E. *Christianity and Sexuality in the Early Modern World: Regulating Desire, Reforming Practice.* London: Routledge, 2000.

Sources

Chapter I

5 © Norman P. Tanner, ed. 1990, *Decrees of the Ecumenical Councils, Volume One, Niceae I to Lateran V*, Burns & Oates, used by permission of Bloomsbury Publishing Plc.

7 *Christian Humanism and the Reformation: Selected Writings of Erasmus*, revised edition, ed. John C. Olin. New York: Fordham University Press, 1965.

9 Excerpts from "A Pilgrimage for Religion's Sake," from "Colliquies," CWE 40, trans. and annotated by Craig R. Thompson © University of Toronto Press 1997, pp. 632–33, 641, 642–44, 650. Reprinted with permission of the publisher.

Chapter II

10 From Dewey Weiss Kramer, trans., *Johann Tetzel's Rubuttal against Luther's Sermon on Indulgences and Grace* (Atlanta: Pitts Theology Library, 2012), 1231. Reprinted by permissions of the author.

11 From Dewey Weiss Kramer, trans. *Johann Tetzel's Rubuttal against Luther's Sermon on Indulgences and Grace* (Atlanta: Pitts Theology Library, 2012), 1231. Reprinted by permission of the author.

18 Excerpts from "A Discussion of Free Will," trans. Peter Macardle and annotated by Macardel, Clarence H. Hiller, and Charles Trinkaus, from "Controversies," CWE 76 © University of Toronto Press 1999. Reprinted with permission of the publisher.

Chapter III

20 From *The Essential Carlstadt: Fifteen Tracts* © 1995 by Herald Press, Waterloo, Ontario. Used with permission.

22 From *The Essential Carlstadt: Fifteen Tracts* © 1995 by Herald Press, Waterloo, Ontario. Used with permission.

23 From *Spiritual and Anabaptist Writers*, by George Huntston Williams, ed., from The Library of Christian Classics (Philadelphia: Westminster Press, 1957), pp. 62–66, 68–69. Reprinted by permission of Westminster John Knox Press.

Chapter IV

28 Excerpts from *Great Debates of the Reformation,* ed. Donald J. Ziegler, copyright © 1969 by Donald Ziegler. Used by permission of Modern Library, an imprint of Random House, a division of Penguin Random House LLC. All rights reserved.

29 Excerpts from John C. Wenger, "The Schleitheim Confession of Faith," *Mennonite Quarterly Review* 19 (1945): 243–53. Reprinted by permission of the publisher.

Chapter V

33 Excerpts from *Institutes of the Christian Religion,* 1536 Edition, Ford Lewis Battles, trans. (Grand Rapids, MI: Eerdmans, 1975), pp. 339–42. Reprinted with permission of the publisher.

39 Excerpts from Thomas A. Lambert and Isabella M. Watt, eds., *Registers of the Consistory of Geneva in the Time of Calvin,* M. Wallace McDonald, trans. (Grand Rapids, MI: Eerdmans, 2000), pp. 29–30, 33, 37–38, 40–41, 67, 103–04, 111, 133, 178. Reprinted with permission of the publisher.

Chapter VII

51 From Gilliam T. W. Ahlgren, ed. and trans., *The Inquisition of Francisca: A Sixteenth-Century Visionary on Trial,* The Other Voice in Early Modern Europe (Chicago: University of Chicago Press, 2005). Pp. 68–71, 156–58. Copyright © 2005 University of Chicago Press. Reprinted with permission of the publisher.

Chapter VIII

54 *Huldrych Zwingli,* ed. G.R. Potter. London: Edward Arnold, 1978.

55 *Huldrych Zwingli,* ed. G.R. Potter. London: Edward Arnold, 1978.

56 From Eric Lund, ed. *Documents from the History of Lutheranism, 1517–1750* (Minneapolis: Fortress Press, 2002), pp. 161–62.

58 Excerpt from pp. 232–8 from Pursuit of Power, Ed. and trans. by James C. Davis. English translation copyright © 1970 by James C. Davis. Reprinted by permission of HarperCollins Publishers.

Chapter IX

61 Reprinted from *Christian Initiation: Baptism in the Medieval West* by J.D.C. Fisher © 2004 Archdiocese of Chicago: Liturgy Training Publications 1-800-933-1800. www.LTP.org. All rights reserved. Used with permission.

62 From J.D.C. Fisher, "Christian Initiation, The Reformation Period: Some Early Reformed Rites of Baptism and Confirmation and other Contemporary Documents," Alcuin Club Collections 51 (London: SPCK, 1970), 35–37. Reprinted by permission of SPCK/IVP.

69 Excerpted from William R. Estep, Jr., ed., *Anabaptist Beginnings (1523–1533): A Source Book,* Bibliotheca Humanistica & Reformatorica 16 (Nieukoop: B. de Graaf, 1976), 32–33. Reprinted by permission of the publisher.

73 Excerpts from "The Funeral" from "Colliquis," CWE 40, translated & annotated by Craig R. Thompson © University of Toronto Press 1997, pp. 772–773. Reprinted with permission of the publisher.

Chapter X

75 From Marie Detière, "Epistle to Marguerite de Navarre and Preface to a Sermon by John Calvin," translated by Mary McKinley, *The Other Voice in Early Modern Europe* (Chicago: University of Chicago Press, 2004), pp. 85–87. Copyright © 2004 University of Chicago Press. Reprinted with Permission of the Publisher.

76 From Katharina Schütz Zell, "Church Mother: The Writings of a Protestant Reformer in Sixteenth-Century Germany," ed. and trans. Elsie McKee, *The Other Voice in Early Modern Europe* (Chicago: University of Chicago Press, 2006), pp. 188, 191–92, 195–97. Reprinted with permission of the publisher.

77 Excerpts from *Luther's Works,* American Edition (Saint Louis: Concordia Publishing House, 1955). Reprinted by permission of Fortress Press.

79 From "Autobiography and Other Writings," ed. and trans. Darcy Donahue, *The Other Voice in Early Modern Europe* (Chicago: University of Chicago Press, 2008), pp. 39–41. Reprinted with permission of the publisher.

80 From Johannes Pfefferkorn, *The Jews' Mirror (Der Juden Spiegel)*, trans. Ruth I. Cape, *Medieval and Renaissance Texts and Studies* 390 (Tempe, AZ: Arizona Center for Medieval and Renaissance Studies, 2011). Reprinted by permission of the publisher.

81 From Johannes Reuchlin, *Recommendation Whether to Confiscate, Destroy and Burn All Jewish books: A Classic Treatise against Anti-Semitism*, ed. and trans. Peter Wortsman. *Studies in Judaism and Christianity* (New York: Paulist Press, 2000), 35, 37, 39–40, 42, 45–46, 48, 50, 61–62, 64. Reproduced with permission of Paulis Press in the format Book via Copyright Clearance Center.

82 Excerpts from *Luther's Works*, American Edition (Saint Louis: Concordia Publishing House, 1955). Reprinted by permission of Fortress Press.

83 Excerpts from *Luther's Works, American Edition* (Saint Louis: Concordia Publishing House, 1955). Reprinted by permission of Fortress Press.

84 From *Concerning Heretics*, by Sebastian Castellio, trans. Roland H. Bainton, Copyright © 1965 Octagon Books. Reprinted with permission of the publisher.

86 Excerpts from *The Great Debates of the Reformation*, ed. Donald J. Ziegler, copyright © 1969 by Donald Ziegler. Used by permission of Modern Library, an imprint of Random House, a division of Penguin Random House LLC. All rights reserved.